LEAN
SIX
SIGMA
SECRETS
FOR THE CIO

LEAN SIX SIGMA
SECRETS
FOR THE CIO

William Bentley

Peter T. Davis

CRC Press
Taylor & Francis Group
Boca Raton   London   New York

CRC Press is an imprint of the
Taylor & Francis Group, an **informa** business

CRC Press
Taylor & Francis Group
6000 Broken Sound Parkway NW, Suite 300
Boca Raton, FL 33487-2742

First issued in paperback 2019

© 2010 by Taylor and Francis Group, LLC
CRC Press is an imprint of Taylor & Francis Group, an Informa business

No claim to original U.S. Government works

ISBN-13: 978-1-4398-0379-0 (hbk)
ISBN-13: 978-0-367-38517-0 (pbk)

Library of Congress Cataloging-in-Publication Data

Bentley, William, 1944-
   Lean six sigma secrets for the CIO / William Bentley, Peter T. Davis.
      p. cm.
   Includes bibliographical references and index.
   ISBN 978-1-4398-0379-0 (hbk. : alk. paper)
      1. Information technology--Management. 2. Six sigma (Quality control standard) I.
Davis, Peter T. II. Title.

HD30.2.B458 2010
658.4'013--dc22   2009029625

Visit the Taylor & Francis Web site at
http://www.taylorandfrancis.com

and the CRC Press Web site at
http://www.crcpress.com

To Joyce, my always happy wife, who continues to endure me even after nearly four decades; and to Brandon and Trevor, my wonderful sons, both with computer science degrees, who continue to be amused that I don't give up trying to understand the world of computers.

—Bill

To Kelly, the pride of my life, who is off pursuing her dreams. Bonne chance. Buena suerte. Viel Glueck. Buona fortuna.

—Peter

Contents

Acknowledgments

We would like to acknowledge Rich O'Hanley who started this rolling; John Wyzalek, acquisitions editor, for pitching the book to the editorial committee and getting us a contract (Much appreciated, John); Teresa Horton, copy editor, who kept us honest; and Rich Halstead-Nussloch, technical editor, for his diligence in reviewing the material (Thanks, Rich).

Peter T. Davis would like to thank first and foremost his co-author for taking this trip with him. He also would like to thank Dorian Cougias, Rabindra "Danny" Jaggernauth, John Kearns, Al Marcella, Tony Noblett, William Prado, Winn Schwartau, Rob van den Eijnden, and Herman Veltkamp for answering a call for help. The provided information shows in this book. Any mistakes, as they say, are mine and not theirs.

William (Bill) Bentley would like to thank Peter, his co-author for being patient enough to wait for him to come around and write this with him, and his wonderful network of Value-Train students and trainers, who are always there to help with his sometimes unusual requests.

About the Authors

William (Bill) Bentley (BSEE, MSEE, Six Sigma Master Black Belt, Lean Black Belt) is the owner and president of Value-Train, a process improvement consulting and training firm started in Atlanta, Georgia, in 2002. Bill's college education is in electrical engineering (advanced automatic control systems) and he practiced that in various roles with Procter & Gamble, Frito-Lay, and Nabisco Brands for twenty years. His last assignment in that career was director of automation for Nabisco Brands. He subsequently managed engineering and software operations for various companies, with his most recent corporate position being president and CEO of MDT Software in Atlanta. He lives with his wife Joyce, two dogs, and two parrots, all of whom get along just fine. He is an avid sailor, motorcyclist, bicyclist, and virtual world advocate.

Peter T. Davis (CISA, CMA, CISSP, CWNA, CCNA, CMC, CISM, CoBiT FL, ITIL v3 FL, ISSPCS, PMP, SSGB, CGEIT) founded Peter Davis + Associates (a very original name) as an information technology governance firm specializing in the security, audit, and control of information. A battle-scarred information systems veteran, his career includes positions as programmer, systems analyst, security administrator, security planner, information systems auditor, and consultant. Peter also is the past president and founder of the Toronto Information Systems Security Association (ISSA) chapter, past recording secretary of the ISSA's International Board and past Computer Security Institute Advisory Committee member. He has written or co-written numerous articles and ten books including *Hacking Wireless Networks for Dummies* and *Securing and Controlling Cisco Routers*. He was listed in the *International Who's Who of Professionals*. In addition, he was only the third editor in the three-decade history of *EDPACS,* a security, audit, and control publication. He lives with his wife Janet, a cat, and a dog in Toronto, Ontario.

Chapter 1

Beyond IT Governance

The CEO's secretary calls and tells you the boss wants to see you immediately. As you stride confidently toward the corner office, you cannot help wondering what's up. You have met all your targets and you believe your users are satisfied—although you have no proof. When you enter the office, you notice the CEO is sitting with the CFO. The air in the room is icy and you get a slight chill. This does not augur well. With the CFO nodding like a bobblehead doll, the CEO explains the financials this quarter are not good and the stock is going to get pummeled. Right now you are thinking of the pointy-haired boss from the Dilbert cartoon. Now the CFO explains that you will need to cut 10 percent from salaries and noninterest expenses.

The Corporate Paradox

Does this sound familiar? This is not an unusual tactic. When times are tough, many organizations retreat and decide to cut costs. Read the paper any given day and you will see that organizations are laying off employees to reduce costs to return to profitability or just to survive. As we write this book, U.S. automakers are laying off workers because they did not foresee the shift in the auto market or increases in gas prices.

When organizations cut staff, financial analysts respond favorably by buying the organizations' stock and forcing the value of the companies upward. This behavior perpetuates the cycle: Hire them when times are good and fire them when times are bad. This behavior obviously has a negative impact on any organization. If your employees think they are the next to go, they will not demonstrate a lot of loyalty. Furthermore, the good ones will look for alternative employment while the

poor ones remain. If that doesn't convince you, read the 2008 Cyber-Ark survey*
that reports a whopping 88 percent of information technology (IT) administrators
admitted they would take corporate secrets, should their organization suddenly lay
them off. This strategy is obviously not always the best. As motivational speaker
Catherine DeVrye warns, "Remember that the six most expensive words in business
are: 'We've always done it that way.'"

Downsizing, rightsizing, capsizing: You know that cutting resources beyond
the point of pain is not the way to succeed. You will have burnt-out staffers and
stressed-out managers who are just trying to keep their heads above water. Forget
trying to rework processes to improve performance when your staff finds it difficult
to just cope.

The Pitch

As you consider the CEO's request, you are reminded of Monty Python's first
film *And Now for Something Completely Different* and you tell the CEO and CFO
you'd like to go in a different direction. You think now is the time for Lean Six
Sigma. Your golfing buddy has been going on and on about it and you'd like to
try it.

Why not focus on becoming better at what you do? By focusing on improving
your processes, you can add to the bottom line. If it costs $100 to handle a call to
the service desk and you can reduce the number of calls from 100,000 to 50,000,
you have just added $5 million to the bottom line. So why not focus on efficiency
and effectiveness? You understand it is necessary to do some belt-tightening to affect
the bottom line, but kick-starting the top line is equally important. You also know
Lean Six Sigma can help improve your processes and stimulate innovation.

You tell them, "I would like to try to use Lean Six Sigma in my area. Lean Six
Sigma is a combination of historical methods for process improvement that focuses
on the bottom line and critical-to-customer requirements. It is a robust business
improvement methodology that focuses an organization on customer requirements,
process alignment, analytical rigor, and timely execution. LSS includes leadership,
infrastructure, tools and methods."

The CEO and CFO have heard the term, but they're not quite sure what it
means. Is Lean Six Sigma really different, or is it just another flavor-of-the-month
program that will disappear eventually? Is it an expensive, complicated approach
oversold by engineers and zealots? Is it the fabled goose that laid the golden egg, as
some suggest, or is it a boondoggle?

---

* http://www.cyber-ark.com/news-events/pr_20080827.asp.

Lean Six Sigma Business Case

You assure them that Lean Six Sigma is not a skinny rock band from northern Kentucky, a fad or a cult, or a fraternity or secret society with secret handshakes—although there are some really neat pins. Rather, it is a flexible quality improvement strategy used by organizations to identify and eliminate variation and reduce cycle time and costs. This method differs from previous process improvement approaches because it uses established engineering principles and is based on the institutionalization of the approach and independent validation of claims of success. You also ensure them that it complements the existing corporate and IT governance programs. You explain how General Electric (GE) used Six Sigma (6Σ) alone to turn around their performance and strengthen customer relationships and how Toyota used Lean Six Sigma to become a juggernaut.

Lean Six Sigma techniques go back to the 1920s with the development of time and motion studies and the principles of statistical quality control. Thirty years later in the early 1950s, W. Edwards Deming and Bonnie Small developed the foundations of modern process improvement methods. Deming developed Total Quality Management (TQM) and exported it to Japan. Small made the analyses of statistical quality control accessible to people who were not professional statisticians and mathematicians through her publication of *The Western Electric Rule.**

Incorporating elements from the work of many quality pioneers, Six Sigma aims for virtually error-free business performance. Six Sigma is a rigorous, focused, and highly effective implementation of proven quality principles and techniques. You can measure an organization's performance by the sigma level of their business processes.

The 14 Principles of The Toyota Way, created by the Toyota Corporation is a management philosophy that includes the Toyota Production System. Guiding principles of The Toyota Way are to base management decisions on a "philosophical sense of purpose" and to think long term, to have a process for solving problems, to add value to the organization by developing its people, and to recognize that continuously solving root causes drives organizational learning.

You add, "According to the American Society for Quality, eighty-two of the one hundred largest companies in the United States have embraced Six Sigma. Lean Six Sigma is steamrolling the nation as well. When companies start paying attention to process improvement, they can realize huge improvements in productivity and profitability. Recent research tells us that efforts like Lean Six Sigma are certainly needed. For example, in the service industry, slow production and rework accounts for between 30 and 50 percent of the actual cost of producing and delivering a service. Think of how much better off any company would be when they pay attention to processes and controls. Sure we would eat up some time and dollars in the near term should we implement Lean Six Sigma, but it will pay big dividends in the long term. For non-Lean Six Sigma companies, the cost of nonconformance is

---

* You can read about the rules at http://tinyurl.com/m2p76u.

often extremely high. Companies operating at three or four sigma typically spend between 25 and 40 percent of their revenues fixing problems. This translates to approximately 67,000 defects per million opportunities! If the rework costs just $10 per defect, an extremely low number, that's a cool $670,000! This is known as the cost of quality, or more accurately the cost of poor quality (COPQ). In companies where the COPQ is unknown, it usually exceeds the profit margin. Think what this could mean to our competitiveness when we're at three sigma and our direct competitor is at four sigma. The dollar cost of this gap is huge. Every time you move up a sigma level, it can easily mean a 20 percent increase in profit margin. GE, a pioneer of the concept, estimates that the gap between three or four sigma and Six Sigma was costing them between $8 billion and $12 billion per year. Traditionally, companies accepted three or four sigma performance levels as the norm, despite the fact that these processes created between 6,200 and 67,000 problems per million opportunities! The Six Sigma standard of 3.4 defects per million opportunities is a response to the increasing expectations of customers and the increased complexity of modern products and processes. Companies operating at Six Sigma typically spend less than 5 percent of their revenues fixing problems."

In short, what sets Lean Six Sigma apart from its individual components is the recognition that you cannot do "just quality" or "just speed," you need the balanced process that can help an organization focus on improving service quality, as defined by the customer within a set time limit.

Simple tools, simple questions, and common sense enhance customer experience, maximize growth, and enhance profitability—regardless of business size and structure.

Lean Six Sigma Benefits

Lean Six Sigma for services is a business improvement methodology that maximizes shareholder value by achieving the fastest rate of improvement in customer satisfaction, cost, quality, process speed, and invested capital. The fusion of Lean and Six Sigma improvement methods is required because:

- Lean itself cannot bring a process under statistical control.
- Six Sigma alone cannot dramatically improve process speed or reduce invested capital
- Both enable the reduction of the cost of complexity.

"While the CEO and CFO mull over what you said, you weigh in with this: Evolving from Japanese manufacturing initiatives like Kaizen (continuous improvement), Kanban (just-in-time or JIT), Toyota Production System (TPS), and 5S (Visual Workplace), Lean is geared toward waste elimination and value-chain improvements. When a company maximizes process flow and flexibility, it can achieve breakthrough financial impacts. Like Six Sigma, it is dependent on process data, but it also requires data integration and forecasting capabilities."

Why Is Its Use Not Rampant?

The CFO asks the obvious question: "Why isn't every business utilizing Lean and Six Sigma?"

You say, "I'm glad you asked. You would think the benefits of an increase in performance and decrease in process variation leading to defect reduction and vast improvement in profits, employee morale, and quality of product would be enough. But the truth is that many companies choose not to implement Lean and Six Sigma because they think it is too complicated. In essence they are saying it's the philosophy of Lean and Six Sigma that doesn't work for them, claiming they do not have the time to build an infrastructure, train staff, and dive deeply into statistical analysis. They say the effort is too burdensome and would slow down their fast-paced world of meeting customer demands. Unfortunately, most of these companies are not actually meeting customer demands because they don't know what their customers really want. Lean Six Sigma is a quality objective that specifies the variability required of a process in terms of the specifications of the product so that product quality and reliability meet and exceed today's demanding customer requirements. Even though they need a systematic approach to making change happen, they can't get past the perception that Lean and Six Sigma is all about statistics and too complex. By eliminating all the emotive statements people tend to attach to problems, you can create a statistical solution and turn that into a practical reality.

"If you went to any IT department, including ours, and asked the first person you met what it was they did around there, they'd respond by saying they were in system administration or application development. With much prodding, they would eventually say retail, manufacturing, government, or finance. IT is insulated in most cases from the customer. People working in traditional functional organizations often have difficulty seeing how their work relates to other departments and, more important, how their work relates to customers. This is especially true for centralized service units such as technology, operations, and finance. Sure if we were Microsoft or Hewlett-Packard, our employees would be in the business of IT. But we're not. Each department in our organization should know where it fits in the organization and how it lines up with what our customers want. Our business architecture needs to become a visual aid linking customers, business processes, and support activities. The picture needs to focus on processes and customers—not departments. The business architecture forms a foundation for many management practices and programs including Lean and Six Sigma. Although the term business architecture sounds theoretical, companies with a clear business architecture, captured in a simple diagram that all employees understand, can accelerate their progress toward their strategic goals.

"Left to their own devices, employees doing work will always think there is one right perspective: theirs. Rarely do people see themselves as working to satisfy customers. The more departments you have—even if there's only one person in each—the harder it is for people to see how work fits together to create customer satisfaction. People need a road map; what the Lean Six Sigma advocates call a 'process map.' Process mapping takes the business architecture structure and Hoshin planning techniques to the next level by accurately depicting both current and future environments. Creating these diagrams is a dynamic and iterative process. It usually helps to flush out non-value-added work.

"Compensation and incentives can be based on measures and aligned with processes. Customer research can be redirected. Products can be reviewed for their effectiveness in the processes that customers care most about. Our technology projects can be redirected, accelerated, or killed. It will also help identify fast failures, indicators that a research program is on the wrong track. Just imagine all the possible improvements that a company could make. From the tape librarian to the application developer, hundreds of processes are waiting to be improved. No matter what we're doing, it's possible to complement scientific knowledge and experimentation with analytical and statistical methods to weed out practices that get us where we want to go faster.

"The heart of it all is very simple. In fact, it's just good business. Start with the customer: no revenue, no company, just the customer. The customer comes first. Always. You need to ask the big questions: Do we actually know what our customer wants? Have we asked? How much effort does it take to produce what our customer wants? Do our people respond to the customer the same way when situations recur?"

It's Not Just for Manufacturing

Your boss challenges you: "But we are not a manufacturing company and IT is definitely not one." You counter: "High-quality claims are not the domain of manufacturing! Anyway, it's a mistake to view Lean and Six Sigma as exclusive to 'hard' manufacturing. Despite its origins in manufacturing, Lean Six Sigma isn't about widgets; its focus is on processes. Every day people go to work and have a process for getting their work done. Every day, chances are, there are better ways of doing it quicker and more efficiently. Quickness and efficiency equal a better product or service, a happier customer, and higher profits for the company. LSS has been very successfully used in transactional and service industries as LSS is a best practice for process improvement.

"Any group operating and maintaining an IT enterprise cannot survive without processes. Our IT function includes a range of activities that includes the planning for, the acquisition and installation of, as well as the operation and support of various hardware and software infrastructure components, including workstations, networks, office-support tools, and communications facilities. We also acquire and modify application software. It also directly applies to software processes, but few organizations have applied it. We also operate a service desk, make changes, manage projects, and occasionally provide business process reengineering services and internal consulting to facilitate business process improvement. These are all processes and they could all stand improvement. These activities sound like simple, mundane matters until you consider our size. We have over 1,000 people working in IT.

"Lean Six Sigma works for all aspects of business, not just manufacturing production. In reality, we might find the payoffs even greater in our administrative areas because traditionally we often neglected these processes. When applied to IT operations, Lean Six Sigma can help us identify valued-added processes, and to measure and improve these internal processes, such as network throughput and reliability, and line-of-business processes where IT has a role, such as how well our online order system is working. The more complex a product or service, the more ways there are to disappoint our customers."

Gaining momentum you add, "Although Lean and Six Sigma both promote continuous improvement, they are separate tools. LSS is not purely about quality, but encompasses much more. Lean is a customer-driven philosophy with a goal of producing what customers want within the shortest lead time, whereas Six Sigma is project-focused. Lean promotes rethinking how to structure the process and Six Sigma promotes refining how to reduce variation of the existing process. Lean aims to drive down cycle times and retaining processes and subprocesses that add value while trimming or eliminating those that don't. Also Lean is an overarching program to eliminate waste, whereas Six Sigma focuses on variation in processes. When we get rid of waste and variation, we can get a more consistent process. The most important thing to remember is that when we eliminate waste, the savings directly impact the bottom line. Think of Lean as improving process speed and think of Six Sigma as improving the quality of the end product. Any end result that can be quantified will benefit from Six Sigma. Ironically, Six Sigma and Lean have often been regarded as rival initiatives. Lean enthusiasts note that Six Sigma pays little attention to anything related to speed and flow, and Six Sigma supporters point out that Lean fails to address key concepts like customer needs and variation. Both sides are right. Yet these arguments are more often used to advocate choosing one over the other, rather than to support the more logical conclusion that we blend Lean and Six Sigma. Simply put, we use Lean to move the mean and Six Sigma to reduce variability around the mean. By wedding the two, we get Lean Six Sigma: an effort to improve both process speed and product quality at the same time. The two methodologies interact and reinforce one another, such that percentage gains in return on investment (ROI) are much faster when Lean and Six Sigma are implemented together.

"If customer satisfaction is the practical problem, using Lean Six Sigma can turn this into a statistical problem we can analyze, using the Six Sigma structured framework, and turn it into a statistical solution that in turn we can change to a practical solution. It doesn't matter whether you're streamlining manufacturing or developing a new application. If you can define what you're going after and quantify those factors that are critical to quality, then you can apply Lean Six Sigma."

It's the Value, Stupid

"In IT, we are always caught up with insatiable demands and lost ROI. Lean Six Sigma could assist us with both those problems. Lean is designed to weed out non-value-adding processes. Lean inspects a process by analyzing each task or activity to determine whether it is value-added, is not value-added but necessary, or is not value-added. A value-added activity is something for which the customer is willing to pay. An example of a value-added activity is the operation of the accounting application. If we outsource this application, then an example of a non-value-added but necessary activity is the payment of the invoice. We must eliminate those activities that don't add value or are unnecessary. Backing out of an update because we didn't properly test it is non-value-added. We should therefore stop doing it. Lean Six Sigma would give us a very precise way to demonstrate the real value of technology, and it would help us improve the way we deliver that value."

The CEO and CFO look a little perplexed and they wonder whether you have been smoking your socks. You decide to use incident management as an example because it has great variation. Users sometimes call the service desk where the operative logs the call, but other users call the system analyst directly in an effort to expedite the issue. To meet the increasing demand for high-quality service, the analyst starts to work on the problem. This makes it difficult to monitor performance and to build consistency into one process. "We don't know how much this is costing the company."

Lean uses systems thinking and considers all of the process interactions while utilizing simple tools. Unlike Six Sigma, Lean does not require a lot of mathematical analysis and works well for mature, slow-growth, or low-transaction businesses.

It's about More than Reducing Costs

You add, "Lean thinking is about smooth process flows, doing only the things that add customer value and eliminating activities that don't. Even though Lean and Six Sigma are wonderful tools, I am not suggesting they are a panacea, but are these not steps that a mature, well-run organization should undertake?

"However, we must ensure that we do not use our Lean Six Sigma effort strictly as a means of reducing costs. Organizations that do so often do so at the expense of service, a critical requirement for most customers. Lean Six Sigma is essentially a comprehensive yet flexible system for achieving, supporting, and maximizing business profits.

"Lean Manufacturing and Six Sigma, the celebrated parents of Lean Six Sigma, are both about making improvements through measurements, but it is about so much more. We cannot simply focus on measurements. To prove my point I want to remind you of The McNamara Fallacy. The McNamara Fallacy, named after Robert McNamara, the U.S. Secretary of Defense in the 1960s, is when you believe that when you can measure things you can manage them. McNamara was obsessed with quantifying the Vietnam War. Unfortunately, by focusing solely on measurements, he tended to ignore what was truly going on. He missed the critical-to-quality aspects of the war. And we all know how that worked for him!

"Lean focuses on eliminating non-value-added and unnecessary tasks. Tasks are value-added when the customer is willing to pay for them. Some tasks like charge-back are non-value-added, but are necessary for business operations. The Lean methodology is focused on the bottom line but does not directly address quality."

Further you explain, "Lean Six Sigma might start in IT, but to reap the full benefits of Lean Six Sigma, we must apply the methodology organization-wide. Lean Six Sigma is about change, so there is a natural resistance to it. A way to soften resistance is by obtaining buy-in at the earliest point on our adoption road-map. Of course, as leaders we must single-mindedly inculcate Lean and Six Sigma into every corner of the organization. Leadership is the key to the success of any plan attempting to change the way an organization does business. Without the support, participation, and leadership of top- and mid-level management and the development of an appropriate infrastructure, any program is destined to become just another fad or the latest flavor-of-the-month program. Lean Six Sigma can fail when top management doesn't understand or won't buy into the idea or employees aren't committed to the process."

You explain that W. Edwards Deming, a leader in quality and the most revered business gaijin in Japan, believed strongly in leadership. Deming (2000, p. 248) summarized the role of leaders in *Out of the Crisis* as:

> The aim of leadership should be to improve the performance of man and machine, to improve quality, to increase output, and simultaneously to bring pride of workmanship to people. Put in a negative way, the aim of leadership is not to find and record failures of men, but to remove the causes of failure: to help people to do a better job with less effort.

"Generally, you'll find four types of managers with respect to Lean Six Sigma: support LSS and get results, do not support LSS but get results, support LSS but do not get results, and do not support LSS and do not get results. We want to find those managers who support LSS and get results and use these people as champions to spread the good word. We need to convince those managers who do not support LSS and get results so that they could get even better results. Those managers who do not support LSS but do get results are the old Theory X managers who believe they have all the answers. We have a lot of those in our organization. We'll need to find these people and work on awareness with them to change their behaviors. Otherwise they will work behind the scenes to undermine our efforts. They are difficult to identify at first. Those who support Lean but do not get results require coaching. Eventually, they might need career coaching. Managers who do not support Lean and do not get results need to move along in one way or another.

"Much of what makes the workplace successful has to do with things that cannot be measured: integrity, team spirit, dedication, and loyalty. Overlooking these things—or dismissing them—is downright dangerous.

"Lean Six Sigma is a business-driven, multipronged approach to process improvement, reduced costs, and increased profits. With a fundamental principle to improve customer satisfaction by reducing defects, its ultimate performance target is virtually defect-free processes and products. Within this improvement framework, it is the responsibility of the improvement team to identify the process, the definition of defect, and the corresponding measurements. This degree of flexibility enables the Lean Six Sigma method, along with its toolkit, to easily integrate with existing guidance. Jack Welch, former GE Chair, said 'An organization's ability to learn, and translate that learning into action rapidly, is the ultimate competitive advantage.'

"Finally, some of the country's largest IT organizations are looking trim and vigorous these days. It's no miracle cure or diet of the month. It's not slash and burn. It's a particular piece of process methodology called Lean Six Sigma."

Fortunately, or unfortunately, the CEO buys your pitch and gives you the go-ahead. Now you must figure out how to make it work with your IT governance and compliance programs. If this is your dilemma, you have come to the right place. We aim to explain the various IT governance guidances and how to use them with Lean and Six Sigma. Believe it or not, there is great synergy here. Almost every major piece of guidance focuses on continuous improvement.

As you will see in Chapter 3, the problem facing you is not that there isn't any IT governance that focuses on process improvement, but that there is too much. As well, the available guidance, although referencing efficiency by recommending the Plan-Do-Check-Act (PDCA) methodology, does not specifically address efficiency. It is left to the reader to determine how to measure efficiency and effectiveness. Prior to the development of LSS, process improvement methods were narrowly focused. They did not address the bottom line in terms of what is critical to the customer and the cost of poor quality.

Also, in the past IT was considered an art and not a science. Outside of the manufacturers, there was little science in computer science. It is imperative in today's world, however, that every organization start to focus on quantitative measures as well as qualitative measures.

We must embed quality into all IT processes. You need to change fundamentally the way your organization conducts business and makes decisions by working on key processes. In Chapter 2, we explore further the concept of processes. For now, suffice it to say we must focus on improving our processes.

Governance Benefits

Admittedly, corporate governance improves business, frequently having a positive effect on investment, market share, sales growth, sales margins, competitive advantage, and avoidance of litigation. A corporate governance program should provide the following advantages:

1. Create a more efficient and effective operation for you
2. Increase your customer satisfaction and retention
3. Reduce the impact of audits
4. Enhance your marketing
5. Improve employee motivation, awareness, and morale
6. Increase profits
7. Reduce waste and cycle times
8. Increase your productivity

This list dovetails nicely with LSS. Lean Six Sigma's main objective is to deliver high performance, value, and reliability to the customer. The primary goal of Lean Six Sigma is to improve customer satisfaction, and thereby profitability, by reducing and eliminating defects. Defects can be related to any aspect of customer satisfaction: high product quality, meeting schedules, or cost minimization. Underlying this goal is the Taguchi Loss Function, which shows that increasing defects leads to increased customer dissatisfaction and decreased financial loss.

All these benefits are available to some degree by merely standardizing processes, but to truly see phenomenal improvements, you must focus on quality management. As you will see in Chapter 3, almost every methodology now embraces PDCA, as the logic is sound. However, these same methodologies stop short by not providing the tools to do it.

Today's customer- and service-driven IT shops are using internal control frameworks as a business tool. Some of these IT shops were forced to look at governance frameworks to meet their fiduciary responsibilities, whereas others do so because they need to improve internal control. Through the use of properly stated quality objectives, customer satisfaction surveys, and a well-defined continuous improvement program, IT shops are using standardized processes to increase their efficiency, effectiveness, and profitability. However, many IT organizations have great difficulty measuring organizational efficiency and effectiveness, despite a bewildering array of metrics that have been proposed and occasionally used. A basic yet powerful set of metrics that gets to the heart of these issues does exist, and at the same time facilitates the application of Lean Six Sigma. It is measuring effectiveness from the perspective of execution that is the objective here. The concerns addressed are cost, quality, and cycle time.

Figure 1.1 illustrates the relationship among some of the guidance we discuss in this book.

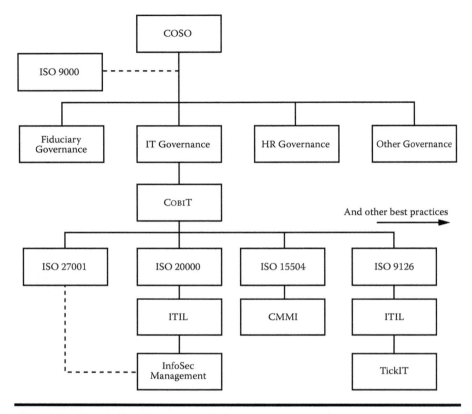

Figure 1.1   Enterprise governance framework.

Prescriptive versus Proscriptive

The CIO must truly understand the myriad frameworks and standards and how they fit together to truly understand how to effectively and efficiently manage IT resources and to maximize the use of Lean Six Sigma in IT. For the purpose of this chapter we refer to these documents collectively as guidance. Guidance is an appropriate term because the frameworks and standards are not prescriptive; they are proscriptive. Proscriptive refers to the codification and the enforcement of rules governing how an organization operates. If it helps to distinguish the difference, think of a prescription the doctor gives; you take it as instructed. If it was a proscription, the doctor would make you stay in the hospital while he or she administered the drug. Prescription is an instruction, whereas proscription is a prohibition.

The Sarbanes–Oxley Act of 2002 (SOX) is proscriptive for some companies, which means when you are a publicly traded company on a U.S. stock exchange, you must meet the rules. Table 1.1 illustrates that the United States does not have a monopoly on fiduciary governance.

Table 1.1 Worldwide Proscriptive Guidance

Country	Legislation
Argentina	Central Bank of Argentina A4609
Australia	CLERP 9
Austria	Austrian Code of Corporate Governance
Belgium	Belgian Corporate Governance Code (Code Lippens)
Brazil	Central Bank of Brazil 3380
Canada	Bill 198
EU	OECD Principles of Corporate Governance
France	LSF (Loi sur la Sécurité Financière)
Germany	Deutscher Corporate Governance Kodex
India	SEBI Clause 49
Ireland	Electronic Commerce Act 2000—Implements Directive 1999/93/EC
Italy	L262/2005
Japan	J-SOX
Luxembourg	Commission nationale pour la protection des données (CNPD)
Mexico	Ley del Mercado de Valores
Netherlands	Code Tabaksblat
Singapore	Code of Corporate Governance
South Africa	King Code II 2002
Sweden	Swedish Code of Corporate Governance
Switzerland	Registre du droit communautaire pertinent pour les accords bilatéraux Suisse-CE du 21 juin 1999 et du 26 octobre 2004
The Netherlands	Archiefwet 1995 & Archiefbesluit 1995
United States	Sarbanes–Oxley Act of 2002

The guidance referenced in this chapter is prescriptive, which means at this time no outside entity can force you to use any of it. Some guidance is very general, applying to any going concern, whereas other guidance is more specific to IT. Table 1.2 shows you a breakdown of the guidance and how you could use it.

A savvy CIO will leverage guidance from each row, realizing that one framework or standard doesn't solve all the issues of a dynamic IT department. She knows that you adopt and adapt and mix-and-match until you have the right control framework. In this manner, she will manage IT assets effectively and efficiently.

As CIO, you must appreciate how the various available guidance dovetails with the organization's Lean and Six Sigma efforts. Your Lean Six Sigma efforts will succeed, and indeed thrive, when you integrate them with other internal control mechanisms, which means you must consider those efforts holistically and not in isolation. Lean Six Sigma is a business-driven, multifaceted approach to process improvement, reduced costs, and increased profits. With a fundamental principle to improve customer satisfaction by reducing defects, its ultimate performance target is virtually defect-free processes and products. Within this improvement framework, it is the responsibility of the improvement team to identify the process, the definition of defect, and the corresponding measurements. This degree of flexibility enables the Lean Six Sigma method, along with its toolkit, to easily integrate with existing models of software process implementation. This is where the IT guidance helps. For instance, Control Objectives for Information and Related Technology (CobiT) provides the process, the base controls, and key goal and performance indicators.

In the software and systems field, Lean Six Sigma can be leveraged differently based on the state of the business. In an organization needing process consistency, the guidance in Table 1.2 can help promote the establishment of a process. For an organization striving to streamline their existing processes, Lean Six Sigma can be used as a refinement mechanism.

Following a Lean and Six Sigma philosophy to create a more customer- and service-centric organization need not be complicated, burdensome, or cost prohibitive. It all begins with understanding what your customer wants from you. The business architecture, Hoshin plan, and process maps support a well-thought-out customer strategy. They help create a strategy aimed at enhancing the customer experience while maximizing growth and profitability. This differentiates an organization from its competition and gives employees direction in how to do their jobs each and every day.

So why delay? There is no time like the present to start your journey beyond CobiT and Information Technology Infrastructure Library (ITIL) with a discussion of processes—the basic component of your business.

Table 1.2   Guidance Compared

Category	Type	Examples
IT governance	Focus on how to manage information and information and communications technology efficiently and effectively.	CobiT, ISO 38500, Val IT
Information management	Focus on how to perform and organize IT management, such as service delivery and support.	Generic Framework for Information Management, ITIL
Quality management	Focus on quality standards, applied to specific IT domains.	TQM, ISO 9000, ISO 10006, ISO 20000, ISO 27001
Quality improvement	Focus on improvement of processes or performance.	IT BSC, ITS-CMM, Six Sigma
Project management	Focus on portfolio, program, and project management.	MSP, PMBOK, PRINCE2
Risk management	Focus on identifying and managing risk.	ISO 31000, M_o_R, OCTAVE, FIRM

Chapter 2

You Say Pro-ses and I Say Pra-ses, Let's Do the Whole Thing Right!

With our apologies to George and Ira Gershwin, it doesn't matter how you pronounce process but it does matter what you do with it. Business processes matter. As mentioned in Chapter 1, organizations are a conglomeration of business processes. These business processes are, in turn, a collection of interrelated subprocesses, activities, steps, or tasks that accomplish or support a particular goal or purpose. In other words, a process is a specific temporal and spatial ordering of work activities, with a beginning and an end, and clearly defined inputs and outputs. Usually, you can decompose a business process into several subprocesses, which have their own attributes, but also contribute to achieving the goal of the process. A process can cross functional boundaries; that is, it could range over several business functions. As a company is an assemblage of processes, it makes sense to focus on improving processes rather than inspecting outputs.

To really become a world-class organization and to meet the myriad laws and regulations impacting your organization, you must recognize that there is an increased requirement for improved process understanding. Understanding is key. W. Edwards Deming talked about a system of profound knowledge and its four constituent parts, one being the appreciation of a system. This appreciation entails thoroughly understanding the overall processes involving the suppliers, producers, and customers of goods and services. As Deming suggests, without appreciation our knowledge is meager. You might have the most compelling vision ever, but as

Colin Powell, former U.S. Secretary of State, once said, "Vision without execution is hallucination."* Execution matters.

Process Components and Characteristics

Before you can study your processes, you need to understand the component parts of a process, illustrated in Figure 2.1.

A process needs clearly defined boundaries—input and output—and consists of smaller parts—activities—that are ordered in time and space. There must also be a receiver of the process outcome—the customer—and the transformation taking place within the process must add customer value. The characteristics of a business process are as follows:

- *Structure:* A process cannot exist on its own; it is embedded in an organizational structure.
- *Definable:* It has clearly defined activities, input, and output.
- *Order:* It consists of activities ordered according to their position across time and in space.
- *Value-adding:* The transformation adds value to the customer, either upstream or downstream.
- *Customer:* There is a recipient of the process outcome or output; that is, the customer.
- *Cross-functional:* A process could, but does not necessarily, span several functions.

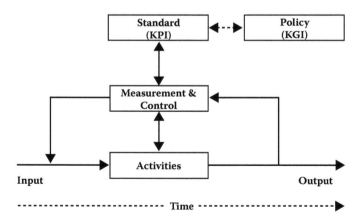

Figure 2.1   The process model.

---

* http://www.industryweek.com/ReadArticle.aspx?ArticleID=14348.

The illustration, definition, and preceding characteristics imply certain things, including a measured set of activities designed to produce a specific output from certain inputs. You might find these tasks broken down into tasks or steps.

The process must transform the inputs; otherwise nothing has happened and there is no value added. Business processes must add value for the customer and should not include unnecessary activities. Sometimes when we document a process we come to the startling realization that we have done nothing with the process. Your internal or external customers do not want to pay for unnecessary activities!

Processes are the necessary structure that determines what an enterprise does to produce value for its customers. The activities transform the inputs into outputs. Ideally, the transformation that occurs in the process adds value to the input and creates an output that is more useful and effective to the recipient either upstream or downstream.

Our definition also emphasizes the constitution of links between activities and the transformation that takes place within the process. A business process begins with the customer's need and ends with the customer's satisfaction. It is the value that we discuss in Chapter 4.

Processes are performing optimally when the result of the process is at the expected value and there is minimal variation. The outcome of a well-designed business process is increased effectiveness (value for the customer) and increased efficiency and more economy (reduced costs for the company).

Types of Business Processes

The business process output is either a product or service. Some processes result in a product or service that is received by an organization's external customer. We call these operational or primary processes. Other processes produce products or services that are invisible to the external customer but are essential to the effective management of the business. We call these support processes, and most IT processes fall into this category. Attempts to meet the requirements of legislation such as SOX show us IT is a key business process, reaching throughout the entity. In addition, we have another secondary type of process: management process. To summarize, the three types of processes are:

1. Operational processes, which constitute the core business and create the primary value stream. We talk about value streams and mapping them in Chapter 4. Examples include manufacturing and sales.
2. Supporting processes, which support the core processes. Examples include accounts payable, recruitment, and IT change management.
3. Management processes, which govern the operation of a system. Examples include strategic planning, budgeting, and value management.

Value chains build on a division of primary and secondary activities. A successful process-based organization demonstrates the absence of secondary activities in the primary value flow created in the customer-oriented primary processes.

A process system is a specialized system of processes. Processes are comprised of other processes. Complex processes are made up of several processes that are in turn made up of several other processes. This results in an overall structural hierarchy of abstraction. If you study the process system hierarchically, it is easier to understand and manage; therefore, process architecture requires the ability to consider process systems hierarchically.

Process Management

Any process needs management or control. With CoBiT 4.1, Information Systems Audit and Control Association (ISACA) provided generic control requirements as shown in Table 2.1. They recommend that you consider these objectives and activities as well as the specific process control objectives and activities to have a complete view of control requirements and necessary activities. The generic control objectives provide the characteristics of any process.

You could define IT processes within your enterprise, but if your enterprise is like others, it performs certain functions such as change management or problem management. In the next chapter, we introduce you to sundry enterprise and IT guidance. For now, we use CoBiT to illustrate IT processes. In Figure 2.2 you can see the thirty-four IT processes specified within the CoBiT framework. ISACA believes these to be the necessary and sufficient set to govern IT in any organization. If you look at the framework, you can see that it roughly follows a system development life cycle (SDLC).

The focus of CoBiT is to work on continuously improving the core IT processes. Change management programs are typically involved to put the improved business processes into practice. ISACA provides an implementation guide to assist you in doing this.

We could, and do, focus on any one of the processes in CoBiT, ITIL, Capability Maturity Model Integration (CMMI), and so on, but to illustrate we focus on only one now. Because of SOX, the Gramm–Leach–Bliley Act (GLBA), Basel II, and so on, IT compliance has moved into everyone's consciousness. The activities of a simple IT compliance process might include the following:

1. Establish the scope of the compliance effort.
2. Assign employees to specific compliance-related tasks.
3. Screen personnel to ensure job functions don't overlap.
4. Communicate and train employees on good compliance practices.
5. Enforce corporate policies and rules about compliance.
6. Prevent policy breaches through monitoring and enforcement.
7. Monitor ongoing compliance efforts and consider improvements.

Table 2.1   Generic Control Objectives

Number	Objective	Activity	Comments
PC1	Process goals and objectives	Define and communicate specific, measurable, actionable, realistic, results-oriented, and timely (SMARRT) process goals and objectives for the effective execution of each IT process. Ensure that they are linked to the business goals and supported by suitable metrics.	In Chapter 5, we talk about coming up with SMARRT, SMART (specific, measurable, actionable, realistic, timely) or RUMBA (reasonable, understandable, measurable, believable, achievable) goals using problem-solving tools.
PC2	Process ownership	Assign an owner for each IT process, and clearly define the roles and responsibilities of the process owner. Include, for example, responsibility for process design, interaction with other processes, accountability for the end results, measurement of process performance, and the identification of improvement opportunities.	The process owner is responsible for the process results and continuous improvement. The process manager is responsible for the realization and structure of the process and reports to the process owner. Process operatives are responsible for executing the defined activities and reporting to the process manager.
PC3	Process repeatability	Design and establish each key IT process such that it is repeatable and consistently produces the results. Provide for a logical but flexible and scalable sequence of activities that will lead to the desired results and is agile enough to deal with exceptions and emergencies. Use consistent processes, where possible, and tailor only when unavoidable.	Most guidance favors the automation of the process to increase the likelihood of repeatability and to reduce process variance.

Table 2.1 Generic Control Objectives (Continued)

Number	Objective	Activity	Comments
PC4	Roles and responsibilities	Define the key activities and end deliverable of the process. Assign and communicate unambiguous roles and responsibilities for effective and efficient execution of the key activities and their documentation as well as accountability for the process end deliverables.	Use RACI, ARCI, RASCI, or RACIO (responsible, accountable, consulted, informed, omitted or out-of-the-loop) charts to show unambiguously roles and responsibilities.
PC5	Policy, plans, and procedures	Define and communicate how all policies, plans, and procedures that drive an IT process are documented, reviewed, maintained, approved, stored, communicated, and used for training. Assign responsibilities for each of theses activities and, at appropriate times, review whether they are executed correctly. Ensure that the policies, plans, and procedures are accessible, correct, understood, and up to date.	Lays down rules, guidelines, and behavior patterns that, when followed, lead to the desired process performance. In business processes, process requirements are policies that must be fulfilled by acceptable procedures. The policy defines the process key goal indicators (KGIs) and the standards define the process KPIs. Processes are described using procedures and work instructions. The procedures define the steps, tasks, or activities necessary to meet the KGIs.

| PC6 | Process performance improvement | Identify a set of metrics that provides insight into the outcomes and performance of the process. Establish targets that reflect on the process goals and performance indicators that enable the achievement of process goals. Define how the data are to be obtained. Compare actual measurements to targets and take action on deviations, where necessary. Align metrics, targets, and methods with IT's overall performance monitoring approach. Effective controls reduce risk, increase the likelihood of value delivery, and improve efficiency because there will be fewer errors and a more consistent approach. | CobiT, ITIL, CMMI, and others provide metrics. Six Sigma gives you the tools to assess the validity of the metrics. |

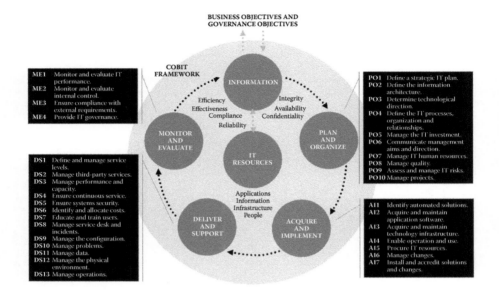

Figure 2.2 The thirty-four CoBiT processes.

Now you have the activities, so you need only decide who owns this process and develop a responsible, accountable, consulted, informed/accountable, responsible, consulted, informed (RACI/ARCI) chart for the activities. Table 2.2 illustrates a typical ARCI chart.

Process management is the specific set of activities of planning and monitoring the performance of a process. It is the application of knowledge, skills, tools, techniques, and systems to define, visualize, measure, control, report, and improve processes with the goal of meeting customer requirements economically, efficiently, and effectively. It differs from program management in that program management

Table 2.2 ARCI Chart

Activity	LOB CIO	LOB BM	SOX Reviewer	Support Operations	InfoSec Management	BM	Subject Matter Expert
Identify new SOX applications.	A	R		C	C	C	I
Manage changes to the SOX application list.				A/R		I	I
Publish the list.				A/R			

is concerned with managing a group of interdependent projects. Simply put, process management is the work that you must do to improve and master the processes you need to provide value to the customer.

Process Mapping

Just talking about processes doesn't help us understand them. Looking at them from 40,000 feet isn't going to do it. You must dig right in and analyze your processes to determine whether they support your key business objectives. When we read through procedure documents and talk to managers and supervisors about the processes, we gain an understanding that is at least one step closer to reality. Should you document processes using this information, you'll find the documentation does not reflect reality. Figure 2.3 depicts this situation. To understand a process, we need two things: the right information and a detailed illustration of the process.

Pictorially the process manager can understand what the process does, where the work occurs, who does the work, and how long it takes to complete the work. Creating the illustration is as simple as asking who, what, when, where, how, and why. To define an existing process (the as-is chart), you need to answer these questions: Who does the work? What is happening? When is it done? Where is it done? How is it done? Of course, the "Why is this done?" question needs answering, but is not necessary to document the process. This is really the value question.

Your appreciation of business processes typically starts with the mapping of processes and subprocesses down to the activity level. An organization can map business processes using a large number of methods and techniques. Business process mapping refers to activities involved in defining exactly what a business entity does, who is responsible, to what standard a process should be completed, and how the success of a business process can be determined. International Organization for Standardization (ISO) 9001 requires a business entity to follow a process approach when managing its business, and to this end creating business process maps will assist. In Chapter 4, we look at different ways to map the process.

| Perception | Reality | Desired |

Figure 2.3   Process states.

Before you can improve business processes, you must first illustrate them. The first step in gaining control over your IT function is to know and understand the basic processes. The hardest task in business process mapping is getting everyone to agree on what the process looks like. The starting point is an illustration of the process. The production of a process illustration is an iterative activity. The more widely circulated the draft illustrations, the more accurate the final "as-is" illustration should be. Once you have illustrated a process, there should be no uncertainty as to the requirements of the business process.

The entity can then work toward ensuring its processes are effective (the right process is followed the first time) and efficient (continually improved to ensure processes use the least amount of resources).

Process mapping has in recent years developed due to software tools that can attach metadata to activities, drivers, and triggers to provide a more complete understanding of processes. For example, you can attach to an activity the applicable data elements, such as key performance indicators (KPIs), times, volumes, documents, files, databases, and compliance requirements, to improve understanding and achieve several business goals simultaneously. Constructive analysis might include the identification of duplicated data elements, duplicated effort, and proof or lack of proof of compliance.

You could use business process mapping to communicate a wide variety of information to a wide variety of audiences. Process mapping has always been a key aspect of business process reengineering, and continuous improvement approaches are seen in Lean and Six Sigma.

The Process Document

In addition to illustrating the process, it is necessary to document the process adequately. A process description might include the content shown in Table 2.3.

Let's look at the components of the process description in the table of contents.

Document Control Information

The document control information includes information about the owner and authors and current and past copies.

Document Owner

The document should include information regarding those individuals or groups responsible for the creation, publishing, and updates made to the document, as well as the ultimate users of the process.

Table 2.3   Process Description Table of Contents

Document Control Information
Document Owner
Change Control
Document Review
Document Approval
1 Process Overview
1.1 Description
1.2 Process Scope
1.3 Process Objectives
1.4 Process Benefits
1.5 Process Overview
1.6 Process Metrics
1.7 Process Principles
1.8 Process Flow
1.9 Process Description
1.10 Process ARCI
2 Roles & Responsibilities
3 Glossary and Definitions

Change Control

You should include information that details the history of changes made to the document along with its associated document version. This information would include the dates and the names of the revisers. It should also highlight the revision changes, so that the reader can find them.

Document Review

You should include information regarding those individuals or groups that reviewed the content of the document for its accuracy, adaptability, and practicality.

Document Approval

Similarly, you should include information regarding those individuals or groups that signed off on the content of the document. Obviously, the accountable person will sign off, as will those shown as having a role in or responsibility for the process.

Description

You should use this section to provide a high-level narrative of the process.

Process Scope

You need to define the scope of the process. Is it restricted to one group? Is it cross-functional?

Process Objectives

In this section, you should outline the value of the process to the business. What problem is it trying to solve? What is the point of the process?

Process Benefits

Process benefits are the value statement. Does this process help meet a law or regulation? Does it help improve overall efficiency? Effectiveness? Does it improve quality? Does it provide consistency of results?

Process Overview

You should use this section to define the major activities or subprocesses for the process.

Process Metrics

Process metrics are essential in providing feedback on business and technical performance, measurement of process effectiveness and efficiency, identification of continuous process improvement opportunities, identification of compliance issues, and aid in strategic decision support. You need live and historical reporting to fully support any given process. When creating metrics, you should address the following four types of metrics:

1. *Performance metrics:* For example, mean time from security event open to security event closed.

2. *Quality metrics:* For example, total security events matched against known errors.
3. *Value metrics:* For example, number of security events processed by more than two groups.
4. *Volume metrics:* For example, total number of security events opened.

Process Principles

You should consider and document the founding principles meant to guide the design and delivery of the process. If you are talking about a security process, you could use any of the following principles:

- Confidentiality
- Integrity
- Availability
- Accountability
- Proportionality
- Transparency
- Cost-effectiveness
- Timeliness
- Integration

That's a good start, but should you not like this list or want more, search out a copy of the Generally Accepted System Security Principles document* for a discussion of other information security principles.

Process Flow

You want to document the flow pictorially. We will see later that there are many ways to show the flow, for example, using flowcharts; swim-lane diagrams; suppliers, inputs, process, outputs, customers (SIPOC) diagrams; or value stream maps.

Process Description

The process description usually takes the form shown in Table 2.4. You use it to define the various activities.

Process ARCI

You should include a RACI/ARCI/responsible, accountable, supportive, consulted, informed (RASCI) chart showing the functions that are responsible, accountable,

---

* http://www.infosectoday.com/Articles/gassp.pdf.

Table 2.4 Process Description

Step	Description	Inputs	Outputs	Role(s) Involved	Enabling Tools
1. Start security event tracking	Client must inform Security Operations of a security event.	Notification to Security	Tracking log	Security Operation LOB	Event management database

supportive, consulted, and informed about the process. Table 2.2 above illustrates an ARCI chart.

Roles and Responsibilities

You should detail the process roles and responsibilities that interested parties should view as the minimum required set of roles and responsibilities needed for the proper operation and management of the process.

Glossary and Definitions

Last but not least, you should define terms and acronyms for the reader of the document. Don't assume that the reader is thoroughly familiar with the lingo. You surely remember the old nugget about what assume means.

That's it. Now you have a properly documented process that would make any ISO 9000 assessor smile.

Process Library

As you document more and more processes, you need to consider how you are going to manage the processes and the corresponding process charts. You will want to create a library of them. A process document and chart library will help to do the following:

- Provide business process transparency, allowing others to understand your processes.
- Document processes and controls to help satisfy legal and regulatory requirements, such as Sarbanes–Oxley.
- Satisfy certification requirements, such as ISO 9000.
- Support audits.
- Serve as a foundation for continuous improvement.

For your process library and continuous improvement program to survive, you must incorporate it into the business culture and it must become a way of life. This requires genuine support and encouragement from executive management, real perceived value in the minds of the operating people, and solid training with clear expectations. When the work makes sense and the people understand what they are contributing to the organization, attitudes tend to improve and innovation thrives. Good training can contribute to a good process library and a good process library can help build a good training program, so let's point your organization in that direction!

Whether you're designing a new product or service, measuring today's performance, or improving efficiency or customer satisfaction, you need to place the focus on your processes to meet customer requirements. Mastering and improving processes is not a fruitless management exercise promoted by fanatical consultants (like us), but rather a crucial step toward delivering real value to your customers.

Nearly 2,500 years ago, Confucius offered the following insights:

■ Man can make System great. It isn't System that makes man great.
■ To expect accomplishment without proper advisement is ridiculous.

You cannot expect different results by continuing to do the same thing; isn't that the definition of insanity? You must adopt a framework, adapt it to your needs, and start measuring the things that matter to your customers. Then you must make improvements.

In the next chapter, we introduce you to an embarrassment of corporate and IT guidance to help you with your improvement program, so you have no excuse!

Chapter 3

An Abundance of Wealth

As a CIO, you are aware of the avalanche of IT best practices falling in your lap. The quantity of best practices is overwhelming and somewhat daunting. Should you want a good example of what we mean, check out the Frameworks Quagmire for software development at http://www.stsc.hill.af.mil/crosstalk/1997/09/frame-works.asp. You either have to laugh or cry when you look at that Web page, and it deals with only a single area of interest to the average CIO!

So what is a best practice? For our purposes, a best practice is a technique, method, process, or activity that some individual, group, or entity has deemed more effective at delivering the desired outcome than any other known technique, method, process, or activity. Best practices can come from national, say the American National Standards Institute (ANSI) or the Canadian Standards Association (CSA), or international, say ISO or Institute of Electrical and Electronics Engineers (IEEE), standards organizations, professional associations, or consulting firms. Most IT shops practiced best practices long before someone codified them. Obviously, the best practice codifiers had to have somewhere to start. For instance, most IT shops back up their servers. No one needed to tell them to do so, especially after they got caught once with their system down.

Most CIOs have bought into the notion that using proper processes, checks, and testing helps deliver a desired outcome more consistently with fewer problems and complications. The standardization and routinization of these tasks can only help to increase efficiency. Often best practices are the most efficient (i.e., they require the least amount of effort) and effective (i.e., they deliver the best results) way of accomplishing a task, based on repeatable procedures that over time have proven themselves to many people. For example, the CobiT methodology was developed after extensive consultation and review of existing guidance and the documentation suggests that the processes and controls they provide are a necessary and sufficient set.

On the one hand, CobiT is a best practice offered by an organization that represents IT governance, audit, and security professionals. On the other hand, ISO is an international organization that codifies and gets approval for many IT best practices, including information security and IT service management systems. Both types of organizations provide a standard way of doing things that diverse enterprises can use for management, policy, and IT processes. The downside to these best-practice-setting organizations is their modus operandi. Due to the consensus-building process they use for approval, we find that their methodologies such as ITIL can become somewhat dated. This is why ITIL went through a major refresh in 2007. We expect "best of class" organizations to be on the leading edge and not on the trailing edge relating to these best practices. We expect world-class organizations to be out ahead of the best practices, creating best practices themselves.

As best practice is often a misused term, we use the term guidance. For instance, many people are starting to use the term best practice to refer to what are in fact rules; hence, our preference for the term guidance. For example, the Payment Card Industry's Data Security Standard (PCI DSS)* was considered a best practice until June 30, 2008, at which time it became a requirement. We also don't want you to confuse guidance with what people sometimes refer to in their organization as a "flavor of the month" management practice. We have all seen fads like "management by walking around" and its ilk. Guidance is different and it is just what it sounds like: It is meant to guide your organization.

This chapter focuses primarily on some of the major IT governance guidance and its relationship to Lean and Six Sigma. You will find that each guidance focuses on the need to define processes and key goal and performance indicators. However, Lean and Six Sigma really help us comprehend whether these processes are effective and efficient.

Soon enough we'll tell you about Lean and Six Sigma, but what is IT governance? Well, we can answer that by explaining that enterprise governance is the efficient and effective use of enterprise assets. To exemplify, fiduciary governance is the efficient and effective use of financial resources. Likewise IP governance is the efficient and effective use of intellectual property (IP). Logically, then, IT governance is the efficient and effective use of IT resources. Wherever you have an asset, you need governance processes. These goals, along with safeguarding of the asset, are the major accountabilities of management.

IT governance by its very essence is supported by disciplines such as:

■ Enterprise architecture.
■ Business process management and optimization.
■ Quality management.

---

* https://www.pcisecuritystandards.org/.

- IT asset management.
- IT portfolio management.
- IT security management.
- IT service management.
- Project governance.
- Project and program management in the enterprise IT context (including software engineering where appropriate).

Table 3.1 shows examples of IT guidance mapped to the preceding list.

In this chapter, we discuss some well-known general and IT guidance and how IT groups can use them with Lean and Six Sigma. However, our survey of relevant guidance is incomplete without a discussion of some general methodologies for managing IT. These tools include the following:

- Balanced Scorecard (BSC; http://www.balancedscorecard.org/): A transformational method to assess an organization's performance from four different perspectives.
- ISO 9000 (http://www.iso.org/iso/iso_catalogue/management_standards/iso_9000_iso_14000.htm): A family of standards providing guidelines relating to quality management.

Table 3.1   IT Governance Guidance

Governance Area	IT Guidance
Business service management	ITIL, Val IT
Business technology optimization	CoBIT, Theory of Constraints, Val IT
Enterprise architecture	Zachman Framework
IT asset management	ITIL, Val IT
IT portfolio management	Val IT
IT risk management	M_o_R, OCTAVE
IT security assessment	ISO 27001
IT service management	ISO 20000, ITIL
Project and program management	MSP, PMBOK, PRINCE2
Project governance	Val IT
Quality management	Balanced Scorecard, CMMI, ISO 9000, TQM

- Theory of Constraints (http://www.goldrattconsulting.com/): An over-all management philosophy to help an organization continually achieve its goals.
- Total Quality Management (TQM; http://www.asq.org/learn-about-quality/total-quality-management/overview/overview.html): A widely used and organization-wide management strategy aimed at embedding the awareness of quality into all organizational processes.

Balanced Scorecards

First used at Analog Devices in 1987, the BSC method began as a concept for measuring whether the operational activities of a company aligned with its overall objectives in terms of vision and strategy. In 1992, Robert S. Kaplan and David P. Norton began publicizing the BSC through a series of journal articles. They followed up these articles by publishing an influential book entitled *The Balanced Scorecard* (Kaplan and Norton 1996).* Subsequently, they and others have published supporting books to help people understand or implement the concepts.

As mentioned in Chapter 1, publicly traded companies tended (or still tend) to focus only on financial results. If someone approached the typical CIO with an IT infrastructure project that showed benefits five years out, the CIO was usually loath to do it. There was great focus on the short-run financial outcomes at the expense of the customer and the future. Hence organizations needed (or still need) another method of looking at and measuring outcomes. The BSC method forces organizations to focus on the human issues as well as financial outcomes by providing a more comprehensive view of a business, which in turn helps them act in their best long-run interests.

Simplistically, the BSC is a framework for measuring an organization's activities in terms of its vision and strategies. The BSC is a performance management tool to execute and monitor the organizational strategy by using a combination of financial and nonfinancial measures. It was designed to translate vision and strategy into objectives and measures across four balanced perspectives: financial, customers, internal business process, and learning and growth. Its design helps managers focus on performance metrics while balancing financial objectives with customer, process, and employee perspectives.

The BSC is simply a one-page tool for translating an organization's strategy into operating terms. Even though its design is simplistic, its use is quite sophisticated. A manager can derive a scorecard by choosing five or six suitable measures for each goal in each perspective and demonstrate some interlinking between these goals by limning causal links on the diagram. Should you prefer, the metrics you employ

---

* http://www.amazon.com/Balanced-Scorecard-Translating-Strategy-Action/dp/0875846513/ref=si3_rdr_bb_product.

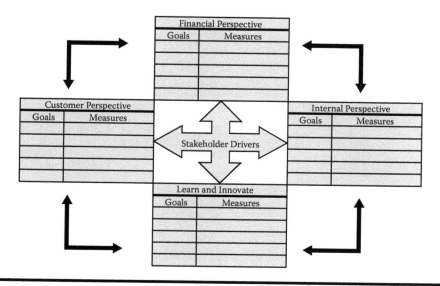

Figure 3.1   Balanced Scorecard.

to populate the BSC are key goal or performance indicators. Figure 3.1 provides a sample IT BSC template.

A criticism of BSC is that the metrics most organizations choose are not based on any proven economic or financial theory, and therefore the BSC is not a scientific method. These critics would argue a scientific method requires a method of inquiry based on gathering observable, empirical, and measurable evidence subject to specific principles of reasoning. However, as you can gather from the preceding and later description, the BSC process is entirely subjective and makes no provision to assess quantities, such as risk and economic value, in a way that is actuarially or economically well founded. However, this does not diminish its value to an IT organization. If nothing else, a good BSC framework allows all employees to see their contribution to the overall goals within the organization. To really transform the organization, you must cascade the BSC framework in your organization. Figure 3.2 demonstrates the concept of cascading. You should have the ability to tie the lowest activity back to the company's objectives through the mapping of the metrics to the strategy. This is a true motivator that does induce continual improvement. In the end, the BSC is a framework, or what we can best characterize as a strategic management system, that claims to incorporate all quantitative and abstract measures of real value to the enterprise.

You can adapt balanced scorecards to any organization or environment. CoBiT, for example, includes an IT scorecard as a method for measuring performance.

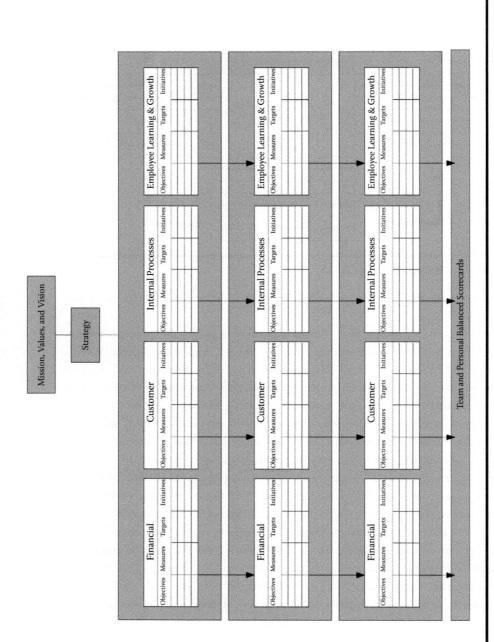

Figure 3.2 Cascading Balanced Scorecards.

Basic Principles of Balanced Scorecard

As mentioned previously, the BSC has four perspectives.

Financial Perspective

The financial perspective examines whether the company's implementation and execution of its strategy contributes to the bottom line. Most CIOs understand this perspective, as we have traditionally used it for assessing the performance of an organization. It represents the long-term strategic objectives of the organization and thus it incorporates the tangible outcomes of the strategy in traditional financial terms. Some of the most common financial measures incorporated in the financial perspective are earned value, ROI, return on invested capital (ROIC), revenue growth, costs, profit margins, cash flow, and net operating income. These are key goal indicators (KGIs) as they are lag indicators.

Customer Perspective

The customer perspective examines whether the company will satisfy customers and thus generate more sales or value to the most desired (i.e., the most profitable or important) customer groups. The measures that a company selects for the customer perspective should measure both the value delivered to the customer (value proposition), which might involve time, quality, performance, service, and cost and the outcomes that come as a result of this value proposition: customer satisfaction and market share. You can focus the value proposition on operational excellence, customer intimacy, or product leadership. Some metrics include delivery performance to customer by date, delivery performance to customer by quality, customer satisfaction rate, and customer retention rate. Again, these are KGIs as they demonstrate results.

Internal Process Perspective

The internal process perspective examines whether the processes that create and deliver the customer value proposition are necessary and sufficient. It focuses on all the activities and key processes required for the company to excel at providing the value expected by the customers both effectively and efficiently. These can include both short-term and long-term objectives as well as incorporating innovative process development to stimulate improvement. Some of the more common measures for the internal process perspective are operations management (by improving asset utilization or supply chain management), customer management (by expanding and deepening relations), innovation (by offering new products and services), and regulatory compliance and social responsibility (by establishing good relations with external stakeholders). Some metrics include the number of activities, opportunity success rate, accident ratios, and overall equipment effectiveness. These are KPIs as they are leading indicators.

Learning and Growth Perspective

The learning and growth perspective examines whether the company has the internal skills and capabilities required to support the value-creating internal processes. The learning and growth perspective is concerned with the jobs (human capital), the systems (information capital), and the climate (organization capital) of the enterprise. Some metrics include research & development (R&D) expenditures, illness and absentee rates, internal promotions, employee turnover, and gender and racial ratios. Again, these are KPIs as they provide some clues as to whether we will achieve our objectives.

BSC Implementation

Implementing a BSC typically includes four processes:

1. Translating the vision into operational goals.
2. Communicating the vision and linking it to individual performance.
3. Business planning.
4. Feedback and learning, and adjusting the strategy accordingly.

BSC will certainly continue to play a significant role in the IT governance arena, although there are competitors such as applied information economics (AIE). However, BSC is still much more widely used than AIE.

BSC and Lean Six Sigma

BSC became a generic brand for business improvement in the 1990s, rather like Six Sigma, although arguably not with the same fanfare. Perhaps this is due to the failure of organizations to understand its contribution to the bottom line. The BSC is a sophisticated strategic analysis and improvement methodology, which could exist on its own, but which you could include within Six Sigma methods. In any case, you might use or reference the BSC in the context of quality and performance improvement.

The BSC identifies, correlates, balances, measures, and drives improvement across a wide variety of factors that your organization would deem responsible for overall organizational effectiveness, and for meeting customer expectations. The tool essentially translates strategy into operational metrics, and typically features current initiatives, business processes, and business results.

In past years, there have been many instances and manifestations of quality improvement programs. We have mentioned at least one: TQM. Scrutiny of the programs will show much similarity and also clear distinctions between such

Table 3.2   Relationship of Balanced Scorecard to Lean Six Sigma

Goal	Objective	Measurement	Target	Initiative
Achieve operational efficiencies with best practices	Reduce identified reactivities within primary processes by 80% over the next three years	Waste volume charts, rework tracking, cycle time	Waste stream reductions of 5% each year, reworks cut in half for next three years, cycle time cut by 75%	Lean Six Sigma

programs and Six Sigma. Similarities include common tools and methods, concepts of continuous improvement, and even analogous steps in the improvement framework. Table 3.2 illustrates how you might make a BSC work with Lean Six Sigma.

For example, an organization might have an IT BSC that shows a KPI of operational improvement. For the IT BSC, the KGIs for a process from CobiT serve as the metrics for the financial and customer perspectives and the KPIs serve as the metrics for the internal processes and learning and growth perspectives.

Theory of Constraints

Dr. Eliyahu M. Goldratt introduced the Theory of Constraints (TOC) in his seminal 1984 book *The Goal* (Goldratt 2000). It borrowed heavily from forty years of management science research and best practice, particularly from PERT (Program Evaluation and Review Technique)/Critical Path Method (CPM) and just-in-time (JIT). Some people imprecisely refer to TOC as constraint management, but this is just a part of TOC. Whatever you want to call it, we think it is a concept most of us in IT can identify with: No one has unlimited resources. We all have constraints: MIPS, servers, time, money, and people. The theory is based on the application of scientific principles and logic to guide organizations on how to deal with these constraints. You can apply Goldratt's theory to operations, finance, distribution, project management, human resource management, strategy, sales and marketing, and most important for us, software development. In fact, Goldratt's (2000) book entitled *Necessary but Not Sufficient* dealt with software development.

TOC basically builds on Liebig's law of the minimum, which states that growth is controlled not by the total of resources available, but by the scarcest resource—the limiting factor. According to TOC, every organization has, at any given point in time, at least one constraint that limits the system's performance relative to its goal.

The constraints are broadly classified as either an internal constraint or a market constraint. For example, either you don't have enough developers—an internal constraint—or no one wants you to run their network because they don't believe you can secure it—an external constraint. To manage the performance of the system, you must identify and manage the constraint correctly. Only by increasing throughput or flow at the constraint—the bottleneck process—can you increase overall throughput.

Because of entropy or change, the constraint naturally changes over time because either you successfully managed the previous constraint or the environment has changed, so you just start your analysis again. This is obviously a continual improvement methodology. The lesson for service and IT is to apply holistic thinking.

Basic Principles of TOC

TOC is not complex: You have a set of basic principles (axioms), a few simple processes (strategic questions, focusing steps, buy-in processes, effect–cause–effect) and logic tools (the thinking processes).

TOC Axioms

In TOC the principles are treated as three axioms, and therefore have no proof, although Goldratt provides credible examples of the rationale why they succeed— derived from his consulting experience—in his books.

Convergence

Convergence or inherent simplicity is the first principle. It states that the more complex a system is to describe, the simpler it is to manage, or that the more interconnected a system is, the fewer degrees of freedom it has, and consequently the fewer points you must manage to impact the whole system. A corollary of this principle is that every organization has at least one constraint active at any given point of time; otherwise it would achieve infinite performance relative to its goal. The more complex and interconnected the organization is, the fewer constraints it will have.

Consistency

Consistency, or there are no conflicts in nature, is the second principle. It states that if two interpretations of a natural phenomenon are in conflict, one or possibly both must be wrong. That is, in an organization with a common goal, when two parts are in conflict, this means that the reasoning that led to the conflict must contain at least one flawed assumption.

Respect

Respect, or people are not stupid, is the third and final principle. It states that even when people do things that seem stupid, they have a reason for that behavior. In other words, you might have some psychopaths and sociopaths, but this principle posits that people are not inherently bad.

Ongoing Improvement Steps

The five key TOC steps for implementing an effective process of ongoing improvement are the following:

1. Identify the constraint (the thing that prevents your organization from obtaining more of the goal).
2. Decide how to exploit the constraint (make sure the constraint is doing things that are unique to it, and not doing things that it should not do).
3. Subordinate all other processes to the decision in Step 2 (align all other processes to that decision).
4. Elevate the constraint (when required, permanently increase capacity of the constraint; for example, buy or get more).
5. If, as a result of these steps, the constraint has moved, return to Step 1 (don't let inertia become the constraint).

The TOC Thinking Processes

The Thinking Processes are a set of tools offered by Goldratt to help managers walk through the steps of initiating and implementing a project. When used in a logical flow, the following Thinking Processes help walk an organization through a buy-in process:

1. Gain agreement on the problem.
2. Gain agreement on the nature of the solution.
3. Gain agreement that the solution solves the problem.
4. Agree to overcome any potential negative ramifications.
5. Agree to overcome any obstacles to implementation.

This, along with the improvement steps, is a PDCA methodology.

TOC and Lean Six Sigma

Like Six Sigma, TOC borrows heavily from preexisting theories and science. Goldratt believes that TOC should not compete with Six Sigma, but that the two are complementary and should work together to create better results and generate and disseminate more knowledge. The two approaches do come to improvement from different directions, although that is not to say that they are in any way incompatible, but they do have similarities. TOC and LSS are logic-driven approaches for analyzing root causes and promoting top-line performance to drive bottom-line growth.

TOC is an approach for managing complex systems, organizations comprised of people working in interdependent, interacting processes. The objective of TOC is to grow a system's capability to achieve more of its goal, now and in the future. The theory focuses on identifying and managing constraints, which you might find are not in the technical limitations of a process (that Six Sigma tools are so good in dealing with), but in the people involved with developing, implementing, and following the policies, procedures, and practices. Hence, a key component of the TOC body of knowledge is the logical thinking and communication tools known as the TOC Thinking Processes. These processes have much in common with our Lean processes, as you'll see later. These Thinking Processes, when used by people with special knowledge about the system in question, go a long way to providing what Deming refers to as "profound knowledge," and providing a way for managers to better predict the outcomes of their actions. Table 3.3 provides a comparison of TOC and Lean Six Sigma.

Although the two approaches are different, they are highly complementary. TOC provides an environment where the players can understand their system profoundly. It strives, with its logistical solutions like operations management, critical chain project management, and replenishment distribution, to stabilize those systems to a degree so that you can see the obvious places to apply and focus your Lean and Six Sigma efforts, and you can predict the outcome of those problem-solving efforts.

TOC-based improvement is built on the fact that bottom-line improvement comes from addressing the system's very few current constraints and looking

Table 3.3 Theory of Constraint and Lean Six Sigma Comparison

Theory of Constraint	Lean Six Sigma
Great for solving issues that are subject to qualitative analysis; that is, it is helpful for dealing with "rock and hard place" dilemmas.	Great for solving technical issues that are subject to quantitative analysis.
Root cause analysis centers on the Thinking Process known as the current reality tree.	Root causes analysis centers on traditional "quality tools" like the fishbone or Ishakawa diagram.
Analysis is appropriate for complex systems, evolved, or self-referencing systems.	Analysis is appropriate for relatively simple (designed) systems.

forward to where the next constraint might arise once you deal with the current constraint. Again, this is consistent with a PDCA methodology.

Project selection, one of the key drivers of Six Sigma success, should take advantage of the profound knowledge of the system afforded by a constraint focus. Your increased knowledge should help you to understand that the best use of Six Sigma is primarily to get more throughput through the constraint (Step 2, exploitation). You can use Lean Kaizen events and Six Sigma projects to drive waste out of the constraint. When the constraint is in an IT process, you should apply projects associated with waste reduction and uptime improvement to its operation. If the constraint is in the market (i.e., should you have more capacity than demand), then internal Six Sigma projects should be aimed at doing things that will make your offerings more attractive to potential customers, typically associated with customer response time and reliability of contracted services or products.

You can use Six Sigma tools and techniques to drive down disruptive variation in nonconstraint system processes that either interfere with or waste the output of the constraint (Step 3, subordination). Again using an IT example, once programming code has passed through an internal constraint process, function, or resource, such as quality assurance (QA), you want to treat it like gold. After all, to replace it will require another trip through the precious constraint—QA testing. Thus, any projects you initiate on downstream processes should focus on serious issues of quality of output and waste reduction. Similarly, any projects you initiate on upstream processes should primarily focus on reliability so that the constraint is never starved for work or presented with poor quality inputs.

With these kinds of projects as the focus of Six Sigma efforts, you should see maximum bottom-line results. Make sure, however, that when the constraint moves as a result of your efforts, your focus moves with it. Just when you're getting good at getting more through the system in terms of quantity, you might need to shift to thinking about speed instead of volume to attract more customers.

A basic premise of the TOC is that the more you can reduce the barriers or constraints to your performance, the closer you can come to realizing your full potential.

Although both Lean and TOC focus on reducing waste and increasing process flow, TOC goes beyond Lean with its focus on throughput. It is nice to reduce waste, but you should center your attention on making more money by selling more service or product (throughput increase), not just by cutting costs. This was the basic premise of Chapter 1.

Process improvement can result in real benefits for your organization by increasing performance, reducing waste, or improving predictability. A lot of process improvement programs are available on the market today. They all work well in different environments and look at problems differently. Whereas Six Sigma aims to reduce variation, Lean looks to reduce waste and TOC focuses on improving throughput of the entire system.

ISO 9000

ISO 9000 is a family of standards for quality management systems. The ISO supports development of the standard and national accreditation and certification bodies administer it globally. An organization independently audited and certified to conform with ISO 9001 can publicly state that it is "ISO 9001 certified" or "ISO 9001 registered." Certification to the ISO 9001 standard does not guarantee the compliance (and therefore the quality) of end services and products; rather, it certifies that the organization applies consistent business processes. ISO 9001 certification does not guarantee that the company delivers services or products of superior (or even decent) quality. It just certifies that the company engages internally in paperwork prescribed by the standard. Indeed, some companies see the ISO 9001 certification process as a marketing tool—and use it as such. An ISO certificate is not awarded forever, as the organization must renew it at regular intervals recommended by the certification body, typically every three years.

Basic Principles of ISO 9000

Figure 3.3 depicts the ISO process model. For our purposes, the key requirements specified in the standards include the following:

1. Procedures covering all key business processes.
2. Monitoring processes to ensure they are effective.
3. Keeping adequate records.
4. Checking output for defects, with appropriate and corrective action where necessary.

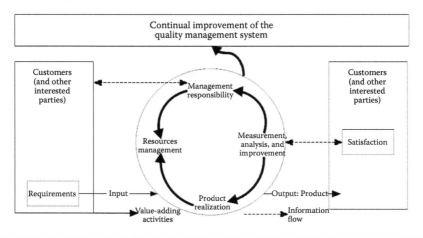

Figure 3.3 ISO 9000 process model.

5. Regularly reviewing individual processes and the quality system itself for effectiveness.
6. Facilitating continual improvement.

Although the standard originated in manufacturing, it is now employed across a wide range of organizations and products. In ISO vocabulary, a "product" can mean a physical object, service, or software.

Although ISO 9000 refers to a series of standards, you might want to look at *ISO 9001: 2000 Quality management systems—Requirements,** a document of approximately thirty pages. This standard specifies the following six compulsory documents:

1. Control of Documents
2. Control of Records
3. Internal Audits
4. Control of Nonconforming Product/Service
5. Corrective Action
6. Preventive Action

In addition to these documents, ISO 9001:2000 requires a quality policy and quality manual (that might or might not include the listed documents). The quality policy is a formal statement from management, closely linked to the business and marketing plan and to customer needs. All employees in the organization must understand and adhere to the quality policy. Each employee needs measurable objectives to work toward.

The ISO 9001 standard is generalized and abstract so you must carefully interpret its parts to figure out how to deploy it in your organization. To illustrate, a CIO might use it as it is generic, but it does not spell out specific requirements for IT. Developing software is not like baking cookies or processing loan applications; yet you can apply the ISO 9001 guidelines to each of these processes because it prescribes business management guidelines.

Over time, various industry sectors have wanted to standardize their interpretations of the guidelines within their own purview. They have done this partly to document their specific requirements, but also to try and ensure that they have more appropriately trained and experienced auditors to assess their requirements. Two IT-related interpretations are the TickIT guideline, which is useful for software development, and TL 9000, or the Telecom Quality Management and Measurement System Standard (from QuEST Forum), which includes standardized product measurements a company can use to benchmark their progress.

---

* http://www.iso.org/iso/iso_catalogue/catalogue_ics/catalogue_detail_ics.htm?csnumber=
46486.

ISO 9000 and Lean Six Sigma

ISO 9000 obliges companies to have standard processes in place that they follow: "Document what you do and do what you document." ISO 9000 involves a third-party registration program certifying that companies follow their documented processes.

Six Sigma is clearly an alternative to broad-based quality initiatives such as ISO 9000, as it works just fine with CobiT, ITIL, the Project Management Body of Knowledge (PMBOK), PRINCE2, BSC, and other operational and valuation methodologies when those methods and measures are customer-centric. ISO 9001 is useful to organizations, however, as it provides guidance on the requirements of a quality management system. As we saw in Table 1.2, there is a difference between quality management and quality improvement, the goal of Lean Six Sigma.

Total Quality Management

A progenitor of Six Sigma is a best practice known as TQM. According to the American Society for Quality, the U.S. Naval Air Systems Command first used the term total quality management "to describe its Japanese-style management approach to quality improvement."

In Chapters 1 and 2, you saw that we characterized an organization as basically a collection of processes carried out to meet the goals of the organization. TQM supports this conceptual framework. The key is that it is a strategy and a management endeavor. Total refers to the idea that the strategy applies to the entire organization, supply chain, or product life cycle. Quality refers to a degree or grade of excellence or worth. Finally, management refers to the plan, organize, staff, direct, and control steps.

In ISO 8402:1994, ISO defines TQM as "a management approach for an organization, centered on quality, based on the participation of all its members and aiming at long-term success through customer satisfaction, and benefits to all members of the organization and to society." Later we discuss the concept of customer satisfaction as it is integral to many of our methodologies, including most notably Lean and Six Sigma.

Basic Principles of TQM

A necessary component of TQM is the specification of a quality management system (QMS). The QMS process, an indicator of business excellence, forms the basis of an organization's ISO 9000, 20000, or 27001 efforts, which requires organizations seeking compliance or certification to define the processes establishing the QMS and the sequence and interaction of these processes. Like ISO 9000, TQM is a management strategy and does not specify the tools for its implementation. Lean and Six Sigma are two tools you can employ in your quality program.

TQM and Lean Six Sigma

Among process improvement approaches like TQM, only LSS requires each of the following activities:

1. Focusing on what is critical to the customer.
2. Emphasizing the bottom line.
3. Validating any claims of success.
4. Institutionalizing the process through extensive training and expertise certification.

TQM, a strategy in which an entire organization is focused on continuous improvement, arose in the 1980s in response to Japanese competition (and the work of W. Edwards Deming). TQM was very *de rigeur* during the 1992 to 1996 period but has fallen out of favor since, although it is evident in ISO 9000 and Six Sigma.

A major aim of TQM is to reduce variation from every process so that you obtain a greater consistency of effort. As you'll see in Chapter 4, this is the goal of Six Sigma. TQM requires that the organization maintain this quality standard in all aspects of its business. Obviously this book concentrates on IT, but you should broadly apply TQM in your organization. You must inculcate TQM or, for that matter, any quality management or improvement initiative, into your organization's culture. This requires ensuring that things are done right the first time and that defects and waste are eliminated from operations.

Six Sigma is similar to TQM in its focus on techniques for solving problems and using statistical methods to improve processes. Whereas TQM emphasizes employee involvement organization-wide, however, Six Sigma emphasizes training experts (the different-colored belts) who work on solving important problems while they advocate to others in the organization.

It would be a mistake to think that Six Sigma is about quality in the traditional sense. Quality, defined traditionally as conformance to internal requirements, has little to do with Six Sigma. Six Sigma is about helping the organization make more money. Refer back to Chapter 1 for a discussion of the savings realized by some organizations. To link this objective of Six Sigma with quality requires a new definition of quality. For Six Sigma purposes, we define quality as the value added by a productive endeavor. For our purposes, quality has two aspects: potential quality and actual quality. *Potential quality* is the known maximum possible value added per unit of input. *Actual quality* is the current value added per unit of input. The difference between potential and actual quality is *waste*. Lean focuses on reducing *muda,* or waste, and Six Sigma focuses on improving quality by reducing waste and helping organizations produce products and services better, faster, and cheaper. In more traditional terms, Six Sigma focuses on defect prevention, cycle time reduction, and cost savings. Unlike mindless cost-cutting programs as discussed in

Chapter 1 that reduce value and quality, Lean and Six Sigma identify and eliminate costs that provide no value to customers: the cost of waste.

Six Sigma discards a great deal of the complexity that characterized TQM. By one expert's count, there were more than 400 TQM tools and techniques. You could spend a lot of time attempting to master 400 tools. Six Sigma takes a handful of proven methods and requires that your Black Belts possess proficiency in the application of them.

BSC, ISO 9000, TOC, and TQM provide just a sampling of the diverse general guidance available to IT shops. Of more interest to a CIO is clearly the IT-specific guidance focusing on IT governance.

IT Governance

As we saw in Chapter 1, IT governance or information and communications technology (ICT) governance, a subset discipline of enterprise or corporate governance, is focused on information and related technology and their performance and risk management. The rising interest in IT governance is to some extent due to the sundry compliance initiatives (such as Sarbanes–Oxley, Bill 198, GLBA, and Basel II), as well as the acknowledgment that IT projects can easily get out of control and profoundly affect the performance of an organization or the attainment of its goals. Many organizations have felt the damaging effects of runaway or failed projects.

Astute organizations realize that they can no longer treat their IT capability as a black box and that is unknowable and unmanageable. They need to treat IT as a crystal box: transparent to the board and C-level executives. Historically, the board and C-level executives often deferred key decisions to the CIO due to their limited technical experience with IT and its perceived complexity. IT governance implies a system where all stakeholders, including the board, internal customers, and others, provide the necessary input into the decision-making process. This prevents a single stakeholder, typically IT, from taking the blame for poor decisions. It also means the organization has a shared strategy and shared results. It also prevents customers and users from later complaining that the system does not behave or perform as expected, or the board from complaining about a perceived lack of IT value.

In Chapter 1, we provided you with a definition of IT governance: the efficient and effective use of IT assets. Of course, there are narrower and broader definitions of IT governance. Weill and Ross (2004; see Appendix E) focus on "specifying the decision rights and accountability framework to encourage desirable behavior in the use of IT." The IT Governance Institute (ITGI) expands the definition to "the leadership and organisational structures and processes that ensure that the organisation's IT sustains and extends the organisation's strategies and objectives." AS 8015, the Australian Standard for Corporate Governance of Information and Communication Technology, defines ICT governance as "the system by which the current and future use of ICT is directed and controlled. It involves evaluating and directing the plans for the use of ICT to support the organisation and monitoring this use to achieve plans. It includes the strategy and policies for using ICT within an organisation." Regardless of how you define it, we should agree that IT governance focuses on the following:

1. Strategic alignment
2. Value delivery
3. Risk management
4. Resource management
5. Performance management

The discipline of IT governance derives from corporate governance and deals primarily with the connection between business focus and IT management of an organization. It highlights the importance of IT-related matters in today's organizations and states that the corporate board should own strategic IT decisions, rather than the CIO or other IT managers.

In a nutshell, the primary goals for IT governance are to do the following:

1. Assure that IT investments generate business value.
2. Mitigate the risks associated with IT.

You can achieve these goals by implementing an organizational structure with well-defined roles for the responsibility of information, business processes, applications, and infrastructure. That is the major thrust of the diverse IT governance guidance.

IT Governance Guidance

As we have seen before, it is not that we have limited or no choices, but that we have many choices to guide the implementation and governance of IT. Some of the more notable are the following:

- AS 8015-2005 (http://www.saiglobal.com/): Australian Standard for Corporate Governance of Information and Communication Technology.
- CoʙɪT (Control Objectives for Information and Related Technology; http://itgi.org/): Another approach to standardize good IT control practices.
- ISO/IEC 27001 (http://www.iso.org): A set of best practices for organizations to follow to implement and maintain a security program. It started out as British Standard 7799 (BS7799 Part 2). Typically organizations use ISO 27001 with another well-known ISO standard (ISO/IEC 27002, formerly ISO/IEC 17799).

- ISO/IEC 38500:2008 (http://www.iso.org): Another framework for effective governance of IT to assist those at the highest level of the organization to understand and fulfill their legal, regulatory, and ethical obligations in respect of their organization's use of IT. ISO/IEC 38500 is applicable to organizations of all sizes, including public and private companies, government entities, and not-for-profit organizations. It provides guiding principles for directors of organizations on the effective, efficient, and acceptable use of IT within their organizations.
- Information Security Management Maturity Model (ISM3; http://www.ism3.com/): A process-based ISM maturity model for security.
- IT Infrastructure Library (ITIL; http://www.itil-officialsite.com/): A detailed framework with hands-on information on how to manage IT successfully.
- Val IT (http://www.itgi.org/): An enterprise value management framework for IT investments.

In this book, we look at CobiT, ISO 27001, ITIL, and Val IT.

CobiT

CobiT is a set of best practices (or framework) for IT management created in 1992 by the ISACA and ITGI. CobiT provides managers, auditors, and IT users with a set of generally accepted measures, indicators, processes, and control best practices to assist them in maximizing the benefits derived through the use of IT and developing appropriate enterprise IT governance and control.

The stated mission of CobiT development is "to research, develop, publicize and promote an authoritative, up-to-date, international set of generally accepted information technology control objectives for day-to-day use by business managers and auditors." Managers, auditors, and users benefit from the development of CobiT because it helps them understand their IT processes and decide the necessary resources and the level of security and control necessary to protect their assets. Managers benefit from CobiT because it provides them with a way to determine and evaluate their IT-related decisions and investments. Decision making is more effective because CobiT aids management in defining a strategic IT plan, defining the information architecture, acquiring the necessary IT hardware and software to execute the IT strategy, ensuring continuous service, and monitoring the performance of the IT function. IT customers and users benefit from CobiT because of the assurance provided to them by CobiT's defined controls, security, and process governance. CobiT benefits auditors and advisors because it helps them identify IT control issues within an organization's IT infrastructure. It also helps them corroborate their audit findings.

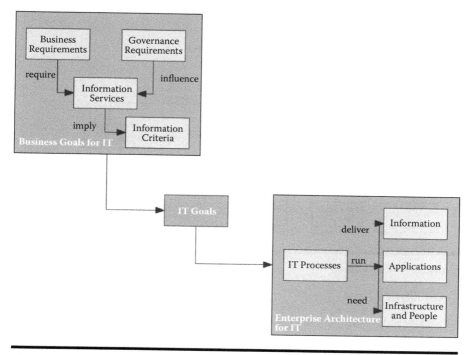

Figure 3.4 CoʙiT framework.

Basic Principles of CoʙiT

Figure 3.4 shows the structure of the CoʙiT framework and its composite parts.

A successful organization is built on a solid framework of data and information. The framework explains how IT processes support organizational data and deliver the information that the business needs to achieve its objectives. This delivery is controlled through thirty-four high-level control objectives, one for each IT process, contained in the four domains. Included are the statements of desired results or purposes to be achieved by implementing the more than 200 specific and detailed control objectives throughout the thirty-four high-level IT processes.

The key to maintaining profitability in a technologically changing environment is how well you maintain control. CoʙiT's control objectives provide the critical insight needed to delineate a clear policy and good practice for IT controls.

The framework also identifies which of the seven information criteria (effectiveness, efficiency, confidentiality, integrity, availability, compliance, and reliability), as well as which IT resources (people, applications, information, and infrastructure) are important for the IT processes to fully support business goals. Figure 3.5 demonstrates the interrelationships of these components.

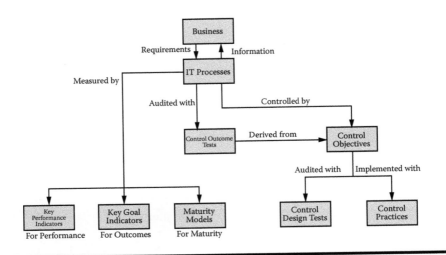

Figure 3.5 CoBiT flow.

CoBiT Structure

As we saw in Chapter 2, CoBiT 4.1 has thirty-four high-level processes that cover more than 200 control objectives categorized in four domains. CoBiT covers the following four domains:

1. Plan and organize.
2. Acquire and implement.
3. Deliver and support.
4. Monitor and evaluate.

Plan and Organize

The plan and organize domain covers the use of information and related technology and how best you can use it in your organization to help achieve the organization's goals and objectives. It also highlights the organizational and infrastructural form IT should take to achieve the optimal results and to generate the most benefits from the use of IT.

Acquire and Implement

The acquire and implement domain covers identifying IT requirements, acquiring the technology, and implementing it within an enterprise's current business processes. This domain also addresses the development of a maintenance plan that an organization should adopt to prolong the life of an IT system and its components.

Deliver and Support

The deliver and support domain focuses on the delivery aspects of IT. It covers areas such as the execution of the applications within the IT system and its results, as well as the support processes that enable the effective and efficient execution of these IT systems. These support processes include security issues and training.

Monitor and Evaluate

The monitor and evaluate domain deals with an organization's strategy in assessing the needs of the company and whether or not the current IT system still meets the objectives for which it was designed and the controls necessary to comply with regulatory requirements. This domain also covers the issue of an independent assessment of the effectiveness of IT system in its ability to meet business objectives and the organization's control processes by internal and external auditors.

CoBiT and Lean Six Sigma

CoBiT and Six Sigma both focus on customer and service quality. They are complementary and you should use them together. You should use the CoBiT framework to increase efficiency, reduce costs, and improve customer satisfaction. You should use Six Sigma techniques to design new processes and upgrade the current ones as part of your continuous assessment program.

You could use the CoBiT Maturity Model for a particular process to determine your capability but it does not provide a precise answer and your selection of a maturity level is pretty arbitrary. Six Sigma provides a more scientific result when determining process capability. You could use the different attributes associated with each maturity level to help define projects in your define, measure, analyze, improve, control (DMAIC) model. CoBiT best practices fit very nicely in the DMAIC model as well as an SDLC. Table 3.4 lists those processes that dovetail nicely with lean Six Sigma.

Common Lean Six Sigma techniques used in CoBiT environments are root cause analysis, voice of the customer (VOC), Pareto Charts, failure modes and effects analysis (FMEA), control charts, process sigma value, and IT scorecard (similar to BSC), for measuring and reporting how well the IT organization is performing.

ISO 27001

ISO/IEC 27001, part of a growing family of ISO/IEC 27000 standards (see Table 3.5), is an information security management system (ISMS) standard published in October 2005 by the ISO and the International Electrotechnical Commission (IEC). Its full name is *ISO/IEC 27001:2005—Information technology—Security techniques—Information security management systems—Requirements* but it is commonly known as ISO 27001.

Table 3.4 Cᴏʙ**iT Processes**

Reference	Process Description
PO1	Define a strategic IT plan and direction
PO4	Define the IT processes, organization, and relationships
PO5	Manage the IT investment
PO8	Manage quality
PO9	Assess and manage IT risks
DS3	Manage performance and capacity
DS4	Ensure continuous service
DS8	Manage service desk and incidents
DS10	Manage problems
ME1	Monitor and evaluate IT processes

For best results, you should use ISO 27001 with ISO/IEC 27002 (formerly ISO/IEC 17799), the *Code of Practice for Information Security Management*, which lists security control objectives and recommends specific security controls. Organizations that implement an ISMS in accordance with the best practice advice in ISO/IEC 27002 are likely to meet the requirements of ISO/IEC 27001.

As with many ISO standards, accredited certification or registration bodies around the world can certify an organization compliant with ISO/IEC 27001. Certification audits are usually conducted by ISO/IEC 27001 lead auditors.

Basic Principles of ISO/IEC 27001

ISO/IEC 27001 certification usually involves a three-stage audit process:

1. A "table-top" review of the existence and completeness of key documentation such as the organization's security policy, Statement of Applicability (SoA), and Risk Treatment Plan (RTP).
2. A detailed, in-depth audit that involves testing the existence and effectiveness of the information security controls stated in the SoA and RTP, as well as the supporting documentation.
3. A follow-up reassessment audit to confirm that a previously certified organization remains in compliance with the standard. Certification maintenance involves periodic reviews and reassessments to confirm that the ISMS continues to operate as specified and intended.

Table 3.5   ISO 27000 Family of Standards

Standard	Title	Description
ISO 27000	Fundamentals and vocabulary	An overview and introduction to the ISO 27000 standards as a whole plus the specialist vocabulary used in ISO 27000.
ISO 27001 (Formerly BS 7799 Part 2)	Specification for an Information Security Management System	Information security management system requirements standard (specification) against which organizations are formally certified.
ISO 27002 (Formerly known as ISO 17799 and as BS 7799 Part 1)	Code of Practice for Information Security Management	Code of practice describing a comprehensive set of information security control objectives and a menu of best-practice security controls.
ISO 27003	Information Security Management System Implementation Guidance	Proposed implementation guide using PDCA.
ISO 27004	Information Security Management— Measurement	Proposed information security management metrics and measurement standard to help measure the effectiveness of information security management system implementations.
ISO 27005	Information Security Risk Management	Proposed information security risk management standard (will replace the recently issued BS 7799 Part 3).
ISO 27006	Requirements for Bodies Providing Audit and Certification of Information Security Management Systems	A guide to the certification or registration process for accredited ISMS certification or registration bodies.
ISO 27007	Guidelines for Information Security Management Systems Auditing	A guideline for auditing information security management systems.

(Continued)

Table 3.5   ISO 27000 Family of Standards (Continued)

Standard	Title	Description
ISO 27008	Guidance for Auditors on ISMS Controls (proposed title)	A guideline on auditing information security controls.
ISO 27010	Information Security Management Guidelines for Sector-to-Sector Interworking and Communications for Industry and Government (proposed title)	A guideline on sector-to-sector interworking and communications for industry and government, supporting a series of sector-specific ISMS implementation guidelines starting with ISO/IEC 27011.
ISO 27011	Information Security Management Guidelines for Telecommunications	A guideline for information security management for telecommunications (also known as X.1051)
ISO 27031	Specification for ICT Readiness for Business Continuity (proposed title)	ICT-focused standard on business continuity.
ISO 27032	Guidelines for Cybersecurity	A guideline for cybersecurity.
ISO 27033	IT Network Security	Replace the multipart ISO/IEC 18028 standard on IT network security.
ISO 27034	Application Security	A guideline for application security.
ISO 2779	Health Informatics—information security management in health using ISO/IEC 27002	Additional information to assist healthcare professionals to implement ISO 27002.

ISO 27001 and Lean Six Sigma

As with any quality management system, ISO 27001 compels companies to have documented standard processes. It also requires them to follow them. It doesn't, though, require these processes to be stable or capable. Our application of Six Sigma techniques and our use of the tools can help us do that.

ITIL

Since the mid-1990s, many CIOs and industry experts have considered ITIL the de facto international standard for IT management. Both IT Infrastructure Library and ITIL are registered trademarks of the United Kingdom's Office of Government Commerce (OGC). However you want to call or pronounce it, ITIL is a set of principles and techniques for managing IT infrastructure, development, and operations. It is a customizable framework of best practices designed to promote quality IT services. In its five books, ITIL prescribes important IT practices and provides comprehensive checklists, tasks, and procedures you can tailor to any IT organization.

As an IT service management (ITSM) framework, ITIL provides a systematic approach to the provisioning and management of IT services, from conception through design, implementation, operation, and continual improvement. ITIL is often considered for use alongside other best practice frameworks such as Application Services Library (ASL), Capability Maturity Model/Capability Maturity Model Integration (CMM/CMMI), Dynamic Systems Development Method (DSDM), Information Services Procurement Library (ISPL), and Information Technology Investment Management (ITIM), and is often linked with IT governance through CobiT or AS 8015-2005.

As you can see in Appendix A, there are other ITSM approaches and frameworks, but many of these are based on or like ITIL. The ISO/IEC 20000 standard (previously BS 15000) is essentially the Service Support and Service Delivery volumes from ITIL version 2. Similarly, the authors of *The Visible OPS Handbook: Implementing ITIL in 4 Practical and Auditable Steps* (Behr, Kim, and Spafford 2004) booklet focus on the biggest impact elements of ITIL. Likewise, vendors also have developed process models loosely or closely aligned with ITIL. For instance, there is the IBM Tivoli Unified Process (ITUP) and the Microsoft Operations Framework (MOF). There are also more limited implementations of ITIL, such as the enhanced Telecom Operations Map (eTOM) from the TeleManagement Forum, which offers an alternative framework for telecommunications service providers. Regardless of the flavor, these documents focus on information management processes.

Basic Principles of ITIL

ITIL version 3 (v3), published May 30, 2007, is a set of five core volumes supported by additional complementary and Web-based materials. ITIL v3 has adopted an integrated service life cycle approach to ITSM, as opposed to ITIL v2, which organized itself around the concepts of IT service delivery and service support. With ITIL v3, there was a repositioning of the framework from the previous emphasis on process life cycle and alignment of IT to the business to the management of the life cycle of the services provided by IT, and the importance of creating business value rather than just the execution of processes. The processes identified and described within the life cycle are supplier and platform independent and apply to all aspects of IT infrastructure. The ITIL v3 core key volumes are:

1. Service Strategy
2. Service Design

3. Service Transition
4. Service Operation
5. Continual Service Improvement

Service Strategy

Service strategy focuses on the identification of market opportunities requiring IT services to meet a need of your internal or external customers. It encompasses a framework to build best practice in developing a long-term service strategy. The output is a strategy for the design, implementation, maintenance, and continual improvement of the service as an organizational capability and a strategic asset. Even though service strategy is shown at the core of the ITIL v3 life cycle, it cannot exist in isolation from the other parts of the IT life cycle. It covers many topics such as general strategy, competition and market space, service provider types, service management, organization design and development, key process activities, financial management, service portfolio management, demand management, and key roles and responsibilities of staff engaging in service strategy.

Service Design

Service design focuses on the activities that take place to turn the strategy into a design document addressing all aspects of the proposed service, as well as the processes needed to support it. Service design includes the design of IT services conforming to best practice, as well as the design of architecture, processes, policies, and documentation. It allows for future business requirements. It covers many topics such as service design package (SDP), service catalog management, service level management, capacity management, availability management, IT service continuity management, information security management, supplier management, and key roles and responsibilities for staff engaging in service design.

Service Transition

Service transition focuses on the implementation of the output of the service design activities and the creation of a production service or modification of an existing service. It relates to the delivery of services required by the business to transition the service into live or operational use, and often encompasses the project side of IT. There is an area of overlap between service transition and service operation. It covers many topics, such as service asset and configuration management, transition planning and support, release and deployment management, change management, knowledge management, and the key roles of staff engaging in service transition.

Service Operation

Service operation focuses on the activities required to operate the services and maintain their functionality as defined in the service level agreements (SLAs) with customers. Service operation specifies best practice for achieving the delivery of agreed levels of services to the consumers and the customers (where customers refer to those individuals who pay for the service and negotiate the SLAs). It is the part of the life cycle where you actually deliver the services and value directly. During this phase, you consider the monitoring of problems and balance between service reliability and cost. It covers many topics such as balancing conflicting goals, event management, incident management, problem management, request fulfillment, asset management, service desk, technical and application management, as well as key roles and responsibilities for staff engaging in service operation.

Continual Service Improvement

Continual service improvement focuses on the ability to deliver continual improvement to the quality of the services that the IT organization delivers to the business. ITIL v3 uses the word "continual," whereas ITIL v2 uses "continuous" service improvement. Continual implies an activity that you can undertake on a phased, regular basis as part of a process. Continuous is more suitable for the definition of activities intended to operate without pause, such as the ultimate goal of availability. It covers many topics such as service reporting, service measurement, and service level management.

ITIL and Lean Six Sigma

Organizations have turned to practices and quality methods that include ITIL and Six Sigma, combining them to measure the quality of service, and improve IT-dependent business processes by focusing on the customers. ITIL and Six Sigma are complementary to each other; ITIL provides a framework for ITSM based on a set of best practices to manage IT services. ITIL and Six Sigma both focus on customer and service quality. ITIL specifies service metaspecifications and ITSM processes. It does this by providing a set of best practices to deliver and support IT services; it does not tell you the quality status of your IT service performance or how to improve it, whereas Six Sigma specifies a set of techniques for improving the quality of services and processes. You can apply the techniques of Six Sigma to identify critical IT areas requiring improvement, calculate process sigma, identify bottlenecks, and test hypotheses. It gives you a proven set of statistical techniques to measure and improve service quality. Six Sigma techniques and tools are useful in the conduct of the ongoing operation of ITIL processes. ITIL requires a quality model like Six Sigma.

You can easily place ITIL best practice activities within the DMAIC model. You could, of course, use ITIL or Six Sigma independently; however, IT executives have found it beneficial to use them together. Many aspects of Six Sigma program and project guidance are applicable to ITIL:

1. Learning, knowledge transfer
2. Integrated management system
3. Fact and data-based decision making
4. Use of technology tools
5. Defect removal focus

Six Sigma is a methodology nearly any organization can use to improve the speed and quality of the components to ensure that they are producing them in a defect-free manner. For example, ITIL prescribes that you have a change management process. Needless to say, this process will be different for each IT organization depending on size, scope, and scale. Once you have defined the change management process and the organization is following it, you can then use Six Sigma tools to ensure that the change management process is free from defects.

You also can use Six Sigma tools to develop a defect-free deployment plan for ITIL—real change management. You could also improve an individual process so that it produces its output better, faster, and with reduced cost or with fewer defects. Processes do not exist in isolation, however: They exist within a unique organization with its unique culture. This implies a process might produce its output, yet not fully mature in terms of how well it is documented or how deeply and seamlessly it is integrated with other processes in an organization. You could definitely use a capability maturity model like CMMI, but maturity models are applied somewhat arbitrarily. However, the Six Sigma methodology and tools are used to integrate the various ITIL processes to produce a defect-free output for the customer or end user.

A process also can fail when it comes under stress. A key indicator for this situation is the bypassing of a certain process whenever a pressure situation arises. We are sure your organization has an emergency fix procedure, but have you considered how many of your changes are emergency changes? A world-class organization will exhibit positive characteristics with respect to change management. A low number of emergency changes is one of them. You could therefore use Six Sigma to improve the adherence to the prescribed ITIL practices as not following the prescribed practice results in defects. In other words, the process needs an environment conducive to its stable operation and you can use Six Sigma tools to measure and create such an environment.

Some changes that might be evident after implementing a new process are accessible lists of people that are available for direct contact and a continuous focus on reducing the cycle time from the point at which an incident is detected to when it is resolved (also known as the mean time to repair [MTTR]). An innovative approach would be for you to use Six Sigma tools to avoid incidents from occurring in the first place.

ITIL has built in continual improvement. For instance, it advocates the service improvement program (SIP), which is aimed at improving the quality of service from a business perspective. The SIP provides the strongest correlation between ITIL and Six Sigma as Six Sigma techniques assist with choosing a good candidate for the SIP, and then measuring its ongoing success.

Some Six Sigma statistical techniques are well established and do not require you to be part of a Six Sigma company to use them. More important, you do not need to be a statistician to understand the techniques either—many tools are available to automate both ITIL processes and Six Sigma techniques. Common Lean Six Sigma techniques used in ITIL environments are root cause analysis, VOC, Pareto Charts, FMEA, control charts, process sigma value, and IT scorecard (similar to BSC). The techniques also show the improved quality from using the ITIL best practices.

In summary, ITIL and Lean Six Sigma help organizations improve the quality of IT service and gain focus on their customers, thereby improving the business bottom line. As you have already read, Six Sigma complements many methodologies, including ITIL. After you have adopted ITIL, you should use Six Sigma process improvement as part of your culture of credibility. You can use the following Lean and Six Sigma techniques and tools to assist in ITIL process optimization:

1. Use Lean to remove waste from your processes.
2. Use DMAIC to improve operational IT processes.
3. Use define, measure, analyze, design, verify (DMADV) to remove defects during design.
4. Use critical to quality (CTQ) to align process improvements with customer requirements.

At this point, it is appropriate to describe the relationship among CobiT, ITIL, and ISO 27002. We could have picked other ISO or IEEE standards addressing other IT management areas but we feel most people intuitively understand the information security paradigm. Many CIOs consider the three mutually exclusive and believe that using more than one is redundant and wasteful. We would argue differently, and recommend that when addressing your organization's security, you consider all three. Most organizations look at their command and control structure or planning horizons hierarchically. With apologies to any military readers, organizations think of strategy, tactics, and operations, with the detail going from general to specific and the time frame going from longer term to shorter term. We can view the guidance in a similar manner. CobiT is a strategic document best used by the CIO and board. ITIL is a tactical document as it addresses tactics typically used by IT service or support managers to improve their areas of control. The ISO 27002 standard provides specific or operational advice on information security. Once you have drilled down through the three layers, you will have implemented best practices, but you might not have done it efficiently or effectively. That is when you use

Lean and Six Sigma to remove waste and to improve the efficiency and effectiveness of the processes. If you are truly on top of things, you will use Design for Six Sigma (DFSS) to design your processes for real breakthroughs in performance.

Val IT

Val IT is another ISACA/ITGI framework for the governance of IT investments intended to extend and complement CoBiT. It is tightly integrated with CoBiT and cross-references its processes to CoBiT senior management processes necessary to get good value from IT investments. Specifically, Val IT focuses on the investment decision (Are we doing the right things?) and the realization of benefits (Are we getting the benefits?), whereas CoBiT focuses on the execution (Are we doing them the right way? Are we getting them done well?).

Val IT is a formal statement of principles and processes for IT portfolio management. It is perhaps the first attempt at the standardization of IT portfolio management principles. So what is IT portfolio management and why do you need it? Well, IT portfolio management is the application of systematic management to large classes of items managed by enterprise IT groups. Examples of IT portfolios you might have are planned initiatives, projects, and ongoing IT services, such as application support. The promise of IT portfolio management is the quantification of previously arcane IT efforts, enabling the measurement and objective evaluation of investment scenarios. Hence, IT portfolio management becomes an enabling technique for organizations to use to meet the objectives of IT governance.

As most CIOs know, IT portfolio management started with a project-centric bias, but has evolved to include steady-state portfolio entries such as application maintenance and support, which consume the lion's share of most IT budgets. The challenge the CIO has for including application maintenance and support in the portfolio is that the IT budget tends not to track these efforts at a sufficient level of granularity for effective financial tracking.

IT portfolio management is analogous to financial portfolio management, but there are significant differences you should know. IT investments are not liquid, like stocks and bonds (although investment portfolios might also include nonliquid assets), and are measured using both financial and nonfinancial indexes (for example, a BSC approach), so a purely financial view is not sufficient.

Financial portfolio assets typically have consistent measurement information (enabling accurate and objective comparisons), and this is at the base of the concept's usefulness in application to IT. However, IT portfolio management is distinct from IT financial management because it has an explicitly directive, strategic goal in determining what to continue investing in versus what to divest from. The agility of IT portfolio management is its biggest advantage over investment approaches and methods.

Management of an application portfolio within the IT portfolio focuses on comparing spending on established systems based on their relative value to the organization. You can base the comparison on the level of contribution in terms of the IT investment's profitability. Additionally, you can base this comparison on nontangible factors such as an organization's level of experience with a certain technology, users' familiarity with the applications and infrastructure, and external forces such as the emergence of new technologies and the obsolescence of old ones.

A project portfolio addresses the issues with spending on the development of innovative capabilities in terms of potential ROI and reducing investment overlaps in situations where reorganization or acquisition occurs. Project portfolio management addresses data cleanliness, maintenance savings, suitability of the resulting solution, and the relative value of new investments to replace these projects.

Resource project management (RPM) involves analyzing and forecasting the talent that companies need to execute their business strategy, proactively rather than reactively. RPM's chief goal is to help organizations make sure they have the right people in the right places at the right time and at the right price. It is a critical strategic activity, enabling the organization to identify, develop, and sustain the workforce skills it needs to successfully accomplish its strategic intent while balancing the career and lifestyle goals of its employees. RPM helps control labor costs, assess talent needs, make informed business decisions, and assess talent market risks as part of overall enterprise risk management.

In general, IT portfolio management as a systematic discipline is more suited to larger IT organizations; in smaller organizations its goals might be formalized into IT planning and governance as a whole.

IT portfolio management follows a simple life cycle as shown in Figure 3.6. The planning phase involves risk profile analysis and a decision on the correct mix of projects, infrastructure, and technologies. It also involves continual alignment with business goals.

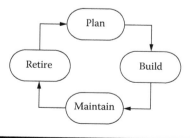

Figure 3.6   Portfolio life cycle.

Basic Principles of Val IT

Val IT allows business managers to get business value from IT investments, by providing a governance framework that consists of a set of guiding principles and a number of processes conforming to those principles that are further defined as a set of key management practices.

Val IT is built on the following guiding principles:

1. IT-enabled investments will be managed as a portfolio of investments.
2. IT-enabled investments will include the full scope of activities required to achieve business value.
3. IT-enabled investments will be managed through their full economic life cycle.
4. Value delivery practices will recognize that there are different categories of investments that will be evaluated and managed differently.
5. Value delivery practices will define and monitor key metrics and will respond quickly to any changes or deviations.
6. Value delivery practices will engage all stakeholders and assign appropriate accountability for the delivery of capabilities and the realization of business benefits.
7. Value delivery practices will be continually monitored, evaluated, and improved.

The three major processes are:

1. Value governance (VG prefix)
2. Portfolio management (PM prefix)
3. Investment management (IM prefix)

Figure 3.7 depicts the three processes, forty management practices, and their relationships.

The major processes have a RACI diagram, indicating the responsibilities of the senior executives, business managers, and information managers, along with the major and minor CobiT control objectives associated with the activity. It is these linkages and assignments of accountabilities that make Val IT a practical ready reference and actionable.

Val IT and Lean Six Sigma

As with CobiT, Val IT nests nicely with Lean Six Sigma. Val IT defines the management practices for value governance, portfolio management, and investment management but it does not provide any guidance on how to ensure they are the best processes possible. It is important to note that although the ITGI developed Val IT to complement

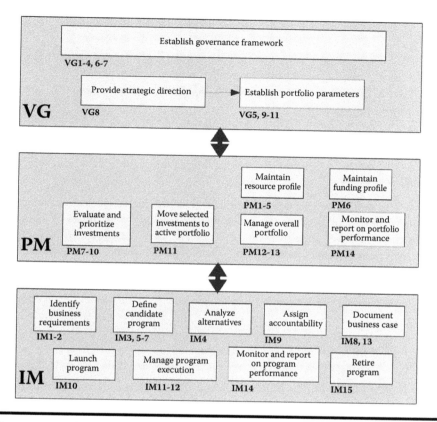

Figure 3.7   Val IT processes and management practices.

CobiT, you can use it on its own. Should you do so, Lean Six Sigma methods become more critical in aiding continual improvement of your value delivery processes.

Providing More Specificity

As we showed in Figure 1.1, we need specific guidance to support CobiT. CobiT, although it does provide high-level guidance on thirty-four key IT processes, it does not offer the level of specificity we need to implement efficient and effective processes, so we must look to lower level guidance for help. Some of the important IT guidance follows:

- CMMI (http://www.sei.cmu.edu/cmmi/): Focuses on a capability maturity model for software engineering.
- IEEE 829 (http://ieeexplore.ieee.org/xpl/freeabs_all.jsp?tp=&arnumber=429 3223&isnumber=4293222): Focuses on information system testing.

- M_o_R (http://www.apmgroup.co.uk/M_o_R/MoR_Home.asp): Focuses on IT risk management.
- PMBOK (http://www.pmi.org/Resources/Pages/Library-of-PMI-Global-Standards.aspx#1): Focuses generically on project management.
- PRINCE2 (http://www.prince2.org.uk/home/home.asp): Focuses on IT project management.
- Zachman Framework (http://www.zifa.com/): Focuses on an architecture framework for IT.

CMMI

CMMI is a process improvement approach that provides organizations with the essential elements of effective processes. It was created by members of industry, government, and Carnegie Mellon University's Software Engineering Institute (SEI). The main sponsors included the Office of the Secretary of Defense and the National Defense Industrial Association. CMMI is the successor of the CMM or Software CMM.

CMMI best practices are published in documents called models, each addressing a different area of interest. The goal of the CMMI project is to improve the usability of maturity models by integrating many different models into one framework. Figure 3.8 shows the CMMI structure.

The current release of CMMI is version 1.2. There are three version 1.2 models now available:

- CMMI for Development (CMMI-DEV): This model addresses product and service development processes.

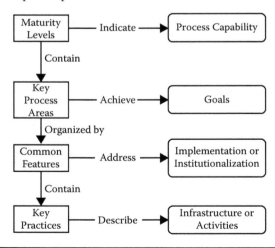

Figure 3.8   CMMI structure.

■ CMMI for Acquisition (CMMI-ACQ): This model addresses supply chain management, acquisition, and outsourcing processes in government and industry.
■ CMMI for Services (CMMI-SVC): This model addresses guidance for delivering services within an organization and to external customers.

There are benefits to using a methodology like CMMI. The SEI published that sixty organizations measured performance increases in the categories of cost, schedule, productivity, quality, and customer satisfaction.

Like other methodologies, organizations must adapt CMMI best practices according to their business objectives. Unlike ISO standards, organizations cannot be CMMI "certified"; rather, an organization is appraised and is awarded a rating of one to five. Appraisals of organizations using a CMMI model must conform to the requirements defined in the Appraisal Requirements for CMMI (ARC) document. The Standard CMMI Appraisal Method for Process Improvement (SCAMPI) is an appraisal method that meets all of the ARC requirements. Appraisals focus on identifying improvement opportunities and comparing the organization's processes to CMMI best practices.

Basic Principles of CMMI

You can appraise CMMI using two different approaches: staged and continuous. The staged approach yields appraisal results as one of five maturity levels. The continuous approach yields one of six capability levels. The differences in these approaches are manifest only in the appraisal itself; the best practices are equivalent and result in equivalent process improvement results.

All CMMI models contain multiple process areas (PAs). A PA has one to four goals, and each goal has associated practices. These goals and practices are called specific goals and practices, as they describe activities that are specific to a single process area. An additional set of goals and practices applies across all of the process areas: the generic goals and practices.

CMMI and Lean Six Sigma

In the software and systems field, you can leverage Six Sigma differently based on the state of your business. In an organization needing process consistency, Six Sigma can help promote the establishment of a process. For an organization striving to streamline their existing processes, Six Sigma can be used as a refinement mechanism.

In organizations at CMM Levels 1 through 3, "defect free" might seem an overwhelming stretch. Accordingly, an effective approach would be to use the improvement framework (DMAIC) as a roadmap toward intermediate defect-reduction goals. Organizations at CMM Levels 1 and 2 might find that adopting the Six Sigma philosophy and framework reinforces their efforts to launch measurement practices, whereas Level 3 organizations might want to immediately use the framework. As organizations mature to Levels 4 and 5, which imply an ability to leverage established measurement practices, accomplishment of improving performance (as defined by defect rates) becomes a relevant goal. The same logic applies to any methodology with a maturity model, such as CobiT.

Many techniques in the Six Sigma toolkit are directly applicable to software and are already in use within the software industry. For instance, you can use VOC and quality function deployment (QFD) for developing customer requirements. There are numerous charting or calculation techniques that you can use to scrutinize cost, schedule, and quality (project-level and personal-level) data as a project proceeds. For technical development, there are quantitative methods for risk analysis and concept and design selection. The strength of Six Sigma comes when an organization consciously and methodically deploys these tools in a way that directly or indirectly achieves customer satisfaction.

As with manufacturing, it is likely that Six Sigma applications in software development will reach beyond improvement of current processes or products and extend to design of new processes or products. This design methodology—DFSS—relies heavily on tools for customer requirements, risk analysis, design decision making, and inventive problem solving. In the software world, it makes sense to heavily leverage reuse libraries of robustly designed software.

Six Sigma is rooted in fundamental statistical and business theory; consequently, the concepts and philosophy are very mature. The use of Six Sigma methods in manufacturing, following on the heels of many quality improvement programs, is likewise very mature. However, the use of Six Sigma methods in software development and other upstream (from manufacturing) processes are only now emerging.

In the past, there have been many instances and evolutions of quality improvement programs. Scrutiny of the programs will show much similarity and also clear distinctions between such programs and Six Sigma. Similarities include common tools and methods, concepts of continuous improvement, and even analogous steps in the improvement framework.

It is difficult to concisely describe the ways you can intertwine Six Sigma with your CMMI initiatives (or vice versa), but Six Sigma and improvement approaches such as CMM, CMMI, personal software process (PSP), or team software process (TSP) are complementary and mutually supportive. Depending on current organizational, project, or individual circumstances, you can use Six Sigma as an enabler to launch your CMM, CMMI, PSP, or TSP initiative. You could use it as a refinement methodology or toolkit within these initiatives. For instance, you might use LSS to select highest priority PAs within CMMI or to select highest leverage metrics within PSP.

Examination of the Goal-Question-Metric (GQM), Initiating-Diagnosing-Establishing-Acting-Leveraging (IDEAL), and Practical Software Measurement (PSM) paradigms, likewise, shows compatibility and consistency with Six Sigma. GQM meshes well with the define and measure steps of Six Sigma. IDEAL and Six Sigma share many common features, with IDEAL slightly more focused on change management and organizational issues and Six Sigma more focused on tactical, data-driven analysis and decision making. PSM provides a software-tailored approach to measurement that may well serve the Six Sigma improvement framework.

Although Six Sigma philosophy and technique came out of manufacturing environments, it also has been used in projects that span the entire functional organization. A reasonable question, therefore, is whether Six Sigma is adaptable for software development and software maintenance.

Software manufacturing deals with the duplication, packaging, and distribution of software. Although software firms should take sufficient care to ensure the quality of these operations, it is really the software development process (software requirements through software quality assurance) that is the source of concern.

There are many parallels between manufacturing and software development, but there are many differences as well. Consequently, one is not surprised that the software industry has come up with its own software methodologies and tool sets.

PSP and TSP are software development process definitions that are compatible with a wide range of software development concepts such as spiral software development, object-oriented software development, and various other sets of techniques, each with certain advantages in modeling software requirements and designs for systems.

Six Sigma for Software, on the other hand, is not a software development process definition; rather, it is a far more generalized process for improving processes and products.

PSP, TSP and CMM are potential choices for software development process definitions that can lead to improved software project performance. However, the full potential of the data produced by these software processes cannot be fully leveraged without applying the more comprehensive Six Sigma for Software toolkit.

Six Sigma programs have proven results, especially in the manufacturing and service industries. A Six Sigma program builds on many of the building blocks of organizational quality that a CMM program would have put in place. However, the program is a lot more rigorous at the highest level. It can deliver extraordinary results, but it requires equally exceptional effort. Several billions of dollars have been saved through these programs. That's why many Indian software companies are looking at Six Sigma as the next logical step after their CMM programs.

You should think of CMMI as the software development version of ITIL—it's a process improvement framework that sets process improvement benchmarks, goals, and measures for software development teams. As we mentioned earlier, Six Sigma is a more generic process improvement methodology that can be applied to multiple types of business processes in addition to IT processes.

CMMI is relevant to our discussion because one of the tools in our bundle—the Maturity Estimator—is based in part on CMMI. The Maturity Estimator tool allows you to understand how well integrated the processes are within the organization. For example, the tool assesses each process in terms of its maturity level and establishes action plans to bring the processes to a higher level of maturity on a prescribed scale. Again, you can use Six Sigma tools to characterize the maturity or process capability of each process by assigning clear data-based measures to outline the level of that capability.

As an example, a CMMI Level 1 or 2 organization won't have the infrastructure to even measure the capability of its processes. In a CMMI Level 3 organization, the processes exist but might not be followed in a rigorous manner. In a Level 4 organization, the process might be followed but doesn't really produce defect-free results.

CMMI and Six Sigma are complementary, as each helps improves key facets of IT operations independently and collectively. Use CMMI to develop world-class process definitions and Six Sigma to execute them with world-class capability.

IEEE 829

IEEE 829-1998, also known as the 829 Standard for Software Test Documentation, is an IEEE standard that specifies a set of document formats for use in eight defined stages of software testing, each stage potentially producing its own separate type of document.

Basic Principles of IEEE 829

The standard specifies the format of these documents, but it does not proscribe whether you must produce them all, nor does it include any criteria regarding adequate content for these documents. The documents are:

- *Test Plan:* A management planning document.
- *Test Design Specification:* Test conditions details and the expected results, as well as testing criteria.
- *Test Case Specification:* Test data specification to use for the test conditions documented in the Test Design Specification.
- *Test Procedure Specification:* Details of all test activities, including any setup preconditions and the steps to follow.
- *Test Item Transmittal Report:* Report on the movement of tested software components from one stage of testing to the next.
- *Test Log:* Completed test case records, including the tester, order of execution, and test results.
- *Test Incident Report:* For any test that failed, details of the nature of the incident, the actual versus expected result, any supporting incident information, and an assessment of the impact on testing of an incident.
- *Test Summary Report:* A management report providing a recap of the test process, including any important information from the tests, assessments of

the testing quality, the quality of the software system under test, and statistics derived from incident reports.

Other standards that might be referred to when documenting according to IEEE 829 include the following:

■ IEEE 730, a standard for software quality assurance plans
■ IEEE 1061, a standard for software quality metrics and methodology
■ IEEE 12207, a standard for software life cycle processes and life cycle data

IEEE 829 and Lean Six Sigma

The IEEE 829 standard provides guidance on how to design software test documentation and provides the basis of any Lean Six Sigma software development efforts.

PMBOK

The Project Management Institute (PMI) published the first *A Guide to the Project Management Body of Knowledge* (*PMBOK Guide*) as a white paper in 1987 in an attempt to document and standardize generally accepted project management principles and practices. The first edition was published in 1996 followed by the second edition in 2000. In 2004, the PMI published the third edition that included major changes from the first edition.

The *PMBOK Guide* is an internationally recognized standard (IEEE 1490-2003) that provides the fundamentals of project management as they apply to a wide range of projects, including construction, software development, engineering, and automotive. The *PMBOK Guide* is meant to offer a general guide to manage most projects most of the time.

Basic Principles of PMBOK

The *PMBOK Guide* is process based, meaning it describes work as being accomplished by a series of processes. This approach is consistent with other management standards such as CobiT, CMMI, ISO 9000, and ITIL. Processes overlap and interact throughout a project or its various phases. The *PMBOK Guide* describes processes in terms of:

1. Inputs (documents, plans, designs, etc.)
2. Tools and techniques (mechanisms applied to inputs)
3. Outputs (documents, products, etc)

The *Guide* recognizes forty-four processes that fall into five basic process groups and nine knowledge areas that are typical of almost all projects. The five process groups are:

1. Initiating
2. Planning
3. Executing
4. Controlling and monitoring
5. Closing

The nine knowledge areas are:

1. Project integration management
2. Project scope management
3. Project time management
4. Project cost management
5. Project quality management
6. Project human resource management
7. Project communications management
8. Project risk management
9. Project procurement management

The nine knowledge areas contain the processes that you need to accomplish to achieve an effective project management program. Each of these processes also falls into one of the five basic process groups, creating a matrix structure such that every process can be related to one knowledge area and one process group.

PMBOK and Lean Six Sigma

There is great interest in Six Sigma within the professional project management community. Usually PMBOK adherents would like to know Six Sigma relates to the PMBOK. Needless to say, Six Sigma and PMBOK do have connections, similarities, and distinctions.

First, you should know that Six Sigma is not just another project management initiative or process improvement program. By now you also should know that Six Sigma is not just a new term for project management, nor is it a mere repackaging of old concepts. It is more than that because it is a robust continuous improvement strategy and process that includes cultural changes and statistical methodologies. Six Sigma is complementary with existing project management programs and standards but differs in significant ways.

Six Sigma is not simply another supplement to an organization's existing management methods. It is a complementary management methodology that is integrated into and replaces the existing ways of determining, analyzing, and resolving or avoiding problems, as well as achieving business and customer requirements objectively and methodically. Six Sigma's set of tools are more broadly applicable than those commonly applied within typical project management. Six Sigma is more oriented toward solutions of problems at their root cause and prevention of their recurrence rather than attempting to control potential causes of failure on a project-by-project basis.

The breadth, depth, and precision of Six Sigma also differentiate it from typical project management. Six Sigma has a well-defined project charter that outlines the scope of a project, financial targets, anticipated benefits, milestones, and so on, based on hard financial data and savings. In typical project management, organizations go into a project without fully knowing what the financial gains might be. Six Sigma has a solid control phase (DMAIC) that makes specific measurements, identifies specific problems, and provides specific solutions that can be measured.

At a conceptual level, many of the management best practices advocated by PMBOK and Six Sigma have a great deal in common; for example, they both identify and communicate with stakeholders; have a sound plan; conduct regular reviews; and manage schedule, cost, and resources. Both seek to establish a sound plan; identify and communicate with stakeholders; conduct regular reviews; and manage schedule, cost, and resources. Both disciplines seek to reduce failures, prevent defects, control costs and schedules, and manage risk. Generally, professional project management attempts to achieve these goals by encouraging best practices on a project-by-project basis, often through the mechanism of a project management office that promulgates policy, provides templates and advice, promotes appropriate use of tools such as critical path method, and perhaps performs periodic project reviews.

From a Six Sigma perspective, most practitioners would likely argue that these types of activities are the province of the project sponsor or champion and the team leader, typically a Green Belt or Black Belt. A Lean and Six Sigma generally best practice is to limit projects (typically less than four months) and to execute them with small, highly trained teams. So, you could argue that appropriate management controls for short projects with Lean Six Sigma professionals is to set individual goals for sponsors, champions, and the belts. Six Sigma practitioners may not welcome additional oversight from a project or program management office, thinking they are roadblocks to the successful conclusion of their project.

In short, we all understand that professional project management adds value to larger projects, but we might not find it clear that the same is true for smaller Six Sigma projects. When Six Sigma projects truly follow the Six Sigma roadmap and faithfully conduct tollgate reviews, you might find it difficult to justify the additional overhead associated with project office controls and reviews.

When looking at the relationship between project management and Six Sigma, you should understand that there is a difference between a new product or process development project (or to enhance an existing product or process) and a

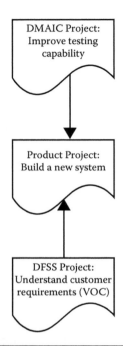

Figure 3.9 Project management and Six Sigma relationships.

concurrently executing Six Sigma project that might parallel, or potentially inter-sect with, the product project. Figure 3.9 illustrates this distinction.

In the future, you might have several Six Sigma projects executing concurrently with a product project and might deliver results that impact or are used by that project. You could charter a DFSS project to understand better the requirements of certain customers, with the intent to deliver that knowledge to the product project team at the appropriate time. Similarly, you might start a process improvement DMAIC project should you recognize that your testing capability is insufficient to deliver the required level of quality within the required time frame. (You might also want to look at the techniques of the TOC and the requirements of IEEE 829 given earlier.) Both Six Sigma projects could have results that impact other product project teams as well, and so are not merely tasks within the product project, but provide organizational value of their own.

Just following the *PMBOK Guide* is not synonymous with following Six Sigma techniques. The *PMBOK Guide* attempts to achieve these goals by encourag-ing sound practices on a project-by-project basis, often through the mechanism of a project management office that promulgates policy, provides templates and advice, promotes the appropriate use of tools such as CPM and earned value, and perhaps performs periodic project reviews. Six Sigma is more typically oriented toward solving problems at the root cause and preventing their recurrence, as opposed to attempting to control potential causes of failure on a project-by-project basis. Six Sigma's set of tools are more broadly applicable than those commonly applied within the discipline of professional project management. Because project management itself is a process, you could use Six Sigma to potentially improve project management. Both sets of practices bring value and you should apply one in conjunction with another.

Too many project management methods have failed not because they weren't adding value, but because you couldn't measure the effectiveness of the methodology or quantify the value added by process changes. Six Sigma provides a structured data-driven methodology with tools and techniques that companies can use to measure their performance both before and after Six Sigma projects. Using Six Sigma, management can measure the baseline performance of their processes and determine the root causes of variations so they can improve their processes to meet and exceed the desired performance levels.

Six Sigma allows managers to take their projects to new levels of discipline and comprehensive commitment. For standard project management ideas, you could approach them ad hoc and implement them as you learn them. You can't do Six Sigma halfheartedly, and that is a good thing. Six Sigma is not for dilettantes. You can't implement it piecemeal. If you're in, you're in deep, and you're in for the long run. Again, that is a good thing because that level of commitment not only gets everyone involved and keeps them involved, but also leads to more substantial and far-reaching change in your processes.

PMBOK is a methodology that fits nicely into the PDCA methodology. The Planning Process Group fits "Plan," the Executing Process Group fits "Do" and the Monitoring and Controlling Process Group fits "Check" and "Act."

We can learn more about the relationship between PMBOK and Six Sigma when we study the process groups. For example, we see tie-ins to Six Sigma's DMAIC methodology. For example, the PMBOK Initiating Process Group relates most directly to the Define phase. This first phase or process includes preparation of a project charter and assignment of a project manager.

We also find that the Six Sigma thought process and toolset mesh well with the Planning Process Group. Six Sigma's DFSS brings a rich toolset to address requirement failures found commonly in project planning, including VOC, Kano classification, needs–context distinction, affinity diagrams (KJ analysis), and other language processing tools that help to reveal hidden or unstated requirements. Six Sigma tools also help to prevent expectations failures caused by poor estimates and inadequate exploration of prioritization and feature selection issues. Six Sigma tools such as analytical hierarchy process, conjoint analysis, and concept selection scorecards promote fact-based conversations between the project team and the customer. Six Sigma's emphasis on predicting and managing capability together with tools such as defect containment scorecards promotes understanding and managing the economic consequences of escaped defects. You can apply Six Sigma tools such as combinatorial methods and Markov chains to the improvement of testing processes. Finally, Six Sigma tools such as Monte Carlo simulation can help within the context of professional project management.

During the Executing Process Group, Six Sigma can complement product project execution primarily in the areas of risk management and in optimization through the application of tools such as the design of experiments (DoE).

Six Sigma complements the Controlling Process Group two ways. First, root cause analysis can help prevent the reoccurrence of problems. Second, during the control step of the DMAIC improvement process, we can institutionalize controls and responses to special cause variation so that reaction to control issues is both rapid and sound.

PRINCE2

Projects in Controlled Environments 2 (PRINCE2) is another project management methodology. PRINCE2 was released in 1996 as a generic project management method. PRINCE2 is a registered trademark of the U.K. OGC. It is a process-based approach to project management that covers the management, control, and organization of a project.

PRINCE2 has become increasingly popular and is now the de facto standard for project management in the United Kingdom and its use has spread beyond that country. In North America, more CIOs have heard of the PMBOK and its accompanying Project Management Professional (PMP) certification. Although the PMBOK is the basis for an internationally recognized standard (IEEE 1490-2003), it is very generic and could apply to a wide range of projects, including construction, software, engineering, and automotive. The PMBOK is consistent with ISO 9000 and CMMI as it is process-based, whereas PRINCE2 is IT-specific. Do not forget the benefits of MSP, OPM3, and Val IT when contemplating the implementation of portfolio, program, and project management.

Basic Principles of PRINCE2

As mentioned, PRINCE2 is a process-driven project management method that contrasts with reactive or adaptive methods such as Agile and Scrum. A PRINCE2 project itself typically has four phases:

1. Starting a project
2. Initiating a project
3. Implementing a project
4. Closing a project

The PRINCE2 methodology defines forty-five separate subprocesses and organizes these into eight processes as follows:

- Starting up a project (SU)
- Planning (PL)
- Initiating a project (IP)
- Directing a project (DP)
- Controlling a stage (CS)
- Managing product delivery (MP)
- Managing stage boundaries (SB)
- Closing a project (CP)

Figure 3.10 shows the processes involved in managing a PRINCE2 project and how they link with each other, creating the normal content of a PRINCE2 project.

PRINCE2 describes procedures to coordinate people and activities in a project, how to design and supervise the project, and what to do when you have to adjust the project should it not go as you planned. In PRINCE2, each process is specified with its key inputs and outputs and specific goals and activities. Divided into manageable stages, the method enables efficient control of resources.

PRINCE2 and Lean Six Sigma

Six Sigma initiatives are mainly driven by the discipline of a project approach. As with the project management framework of PRINCE2, the logic of working through the methodology in sequence, and tailoring it to circumstances, is the key to success.

Project management is a complex discipline and it is wrong to assume that blind adherence to the PRINCE2 methodology will result in a successful project. By the same token, it is wrong to assume that every aspect of PRINCE2 applies to every project. For this reason every process provides a note on scalability. This

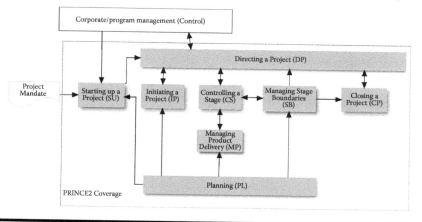

Figure 3.10 PRINCE2 process model.

note provides guidance to the project manager (and others involved in the project) on how much of the process to apply. This allows the project manager to tailor PRINCE2 to the needs of a particular project, and it also allows the manager to omit essential elements of PRINCE2, resulting in a PINO project: PRINCE in name only. To counter this, the APM Group, which specializes in PRINCE2 certification, has defined the concept of a PRINCE2 Maturity Model. The PRINCE2 Maturity Model is similar to the CMMI and CobiT maturity models in that it does not provide much precision and is very arbitrary.

PRINCE2 advocates product-based planning, which means that the first task when planning is to identify and analyze products. Once you identify the activities required to create these products, then you can estimate the effort required for each and can schedule activities into a plan. The approach taken to ensure quality on the project is agreed on, together with the overall approach to controlling the project itself—the project controls.

There are many challenges facing project managers: data gathering and analysis, problem solving, prioritizing activities, allocating scarce resources, understanding and evaluating existing processes, assessing project and product risk, developing and tracking standard measurements, and making quantitative evaluations. The Six Sigma methodology provides tools and techniques to help a manager successfully meet these challenges. Success means understanding what the methodology is, how it is applied, and how it is used.

Six Sigma is a robust continuous improvement strategy and process that includes cultural methodologies such as TQM, process control strategies such as statistical process control (SPC), and statistical tools. When done correctly, Six Sigma becomes a way toward organizational and cultural development, but it is more than a set of tools. Six Sigma is the strategic and systematic application of the tools on targeted important projects at the appropriate time to bring about significant and lasting change in an organization as a whole. In the end, it is clear that Six Sigma complements and extends professional project management, whether it is the PMBOK or PRINCE2 methodology, but does not replace it. Together the project management and quality improvement disciplines make important contributions to successful business outcomes.

Zachman Framework

Originally conceived by John Zachman at IBM in the 1980s, the Zachman Framework is often referenced as a standard taxonomy for developing and documenting the basic elements of enterprise architecture. You can use the taxonomy to organize architectural artifacts by artifact targets (for example, business owner and builder) or by issue (for example, data and functionality). These artifacts can include design documents, specifications, and models. In its original incarnation, it used a two-dimensional classification model based on the six basic interrogatives (what, how, where, who, when, and why) intersecting six distinct stakeholder groups (planner, owner, designer, builder, implementer, and worker). The intersecting cells of the framework correspond to models that, when documented, can provide a holistic view of the enterprise.

According to Zachman, he derived this taxonomy from analogous structures found in older disciplines, such as architecture, construction, engineering, and manufacturing, that classify and organize the design artifacts created in the process of designing and producing complex physical products, such as buildings or airplanes.

Basic Principles of the Zachman Framework

The Zachman Framework addresses the enterprise as a whole, it is defined independently of tools or methodologies, and you can map any issues against it to understand where they fit. Unfortunately, the large number of cells is generally considered an obstacle for the practical application of the framework. You will also find that the relations between the cells are not that well specified. Figure 3.11 depicts the Zachman Framework.

The framework does not prescribe models you have to build before you can deliver an implementation. Only you (or your adaption of the methodology) can determine what models or parts of models you are actually going to build. On the

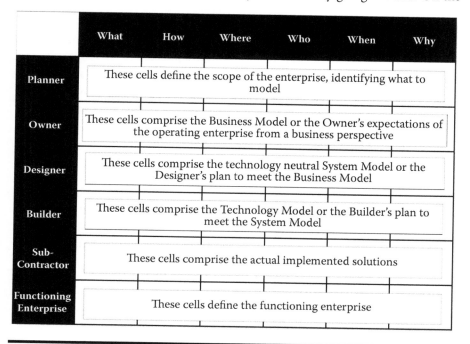

Figure 3.11   The Zachman Framework.

other hand, the framework, by definition, identifies the total, comprehensive set of models relevant for describing your enterprise.

Think of the Zachman Framework as reusable Lego pieces. In the same way that you can use the Lego pieces as building blocks to build a castle, you can use the cells in the Zachman Framework as the building blocks of your enterprise.

The framework columns, which have no order of importance, represent unique abstractions of the enterprise to reduce the complexity of any single model that you might build. The cell models are described as primitive models, because there is only a single variable for each. You need composite models, which are made up of two or more variables, in the design of solutions to satisfy business requirements. Zachman maintains that primitive models are necessary for reusability and for engineering commonality across an enterprise, and that only primitive models can be considered to be elements of architecture.

Each cell model in each column constrains the content of the cell below it. This ensures alignment between the intentions of enterprise owners, as represented by row 2 of the framework, and with whatever is implemented to build the enterprise, as represented by row 5 of the framework.

The granularity of detail in the Zachman Framework is a property of any individual cell regardless of any row. Depending on the requirement, planning, or implementation, a cell model might have relatively little detail or an excruciating level of detail. The Zachman Framework does not prescribe how you create any cell model, including any notation or level of detail. This is left to organizations to determine, based on the methodologies they have adopted.

You can use the Zachman Framework at different levels of your organization. For example, you could use the framework at the enterprise level to provide artifacts for the entire enterprise. You could then create a separate framework at the level of a single division within your enterprise.

Zachman and Lean Six Sigma

Why is it so hard to get tried and true quality improvement disciplines such as Lean and Six Sigma to work effectively in service industries? It is not that they don't have processes requiring improvement. Most service organizations that have tried importing these manufacturing strategies are still looking for break-throughs, and some are still tabulating the cost of failure. It is our opinion that before you jump on the continuous improvement bandwagon, you must check whether your business architecture is fit for purpose. Otherwise, you're throwing good money after bad. When you're doing the wrong things for want of an architecture, you don't need tools to do it more efficiently and effectively. You need something to get you going in the right direction. Hence, you really need a comprehensive enterprise architecture.

Adopt and Adapt

So there you have it: an abundance of answers, an overabundance of opportunities, a plethora of possibilities, and a cornucopia of choices. You can make good progress by adopting some guidance, adapting it to your organization, proselytizing your staff, and reconciling your guidance with the use of Lean and Six Sigma. The right guidance and Lean Six Sigma together become the armamentarium of the CIO. The right guidance is the one that produces consistently good results in your organization. Adopt DMAIC as your organization's PDCA problem-solving method.

As you ruminate on the right guidance, you must differentiate between a catalyst and an elixir. You use an IT framework as a catalyst; that is, a framework such as CoBiT will increase the rate and impact of change in your organization. Unlike your process inputs (or reagents), the framework (or catalyst) is not consumed in the delivery of your service or product. So your framework and its processes can participate in many input transformations.

On the other hand, many impatient CIOs want to act as alchemists. The alchemists sought an elixir or panacea, the substance once believed to transform base metals into gold or to prolong life indefinitely. The use of a framework, such as CoBiT, or a method, such as Lean, will not automatically transform lead into gold—or prolong your corporate life expectancy. It is a catalyst, not a magical cure or elixir. If you are looking for a catholicon, you'll be disappointed, as there isn't one other than hard work and persistence. You need to move from your staff implementing a program to line managers routinely solving problems important to your organization. Then you will truly realize the benefits. This is the real ichor of your enterprise.

Chapter 4

What Is Lean Six Sigma?

Six Sigma is a fairly rigorous methodology for solving business process problems. Although it can solve many kinds of problems, it was originally designed and so is frequently used when solving problems where the essence of the problem is inconsistent behavior from a business process; that is, where there is too much variability in performance. Many of the Six Sigma tools are designed to assess and reduce variability.

The first kind of problems that Six Sigma was applied to were quality problems in manufacturing processes; however, its usefulness soon became apparent to the business world and the use of Six Sigma has spread across supply chains, disciplines, industries, and continents. It is now a mainstream problem-solving technique that belongs in any good problem solver's toolkit. The hallmark of the Six Sigma approach is to (1) use a formal series of steps to solve the problem so you do things in the right order and don't leave any steps out, and (2) make all decisions using data. Six Sigma is essentially the use of the scientific method that we were all taught in high school, to solve business problems. Its elements are not revolutionary, as most of the tools that are used have been around for decades and in some cases a hundred years. What was revolutionary about it was the application of a rigorous scientific thought process to everyday business problems where experience and judgment have historically been considered the essential tools for managers and problem solvers. In a pure Six Sigma environment, your opinion has almost no value. In fact, not only does your opinion have no value, but neither does the opinion of your boss, or of his or her boss, and on up the chain of command. In this environment, power shifts to those people who can make sense of data and use it correctly. Those are the people who can correctly describe what is happening and who can determine what root causes for unwanted behavior really are. Those are the people who are able to make good judgments about what to do to solve a problem. This can be downright scary in a traditional-thinking organization. The more rigid and hierarchical the organization is, the more disruptive such problem solving is likely to be and without significant cultural issues being addressed first, the less likely that a Six Sigma approach will ever take hold. It will simply be too scary for the entrenched management structure to deal with to discover that all of their "experience" might be wrong.

Lean is another methodology for solving business process problems. Like Six Sigma, it also arose out of the manufacturing world, where problems are visible and "in your face." Lean is focused on the elimination of waste, rigorously defined in the Lean world as anything that does not add value to the final product or service. When we look at the details of this later, we will see that most of what your business does is waste. In fact, in a typical business, around 99 percent of everything that is done will fall into the waste category. This can be very scary for the workforce who is being introduced to Lean! Lean can be considered a tool to make an operation more efficient, by driving waste out of it.

The question was, though, "What is Lean Six Sigma?" It's simply a combination of these two methodologies. Each has its strengths and weaknesses, but combined they are a powerful way to address a wide variety of business operation problems. These two systems were developed for different purposes by different groups. Six Sigma was developed by a team at Motorola and Lean was developed by Toyota. For twenty years they have been almost competitive philosophies, but recently, people have realized that when used together, they are quite powerful and useful. Note that there are no real standards bodies for either of these methodologies. There are various groups who would like to think they are the keeper of all knowledge or the best, or the most experienced, and so on. The fact is that these are best thought of as open source process improvement techniques with details that are freely sharable among groups. If that is the case, why do we need a book for it? Plenty of books have been written about Lean, Six Sigma, and the combination of the two. What is missing is a clear application of the techniques to the world of IT. That's what this book is about, so although we assume that Lean Six Sigma is new enough to you that we need to go over the fundamentals, we do it in a way that shows how it applies to the world of computers, networks, and software, commonly known as the IT world.

Understanding Data

Listen up! It is not about computers, or networks, or software; it is about what those systems can do for the decision makers—it is mostly about the data! This book is about process improvement and problem solving in an IT environment. Sound problem solving and process improvement requires data. It requires very specific data. It needs data that demonstrate how important process measurements are doing and what possible or known root cause elements are also doing. IT systems exist for many reasons—accounting, order entry, purchasing, communications, and so on.

IT organizations that are ineffective have lost track of why they are there and have come to believe that they are important just because they are there. Wrong! They are important because they do something better, faster, or more securely than the alternatives. Because all medium- and large-sized companies have IT infrastructures these days, and many small companies do as well, and because many of the essential data needed to run a business flows through the IT infrastructure, the IT organization is in a unique position to play a pivotal role in business problem solving and process improvement. So why is it that, as a rule, IT is often considered to be "in the way" and part of the problem instead of part of the solution to the problem solvers? Why indeed! It's simply because they do not recognize their pivotal role in this part of the business, are not trained to do it themselves, and are so often focused on their infrastructures rather than why the infrastructure is there. They often have little understanding of what data are actually flowing through their systems or the impact that their systems have on the data quality or timeliness, and therefore the usefulness of it. Because data are so pivotal to problem solving, this chapter is a primer on data.

Continuous Data

Continuous data represents measurements that can take on an infinite number of possible values. Typical examples are anything you might use an instrument to measure. Time, distance, height, weight, price, and volume are all examples of continuous data types. What do we mean by an infinite number of possible values? Simply that there is no limit to how many possible values exist for each measurement. Take weight for instance. How many different values are possible for the weight of a pencil? An infinite number of them! Let's say an average pencil weighs 20 grams and we want to weigh a pencil and record it. The pencil might weigh 19 grams. It could weigh 21 grams. The actual weight will probably fall into a fairly narrow range because pencils are fairly consistent things. But we do not have to limit ourselves to whole integers. Let's use a very precise scale. Maybe it weighs 19.32 grams. Lots of possibilities, huh? What if your scale can only read to within two decimal points like that last example? Does that mean that twenty pencils, all weighing 19.32 grams all have identical weights? No! If we had a better scale, one that read to four decimal points, we might find that one is 19.3216 grams, another is 19.3257 grams, and so on. There are really an infinite number of possible values despite our ability to sense them. This is characteristic of all continuous data. Statisticians often call this variable data, which is confusing to IT professionals because to them variables are names of things in a piece of software. Because of this we use the term continuous data in this book, but keep in mind that other books will call these variable data.

Attribute (or Discrete) Data

Discrete data represents measurements that only have two possible values—true or false. IT people love this kind of data, at least at first. Their world revolves around true–false things and deep down inside of all IT systems everything is either true or false, a one or a zero. Typical examples are defects. All defects are true–false determinations. Is this defective? Yes or no, please. Maybe is not allowed. Many, if not most, service processes characteristics are represented by attribute data. Was the project done on time? Was the project within budget? Is this code right? Is this check box in the right place? Was the hotel room clean? You can probably see flaws in this description already, so let us give you some more complicated ones. Rather than asking, "Is this code right?" we look at a number of features within the code and assess each one of them: "Does it run as fast as it should?" or "Does the interface meet customer specs?" and so on. We can often keep subdividing the measurement into smaller and smaller pieces like this, but at each stage, if the allowed answers are only yes or no, it is attribute data.

Attribute data are often summed so it is represented by numbers that look suspiciously like continuous data. "I have twenty defects in my code" looks like the same kind of statement as "My pencil weighs 20 grams." To the eye of the data analyst, however, these are very different kinds of data. The pencil weight is only one of an infinite number of possible weights the pencil could have, but the defect count is the sum of exactly twenty individual and exact yes–no decisions.

Let us give you one more example of attribute data that might on the surface seem to be continuous data. Question: What brand of router is that? Answer: A Cisco WS2740. Is this an example of attribute or continuous data? It is an attribute. This can be made clearer if we ask the question the right way. Is this a Cisco WS2740? Yes. So if we're tallying all of the routers in our company, we're asking a series of yes–no questions for each possible brand of router that we have in the firm.

Most reports and databases have some of both. Learn to distinguish between them and start to become aware of the differences and you'll be better at dealing with data.

Sometimes you have a choice of whether you will collect attribute or continuous data. If process understanding is your goal, always choose continuous data because they contain more information than attribute data. You can always convert a continuous variable into an attribute variable if you need it, but you cannot do the reverse, which is to convert an attribute variable into a continuous one. Here is an example. Suppose you want to record the on-time performance of your software development projects. Each project has a start date and a due date. You really have two choices: You can record whether the project was done on time or not, a yes–no attribute, or you can record how many days late (or early) it was for continuous data. It's much better to record the continuous data. If all you do is record the attribute, consider the following. Looking at the last twenty projects from two software departments, each department had four projects on time and sixteen projects late (we try to use realistic examples). Are these two departments of equal quality with respect to their on-time performance? Using this attribute data it would seem that they are. But what if we recorded the continuous variable of days late for each project instead? A project that is 1 day late and one that is 300 days late are both recorded as simply late when that is recorded as an attribute, but as a continuous variable, the difference is very apparent. Using continuous measurements, these two apparently equal departments can be seen as drastically different when one reveals that its sixteen late projects average 4 days late and the other averages 200 days late. Always use continuous variables when assessing process performance whenever it is possible to do that.

Inputs versus Outputs

Any business process can be considered and modeled like a simple machine (see Figure 4.1). As you saw in Chapter 2, the process turns inputs into outputs. The inputs come into it and the outputs come out of it.

No matter how complex your operation is, you can draw a box around it and find out what comes in and what goes out. You can look at your complex process in more detail and see that it is made up of lots of smaller processes. Each one of those can be modeled the same way, as inputs being processed into outputs. How it does this is determined by the details of the process. Some of those details of how the process works are affected by variables. Some of the variables are internal to the process, perhaps how hard you work, or work policies you have, or the speed of networks. Other variables are external to the process and are called environment variables. These might be working conditions, temperature, external noise, and so on. When you look at it with enough detail you will see that the output of one process is often the input to another process. In Figure 4.2, both outputs of Process 1 are inputs to Process 2 and there is an additional input to Process 2.

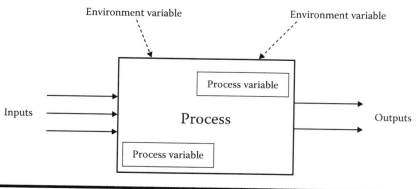

Figure 4.1   A simple process diagram.

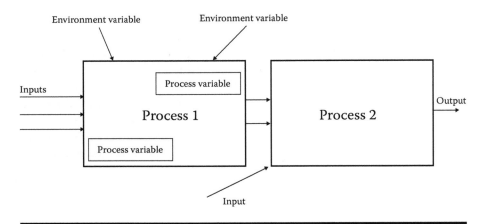

Figure 4.2   Two interconnected processes.

If you do that, you realize that if we simply mention a measurement and ask whether it is an input or an output, that question cannot be answered unless we know what process we're talking about. It could be an output of one process or an input to another process or both at the same time. This is why we take pains to keep inputs and outputs clear when we are dealing with measurements about our processes.

Another reason we keep inputs and outputs clear is that process improvement projects are all about improving outputs. Sometimes on a complex project it's easy to get bogged down and confused about what the goal is, but the goal is always to improve some aspect of a process output. A reasonable question to ask might be "Why bother with inputs when it's the output I really care about?" The answer is simple. If there were a big knob on your business process that said "Make this output better," or larger, or smaller, or less variable, or whatever your goal is, then you would simply turn that knob, the output would change, and you would be done. You wouldn't be reading this book if that knob existed. You would turn it, watch things get better, then go sailing for the rest of the day. Because that knob doesn't exist, we have to find out what causes outputs to behave the way they do. That's what quantitative process improvement—Six Sigma in this case—is all about. We find out and confirm the relationship between inputs and outputs. We keep doing this until we find inputs that we can change, then we do it and watch our process improve. Then we can go sailing.

Data Collection Plans

A data collection plan is simply a project organization tool to organize the collection of data that you need for your process improvement project. Figure 4.3 is an example but they can take any format that is useful to you. The plan is not needed

Data		Operational Definition and Procedures			
What	Measure type/Data type	How measured?	Related conditions to record	Sampling notes	How/where recorded
Data Collection Plan - Record Retention and Purges					
File Growth	Bytes	Reports are currently run	CS files are purged. Growth is due to TOLLXYZ	Use TOLLXYZ calculation to determine CS files growth	XRAMS
Transaction Files	Data records – Multiple files	Sample Query	Date range	File not in use by all databases at beginning of purge period	XRAMS
TOLLSBC	Data records – Multiple files	Program	Date range	Determine what else this program purges	XRAMS
Customer Comments	Data records – Single file	Sample Query	Date range and customer type	Custom purge program needed	XRAMS
Collections History	Data records – Single file	Sample Query	Date range and other variables	Multiple purge programs need to be written	XRAMS
Provisioning Transaction Master	Data records – Single file	Sample Query	Date range and transaction type	Custom purge program needed	XRAMS
Services File	Data records – Single file	Sample Query	Date range and service status		XRAMS
ARTRN	Data records – Single file	Display Database Size	Retired file		XRAMS
Customer Trace/Triggers	Data records – Single file	Query	Date range		XRAMS
Work Orders	Data records – Multiple files	2003 report and Query			XRAMS and PSSC
Telephone Stmt Images	Data records – Multiple files	Run small site	Date range and no reports are created	High risk. This is running with different dates than video stmts	XRAMS

Figure 4.3   A data collection plan.

for a simple project with one or two people working on it and clear and limited data to collect, but as the project gets more complex and as more people get involved, or especially if you want to delegate the data collection to someone other than yourself, the plan is a good idea.

Not everyone will have the same ideas about the specifics, so the act of writing this plan will help clarify things. The devil really is in the details, and when it comes to collecting data you need to be very precise about when you start, what counts, what precision and format it needs to be in, and so on.

If your data-based business improvement project is substantial or in some cases even if it isn't, you might need to collect lots of data from different sources. A good way to organize this effort is to create a data collection plan. This is nothing more than a project organization tool focused on the data you will need to acquire. Consider this plan a living document during your project because you are unlikely to have a complete list of all the data you need right at the start. A living document is simply one that is expected to change over the life of the project, so be sure to keep track of which version you are looking at by versioning it.

At its most basic, a data collection plan is simply a list of what data you will need along with information designed to make it clear. There is no standard data collection plan. We make them according to the needs of the project. Feel free or

Sample Data Collection Plan

Metric	Metric category	What is measured?	Where is the data?	How is data collected	When is the data collected	Start date
	(Cost, quality, cycle time, customer satisfaction, etc.)	Units numerator/ denominator	Source and location		Interval or frequency	To collect
Trouble ticket volume	Cycle time	New calls per day	XYZ database	From ABC report	Daily	4/1/2011
Trouble ticket volume	Cycle time	Hours/ticket	XYZ database	From ABC report	Daily	4/1/2011

End date	Baseline	Baseline time frame	Is process cyclical? Does baseline capture cycle?	Does baseline capture cycle?	Target	How was target developed
To collect	(if avail.)	(used to calculate baseline)			(if avail.)	
8/1/2011	n/a	n/a	no	n/a	none	n/a
8/1/2011	n/a	n/a	no	n/a	6 hrs	By client contract

Figure 4.4   Another sample data collection plan.

add or remove columns as you see fit. The best way to describe one is to use an example. Figure 4.4 is an example data collection plan with a few entries to give you an idea.

Newcomers to data collection often skip this step as trivial, but it is far from that on a complex or large project. The exercise allows you to tell at a glance what you need, defines when you need data for, specifies the measurements units (very important), and gives you a document that when done properly, allows you to have someone else get the initial project data for you and to have some confidence that it will actually be useful.

One of the hidden benefits of preparing a data collection plan is that it forces you to start thinking about details early in the project. You all know the saying "The devil is in the details," right? Well he (or she) sure is. Let us give you an example. Let's say that your project is to reduce the time that it takes to resolve a trouble ticket in a call center that takes trouble calls for a software company. The primary metric is then the time between the opening and closing of a ticket. That sounds simple, doesn't it? However, as we start looking at what data we have, we find that there are lots of reasons that people call this call center; they aren't all software trouble calls. Will we look at all of them or only certain ones? If only certain ones, is it clear for which categories we should collect data? Should we also collect data for the other types of calls simultaneously? When exactly is a trouble ticket opened? When the first call is logged? When the operator starts filling out the trouble ticket? When he or she finishes filling it out? When it has been approved and reviewed by a supervisor? What if there are missing fields in the form? Is that ticket started only after all fields are filled in, even when it takes hours or days to do that? These might seem like easy questions to answer, but in many cases they are not. It is easy to specify a problem at a high level. It is easy for a manager to simply order us to reduce the time tickets are open, but it is much harder to be precise about what that means, and a precise definition is necessary to collect the data. If there are going to be disagreements about this, it's best to air and resolve them early. Besides, creating this level of definition early allows multiple people to collect data and have all of the data be internally consistent.

Let's go over some of the elements of the sample data collection plan that is covered in more detail in the next section.

- *Metric:* The name of a variable you want to collect data on; for example, trouble ticket volume.
- *Metric category:* Categorize the kind of variable it is if this is a large project with lots of different kinds of data; for example, cycle time. Use this as you see fit or not at all.
- *What is measured (units):* Here is where you start to get specific. State the units. This is sometimes a ratio of two things. Be specific to avoid confusion. An example is new calls per day. Stating the units is extremely important and will help to avoid confusion later on, or even worse, terrible errors. One of us once did a project for a political party client, for which they sent health care data. One of the values was the number of people without any health insurance. Nowhere in the material that they sent were the units of those data stated. *They* knew the units, but didn't communicate that. In making cost calculations, it was assumed that the numbers they sent were thousands of people without insurance, but that was wrong: It was millions of people without insurance! Needless to say, the cost estimates were all off by a factor of a thousand. To make matters worse, while it was clearly stated in the report to them that the units were not known and assumed to be thousands, nobody ever bothered to really read what the report said. They simply grabbed the cost figure and published it, questioning it weeks later when political opponents began to snipe at it. They still didn't read the report, of course; they called, so the author was able to point out which page had the assumptions behind the calculations. Don't let this happen to you!
- *Where are the data?* Why make people guess when you already know it? Write it down! This is especially important if there are multiple sources of data. Specify which one to use. Find out if you don't know, or make it part of the data collection exercise to determine which one is best. This is discussed further later in this chapter.
- *How are data collected?* This is another optional field where you have a chance to specify the data source in more detail if needed.

- *When are the data collected?* This really indicates how frequently measurements should be taken. Every minute? Hourly? Weekly? Monthly? Do you need averages? Medians? Modes? If the data you need exist in a database, it might be fine to collect everything you can get and summarize it later into per minute, per hour, or per day categories, but this also might result in overwhelming you with data you don't need. If you are collecting the data manually, you want to be sure you have what you need, but no more than that, as manually collected data are a lot more expensive to collect than pulling a report out of a database. Manually collected data and frequency of data collection are discussed later in this chapter.

- *Start date and end date:* These are the dates of the oldest and newest data needed.

- *Baseline:* If this data element has a typical value, some people like to put it here. This might be a historical average, a target value, or a contracted specification. The value of having it in the table is as an example. If the data collector knows that a typical value for this data element is 12, or that it should be in a range from 10 to 15, and values are in the thousands, he or she will know right away that something is wrong and can check it. You won't always know a baseline value, so just leave this blank if you don't know one.

- *Baseline time frame:* If you have a baseline value, it's often helpful to know over what period of time it was calculated. Put that here. Again, this is simply so that the person doing the data collection has a better understanding of what he or she is looking for.

- *Is the process cyclical?* This is very important and often overlooked. Some processes have natural cycles to them. If you know that, state it here and state what the cycle is. If you aren't sure, estimate it. Why is this important?

- *Does the baseline capture the cycle?* This is just a yes–no question to remind you that for your data collection to be meaningful, if there are natural process cycles, the data collected to determine the baseline need to be long enough to see those cycles. This seems like an overly simple and unnecessary question, but often data are collected without a good knowledge of process characteristics and then are assumed to be representative. If you didn't collect the data yourself, don't assume that whoever did knew anything about natural process cycles.

- *Target:* This is simply the "perfect" value of this measurement. If there were no variability in this process, and you could have this value be the same every time, what would it be? You don't have to have a target. If you are collecting data on a CTQ variable, you will always have specification limits, which are the limits beyond which this characteristic is considered to be defective, but you don't always have targets. There might be no perfect value.

- *How was the target developed?* If there is a target, it is often useful to know where it came from. From the customer? Historical? The boss told me that's what she wanted?

Check Sheets

If you are reading this book, you are probably involved in the management of IT organizations. A lot, and perhaps most of the company's data is in one of the systems you manage. If someone needs data for a process improvement project, there is a good chance they will have to come to you, right? A project by definition is a one-shot event. It hasn't happened before and is unlikely to happen again, at least not exactly in the same way, so there is no reason to assume that the specific data that the LSS project manager needs to analyze is in your database, in the right format, with an interface that makes it easy for the manager to access it. In fact, it's unlikely. Yet the data are probably in there someplace, so the manager comes to the IT department to find it. That's where the fight starts. If you are connected with reality, you know how your organization is perceived with your in-house customers. If you are not, you might turn enough shades of pink to make Max Factor take notice if you could be a fly on the wall and hear what your internal customers have to say about you. In at least 50 percent of the projects we have worked on, the top complaint of the project team and the main reason for project delays or even cancellation has been lack of ability to get the data out of the IT organization in a useful time frame. How ironic that in the twenty-first century, sometimes called "The Information Age," we cannot get the data we need inside of our own companies.

There are plenty of reasons for this of course. Here are a few:

- The data don't exist.
- Just because I can envision the need for certain data today doesn't mean it was envisioned in the past, collected, and stored.
- Nobody knows where it is.
- Organizations can get pretty complicated and it might not be obvious which database has what I need.
- Company policies might not let me view it. This is a tragedy. I've been authorized, indirectly by the CEO, to solve a problem and I need data to solve it, but some other bureaucratic path in the company, also authorized by the CEO, decided that I have no right to it. There is often no fast and easy mechanism to resolve this. Companies with problem-solving mentalities deal with this effectively. Others use it as a crutch.
- The law might not let me view it. Privacy laws have increasingly been getting in the way of good process analysis by providing reasons why confidential data cannot be shared. This is a false reason. There is always a way to do this safely, but it's frequently used as an excuse.
- I might need an application or report written by the IT department to create or retrieve the data. In most of the cases where projects cannot get the data they want, it is because the IT groups are overloaded. It's not that they refuse

to help, it's that the data request becomes a low priority and so is scheduled to be done in a few months, or even years.

■ Maybe we are lucky and none of these reasons apply and we get our data quickly, but the data are in an unusable format. Either they can only be printed, or exported to a format that will cause us lots of extra work to use.

■ Maybe we are even luckier and we get the data we want and in a usable format, but the data source is unreliable and unverifiable. We aren't sure we can trust it. Untrustworthy data can be worse than no data at all.

There are plenty more of these, but this is enough to make the point. So what is a results-oriented problem solver to do when faced with the IT blank data wall? The answer is sometimes very simple: Collect your own data! The fact is that very significant process decisions can be made with sampled data. We don't need all the numbers. Simple random sampling can provide all the insight that is necessary for anyone with a modicum of statistics knowledge. The samples do not have to be large. A hundred measurements can be quite enough data for many corporate process decisions, and this number can often be collected by hand in a day or two. We can use a project team member or hire a temp to do this much cheaper than we can create an IT project to write a custom report to get it out of a database for us.

Here is where a check sheet comes in. It is simply a form that you use to define just what data to collect, how, and when, and it provides a place to record it. Figure 4.5 is a simple check sheet example. It is for collecting root cause data for a problem we are trying to solve.

In this case a data entry operator is being asked to record characteristics of problems found on data forms the operator is entering into the company database. As the operator inputs the information on the form, sometimes there are reasons to stop and suspend that record while he or she investigates to solve the problem. Just what are those problems and with what frequency do they occur? A simple check sheet filled out easily by the data entry operator for a week or so gives us everything we need. It is not very invasive, we can control the data collection process, and we don't have to bother the busy IT department. Of course, we are writing this book

Data entry problems, 200 forms processed	
Not readable	√√√√√
No signature	√√√√√√√√√√√√√√√
Missing date	√√√√√√√√√√
Missing operator	√√√√√
Wrong prices	√√√√√√√√√√√
Item not in database	√√√

Figure 4.5 A simple check sheet.

for IT organizations. You know what we're saying is right. Please don't trap yourself into long and expensive data collection problems when trying to solve problems in your own organization when a few simple check sheets can help you do it. Solving important business problems is no time to let pride force you to do it the hard way.

One of us recently helped an IT group evaluate a new spam filter for their e-mail system. Their company received millions of e-mails a day. A new spam filter vendor claimed their system was better than the company's existing one. The IT group was interested, but had to test it. The two spam filters were put in parallel with all e-mails going through each one. Each filter removed the e-mails it thought were spam and let the others pass. To assess the comparative performance of the two filters, we needed to examine e-mails that passed to see what percentage of them were still spam, and e-mails that were filtered out to see what percentage of those were good e-mails. How do you do that? The best way is for a human to look at them and decide if the filter did the right job. But how do you look at millions of e-mails a day? You don't. Instead you take a random sample and look at the sample. To do this a checklist was developed for the temps who would look at the e-mails so they could collect data on not only the numbers they found, but also on the characteristics of good ones filtered out and bad ones passed. This solution was simple, could be implemented quickly, and only required a few low-cost temps for a few days.

Checklists are simple, low tech, easy to implement, and a practical tool to be considered for any process improvement project.

Basic Sampling

In the last section, we mentioned sampling. Let's talk about sampling, what it is, and why we do it. Despite the long list of reasons offered earlier for why you can't get the data you need out of the company databases, sometimes you can! Not only that, but in this so-called information age we live in, you can get staggering amounts of it. Sometimes the process improvement team hits the data jackpot! First we need some definitions.

A *population* is all of the data for the problem scope. It's a relative thing. If the scope of the problem definition is errors in invoices in the past three years, then the population of invoices would be all of them for the past three years. If the scope of the problem is the errors in capital purchase invoices in the past three years, then the population includes only those. A *sample* is simply a subset of the population. Samples are often randomly selected but not always. Because this chapter is about basic sampling, we just discuss the common random sampling techniques.

I had mentioned earlier that sample sizes can be quite small compared to the population. In fact, often the sample size doesn't depend on the population size at all. This is often a surprise to those new to statistical data handling. If I want to know what proportion of the country will vote libertarian in the next election, I can estimate it quite well with a random sample. That sample will be on the order of a few thousand people that I have to poll. This is true whether I'm talking about a country of 1 million people or 300 million people. The sample size needed in both cases would be the same!

There are lots of good reasons to sample so let's discuss those first.

- *Availability:* I can't get all the data so I have to take a sample.
- *Cost:* All of the data are too much for me to analyze. Samples are cheaper to deal with.
- *Boredom:* Even if I can get all of the data, if manual analysis is needed, it's boring, and therefore error prone to handle huge amounts of data this way.
- *Accuracy:* Sampling can be more accurate than looking at all the data. You aren't going to want to believe this, but in some cases it's true.
- *Statistical:* Some statistical inferences work better with sampled data and some require that we sample data for them to work.

How do you take a sample? First you have to know something about the population from which you are sampling. If you know absolutely nothing about the process you are investigating, your initial work will be at least partly designed to give you some understanding of it. One major thing you need to understand is the degree to which there is stratification of data categories within your population. What do we mean by stratification? Let's call it subcategories instead. We'll use an example. If we are working to improve the company's bill-paying process and want to sample bills for errors, we might decide that we have to select a sample of them for analysis because the errors we are looking for won't be detectible in the database. We are in a big company that pays numerous bills and it would be very expensive to examine every bill, so we'll take a random sample and have people examine those for errors. But can we assume that all of our bills are similar? If so, we have a homogenous population. What if we have bills that are for very different kinds of things, like you probably have? These might be a few categories:

- Professional services
- Maintenance supplies
- Communications
- Leasing and capital purchases

These categories could represent vastly different kinds of bills with very different opportunities for billing errors. Also, some might be very small, and some might be for millions of dollars. Should we let random selection decide which ones we look at? Our intuition would say "No." Intuition is frequently wrong when it comes to analytical analysis, but in this case it is right on. A good way to sample a population like this with very different subcategories, or strata, is to sample within each category to be sure they are all represented. We might take a percentage of each category, for instance.

This isn't a statistics book, so we won't attempt to teach you how to do all of these things in detail, but will provide a few examples for illustration. You might have people in your organization who are Six Sigma Black Belts, or who didn't fall asleep in their applied statistics classes in college who can do this for you, or you can find them as consultants. We do this work all the time and stay on call for some of our clients just for that purpose.

Another kind of stratification comes in the form of data lumpiness. By that we mean that in this case, our invoices might be processed in batches or in some fashion that is not randomly distributed. This is likely in a business process like this. Let's say that all of the capital purchase invoices are processed on Tuesday afternoon, for instance. A true random sampling might happen to miss that time period just out of random chance, and if it did, an entire important category of information would be missing from our analysis. One of us lives on a little neighborhood lake that is stocked with three kinds of fish. He doesn't fish, but knows this because he happened to see the State Fisheries truck stocking the lake one year and stopped to talk to the truck driver. It isn't every day that you get to see 10,000 live fish poured out of a truck. They seemed happy to get out, too. Fast forward a few years when the author was chatting with his neighbor who loves to fish and does it all the time on the shore of his property, never in a boat, which he doesn't own. The author asked him how many kinds of fish were in the lake. He said "Nothing but bass." The author asked him how he knew and he replied that he had been fishing this lake for six years and that's all he had ever caught.

The neighbor had taken what he thought was a random sample of fish out of the lake over a long period of time and came to the wrong conclusion. Why did his random sample fail? Because the three kinds of fish (at least—there might be others that are not stocked) behave in different ways. The trout like moving water, so they hang out near the three stream inlets to the lake and maybe at the outlet. The bass like quiet water and like coves with logs and things like the place the neighbor can reach with his fishing gear. The perch like open, deep water, so they are always hanging out in the middle of the lake. A little advance knowledge of what the population was would have helped him to take a better survey, if that was his intent. To assess what fish are in the lake, you need to have an idea of what we just described and sample in all those areas to be sure you reach all of the subcategories of fish. The same is true of any population we need to sample. How do we find out what the population is when the point of the sampling is to find out and we need to know what it is before we sample? That seems like a tail-chasing exercise. For a scientist studying a brand new field, this might be a tricky problem, but for a business process improvement project it's quite simple. We talk to the subject matter experts (SMEs) for that process and ask them ahead of time. Or we can do a small presample to learn what is there, then use that information to design a more formal, larger sample. No SMEs for your process? Well then, frankly, you are screwed.

All process improvement requires that you have people who know how your process currently operates. We combine their process knowledge with problem-solving expertise to improve it. If you have no process knowledge, I hope you are making plans now for your next job.

Let me talk about a specific kind of sampling often done to create control charts. Control charts are a fundamental tool of process analysis that is discussed later in the book, but while we are discussing sampling, we want to mention them here. A control chart is a picture of how a process varies over time. It is a very formal process analysis and requires that we collect small random samples of process measurements at equally spaced intervals of time. Note the emphasis on equally spaced intervals. This kind of data is sometimes hard to find in company databases, so often has to be collected for this purpose. One of the reasons we mention it here is that control charts are designed to use sampled data. In other words, they will not work with all of your data. In statistics there is a characteristic of sampling called the Central Limit Theorem (CLT), which, in a nutshell, says that no matter what histogram shape your raw data are in, the shape of the samples will tend to be a normal histogram. This fact allows us to do the statistical calculations that are part of control charts and is an example of what we meant when we said that sometimes we have to sample even if we have all of the data and they are free to use.

How do you get a random sample? One thing you don't do is ask everyone in your office to pick a number. People are terrible at creating random anything because our brains just don't work that way. They force us into patterns, often unconsciously. The only way to take a random sample is to use a random number generator. Microsoft Excel has several such functions. One useful one is RANDBETWEEN(X,Y), which returns an integer between X and Y where those are two integers and Y is greater than X. For example, we need to sample daily invoices for auditing. Assume we want to take a random sample of ten every day. Every day we process *n* invoices and *n* can vary. Put the invoice numbers in a spreadsheet and serial number them from 1 to *n* each day. Write the RANDBETWEEN function in twenty cells setting X = 1 and Y = *n*. You will then have ten integers, each between invoice 1 and invoice *n* for that day. Pick those invoices to audit. Press the F9 key to recalculate the spreadsheet every time you need to repeat this sampling and you'll get all new random numbers. This way there is no bias in your selection of which invoices to examine. Table 4.1 shows a screen shot of this spreadsheet example that has thirty invoice numbers and ten randomly selected ones to choose for analysis this way.

By the way, all of the examples in this book can be seen as downloadable files at www.value-train.com/CIOSecrets.

Measurement System Analysis

Your database contains millions, or maybe billions, or even trillions of values. Do you know how each data value was collected? Do you know how? Under what

Table 4.1 Randomizer

Index	Invoice #	Index	Invoice #	Random Index Numbers
1	25357	16	22599	8
2	21550	17	30257	27
3	27724	18	29628	29
4	26750	19	33987	1
5	21471	20	21813	11
6	32619	21	31992	8
7	21362	22	31665	7
8	26003	23	31713	17
9	29872	24	27016	15
10	32510	25	33620	9
11	26066	26	30012	
12	32151	27	34147	
13	34978	28	26177	
14	28715	29	27170	
15	21794	30	29074	

conditions? How can you be sure that any of it is right? What does "right" mean? We don't mean to be paranoid, but the fact is that when most of us see a number on a report, we tend to assume it is right. Managers who look at operations or financial reports all the time know this isn't true. There are all sorts of errors in the data collection that organizations do to run their business. Once it's on paper or in the database, however, finding where the errors are and fixing them can be a daunting task. Getting all of your data correct isn't the subject of this book, but because the subject is how to improve IT business processes, and because many of the techniques we use to do this involve making decisions from data, we are going to have to ask this question: Can we trust the data that we are using to make this decision? Any IT professional is aware of techniques to ensure that data that enter a software application are reasonable. The CobiT framework even provides six application control objectives for you (CobiT 4.1 Framework p. 16). You can do type checking, range checking, and many other techniques. So let's assume for now that all of the reasonable things that can be done are being done. Does that mean the data are all correct? Of course not! Here is a simple example. A lab technician is conducting tests on process data and enters the data into a database from a terminal in his lab. The data entry screen has sophisticated data validation methods used so that he cannot enter ID numbers that are the wrong format, he cannot enter dates in the wrong format, he cannot enter dates older than today, all values are checked to be sure they fall into the proper range, and so on. He takes temperature readings from two vials and enters the vial ID and temperatures into the database but he switches which temperature goes with which vial. That is an undetectable error. All of the values are within proper ranges and there is no way that a piece of software can tell that the technician made that mistake. So now the wrong values are in there for all of recorded time. Fast forward a year and you are conducting a process improvement project involving those data. Those wrong data are now part of the data you use to create a control chart or other analytical view of what is going on, and there is no way that anybody can detect it so it will have an effect on your results. Although there is no way that particular error could be detected, there is a way that you can evaluate the overall quality of the data you are using. How can that be? There are errors in the data and we cannot find them but we can quantify how many there are and how it affects our results? Yes! It seems like magic, but yes you can. This technique is called Measurement Systems Analysis (MSA). This technique was developed in manufacturing decades ago, when it was called Gage R&R (it is sometimes still called that but today, most data are not collected using gauges, so that terminology is not very current and seems old fashioned, although it still shows up in software packages and books. We are not doing our part to eliminate it either because it is in this book, too).

Although Gage R&R may be a quasi-obsolete term, it is descriptive. The two Rs stand for repeatability and reproducibility, which are the two kinds of fundamental measurement errors.

Let's assume for a moment that people are involved in the measurement, like in the lab technician example. These two error types answer these two questions.

■ When multiple people make this measurement over multiple vials, will each of the people get the same results?
■ If the same person makes the same measurement multiple times, will that person get the same results?

In any real system the answer is almost always "no" to both of those questions, but the real question is how much error will be introduced in each case; by the fact that a single person can make the same measurement multiple times and get different answers, and the fact that multiple people can make the same measurement and get different answers.

In addition to these two error types, there is a third common measurement error called calibration error. In the lab example, the technician got the temperature reading by looking at a digital thermometer. When it says 105 degrees Celsius, she writes down 105°C. How do we know the actual temperature of the vial is 105°C? Could the thermometer be biased? Could it be reading a few degrees high or low? What if the thermometer is a mercury type and the technician is reading it off a scale? A tall technician and a short technician would look at the scale from different angles and would report slightly different temperatures because of the parallax effect of their viewing angle. When data are reported consistently higher or lower than actual, that is called a bias and that is also detectable. So bias and repeatability errors are both detectible. Bias is a systematic error and is easily accounted for once it is known. The other two are usually random errors and so have to be dealt with statistically. There is that word again . . . *statistics!* Sorry, but in a world full of randomness, people who don't know how to deal with randomness in an analytical way are at a disadvantage, because those who do understand can make better decisions despite the random nature of many business inputs and outputs. Whether you like Six Sigma techniques or not, one of the positive by-products of its widespread use has been the rise in understanding of how to use applied statistics to help understand and solve common business problems.

We aren't going to give you an MSA course here, but we do describe the essential steps and what can be done with it. Not all data-based process improvement projects use MSA, but projects that are critical and where the team has any question about the data sources should investigate it as a tool. Here is how it works.

MSA is an analysis that is done on data collected from an experiment. The experiment is a measurement experiment. Whatever the measurement is that you wish to test, you design a short experiment to take those measurements repeatedly and with different people or data collection sources if there aren't people. These data will allow you to check for the two kinds of measurement variability we described—repeatability and reproducibility. If they are present, analysis of the experiment data will allow you to quantify how much is present, and give you enough information that you can use it to adjust the conclusions that you previously might have made from the raw data itself. Some examples of conclusions that you might change are given in Table 4.2.

Note that in both examples, the adjusted values are better than the original ones. This is almost always true. Measurement errors can be thought of as a source

Table 4.2 Conclusions That You Might Change

Conclusion Made from the Raw Data	Adjusted Conclusion After MSA Analysis
The standard deviation (variability) of our invoicing error rate is 6.4 errors per thousand.	The standard deviation (variability) of our invoicing error rate is 5.8 per thousand.
We can expect to see 25 errors per thousand database entries.	We can expect to see 19 errors per thousand database entries.

of variability that is added to the actual process variability. In effect, you can never see the process, you can only see the process data, so the process always looks worse than it really is when viewed through imperfect data. Therefore, doing an MSA will almost always correct the values in a direction to make them look better. We're talking about variability issues here now, remember! These are random errors because of mistakes, and so on, not bias problems or intentional fraud. That's another topic.

Not all measurements can be easily subjected to an MSA analysis. Remember this analysis requires that an experiment be run and that usually means that the same thing be measured multiple times. You cannot always measure a one-time event multiple times. Some things change with time and so are never the same for long enough for a second measurement to be the same. Some measurements are destructive. Sometimes, though, a clever team can find ways around some of these problems when the issue is important enough. Here is where experience pays off. Anyone can solve a simple problem with a little training. The really tough ones take some horsepower and creativity.

Chapter 5

Understanding Lean

Lean is short for Lean Thinking, which started as Lean Manufacturing and is sometimes called Lean Enterprise. If it is flavored with examples and oriented to a particular industry, it might be called Lean for Health Care or Lean for Government, or whatever. What it is called depends on who is selling what. To be efficient and cover all bases, we simply call it Lean in this book.

Lean is an adaptation of a system developed by Toyota called the Toyota Production System (TPS). It was developed as a way of thinking and set of tools for making manufacturing processes more efficient. It worked spectacularly well for Toyota and the other Japanese companies who used it, so it spread around the globe, first as TPS, and later as Lean. It has also spread into many areas of business beyond manufacturing, including health care, finance, and supply chain management.

So what does it mean in Lean language to make a business process more efficient? Lean focuses on waste and strives to eliminate as much of it as possible from the process being improved. Waste is classified somewhat rigorously as falling into several categories that we describe shortly. A Lean team looks for waste in all of these categories and systematically proceeds to reduce it. Rarely, if ever, can all the waste be eliminated, but the more you can remove, the better the process will behave. The Lean philosophy that drives the definition of what waste is is called value. Every process consists of a group of operations, or process steps, that are arranged in some fashion so as to turn process inputs into process outputs. There are many process steps in most business processes, but only some of them add value. Value is defined as changing the input to the process step in such a way that the end customer, if they were paying for what you do in an "a la carte" fashion, would agree to pay for what that step does. To add value, an operation has to change the service, part, or information that is flowing through the process in some way that is useful to the end customer. Although many operations add some value, we'll see as we get into it that those same operations also do things that add no value. Anything that we do that does not add value to the thing that is flowing is waste. When we make a map of a business process and identify the process steps and measure how much of what we do adds value and how much adds no value (is waste), most people are initially stunned to discover that as a percentage of the total work that is done, often less than 1 percent of what we are doing is adding any value. In some extreme cases, we've seen the value-added percentage be as low as .01 percent! This can be not only shocking, but demoralizing to managers who thought they were doing a good job. If you think managers are shocked, when you let your employees see this, they will quickly extrapolate that if management's goal is to be efficient and if that means doing only value-added work, and if only 1 percent of what is done now is value-added, then when the Lean program is done, the company will be able to operate with only 1 percent of their workforce, so 99 percent of the people will lose their jobs. This is not true, of course, but it will be thought and will be feared, so it needs to be addressed early on. The fact is that typical improvements in this value-added percentage tend to be modest on this scale. Perhaps a company that starts out having 99 percent non-value-added (NVA) work will end up after their Lean program has a chance to work, with 96 to 97 percent NVA work. Although this might not seem like that much, look at the value-added side. When you go from 1 percent of your efforts producing output to 3 to 4 percent of your efforts producing output, you have tripled or quadrupled your effectiveness. That's impressive! Gains from a Lean program can do exactly that.

To grasp why this is true, you need to understand how we are looking at and measuring workflow and efficiency. The primary tool used to evaluate process efficiency in Lean is a value stream map. We show what these are and how they work in a later chapter; for now, let us describe at a high level why eliminating waste is good. To do this, we're going to use an example of a fulfillment center operation. The example is a simple operation. The center receives orders for software packages and assembles and ships the software. When we look at a process from a Lean perspective, one of the first things we need to do is find out what is flowing, in this case, software packages. Let's assume that the software is already on a CD, in a sleeve, and marked and ready to go. The CDs are sitting in inventory. All inventory is considered waste in Lean. If you were to send a bill to your customer for $2.00 for the cost of having their software hang around in a pile for two weeks, would they want to pay it? Of course not. Remember this: All inventory is waste in Lean. When the order comes in, a person picks one of the software packages from the storage place. They also get a box to put it in. The box is sitting on a shelf waiting. That's more waste. Try sending a bill to your customer for $.50 cents for having a shipping box hang around for a month. Perhaps some paperwork has to go into the box and you print this on demand. The printer is in another office, so enter the order information on a data entry terminal and walk over to get the printed packing slip. Your walk was all wasted time. All movement in lean is waste. Again, send a bill to your customer for all the walking around you did, say $1.50 for walking around to get stuff. They won't approve that, either. Now you have all you need but you need a supervisor to inspect and initial it before you can mail it. The supervisor left early today for his son's baseball game so you wait until tomorrow. Another bill goes to the customer for $1.10 for waiting time for the supervisor's time off. That won't fly either!

Finally, you have a package ready to ship and put it in the outgoing mail bin, where it sits waiting for the package delivery company to pick it up. They only pick up once a day, so there it sits for another seven hours. You get the idea. The way we would calculate the efficiency of this operation is to look at all the time the software and its component parts, the box, and so on, have been waiting from the time it was first created until the time it left the building for transit to the customer. Typical times for that might be 240 hours or ten days. During those 240 hours, how much value-added work was done? Well, we picked the right product and picked a box and made an invoice and assembled them. Those times might add up to about ten minutes. That's it. We did ten minutes of value-added work over a 240-hour time period on this process, which is horribly inefficient. You are going to want to shoot all kinds of holes in this analysis, but wait until we have explained more about Lean before you aim your gun. By then we hope you'll reholster it and come on board as a problem solver with us. I'll introduce one other concept here just to make you feel better about this horribly inefficient process that might be typical of some of yours, and that is the topic of lead time. Lead time is the time it takes to get an item through our process; in this example it was ten days. Most of the time the product spent waiting like most things do. Here is a fact that we're going to ask you to simply accept. If you cut your lead time in half, you will double your throughput rate, and if you can cut your lead time in half with the same amount of labor you will double your production with no increase in labor cost. In so many cases we can do this with no capital cost, either, by simply being smart about how we redesign our processes. That's what Lean allows us to do—increase the throughput of our most important processes with the same or less labor.

The problem with management is that we often look at and try to optimize the wrong thing. We so often focus on our people or our equipment. If we focus on people, we ask questions like "How hard are they working?" and "Are they doing the right thing?" People are not unimportant, but they are not the most important thing to focus on when trying to build efficient business processes. If we focus on our equipment, we ask questions like "How busy is the equipment?" or "What is the uptime?" If we don't get high enough numbers for our people or equipment utilization, we launch into improvement projects to make them better. What we hope you will at least start to realize after reading this book is that before we focus on people or equipment, we should focus on how our process is doing. For that, we need to make process measurements that focus on the things that are moving through it that our customer wants. Our customers don't care if our equipment or people are busy or idle and they won't reward us by paying us if we improve any of those measures. They will reward us for providing what they need quickly, however, and to do that we need to focus on how well our business process does that—how quickly it converts inputs into outputs that we can put into the customer's hands. We need to focus on the thing that is flowing, in this case the software packages. We can assure you that the person fulfilling those orders was busy all day long and felt like she worked hard. Her manager might have even given her some extra time off for working so hard for the company. The fact remains, however, that the process she is working in is inefficient and she is doing little to make it better.

Lean and the Socratic Method

We have already introduced Six Sigma as a problem-solving approach that focuses on process data and is project oriented. Six Sigma uses some tools that are not easily learned by many people, so the improvement projects are usually led by Six Sigma experts, called Black Belts.

Lean, by contrast, is more of a Socratic method of thinking about our processes every day. Although we will find projects to do within the context of a Lean effort, it is really more focused on changing the way managers and employees think about their processes and how they do their jobs. In a Lean thinking environment, we give them tools to evaluate performance, like the value-added percentage measurement, and then have them ask every day, "How can I do this better?" To avoid getting trapped in the problem we mentioned in Chapter 4 about improving the wrong thing, Lean companies first do some systems-level analysis so that they know what the right things are to improve, but then they let their employees do a lot of the rest of the work.

The Socratic method inspires involvement and often creates great excitement when done right. To do it right, a few elements need to be present. First, management and employees need to share common goals and objectives. In a hierarchical organization, like most commercial companies are, shared goals with employees might seem to be a little out of reach in some companies, but at least we can be sure that the employees accept and agree to work toward management's goals. When going out of business is one of the alternatives, staying in business is a great shared goal. You also need to agree on the problem to be solved, need shared access to the information necessary to analyze it, need to agree on how to interpret those data (analysis standards), and need to share any special concepts that form the underpinning of the improvement goal, such as the one we mentioned earlier that all inventory is waste.

If you have heard of the Socratic method before, you know that it is all about learning by questioning. When I use the Socratic method to teach I don't tell students an answer, I just ask them a series of questions and let them figure it out themselves. It forces them to think and to be involved. My job as a teacher is to guide their thinking by formulating questions all around the problem and keep them from going too far off-track, until they finally get it and say, "A-ha!" This teaching method is much better than lecturing but it is time consuming, so in our hurried world, it isn't used as often as it could be. The same technique can be used with teams that do problem solving. A facilitator asks the teams questions about why they do things, why items are in certain orders, why certain procedures are needed, and so on. They question everything! The Socratic method of problem solving permits nothing to be sacrosanct, so every tenet of how you do business can be challenged, and usually is. Every time you come across something that stops progress you can ask why it is needed, how it can be eliminated, how can it be sped up, and so on. Employees love doing this because so much of our lives are spent in processes where we are told what to do and when—the "shut up and draw" approach. To be able to challenge everything is liberating. It also brings with it great responsibility, however, because if you challenge why something should exist, it is then up to you to find a better way and justify it! Problem-solving teams have no fence to throw their ideas over for someone else to find a solution. It's their job to find the solution!

A Lean approach to process improvement does all of this. It involves the entire employee base and it teaches core Lean concepts so that everyone understands them. Management sets improvement goals and inspires the employees to meet or beat them, involving all employees in the process and providing frequent problem-solving sessions called Kaizen events, discussed next. We hope you can see that the combination of employee-led waste reduction teams (Lean) and project-led quality teams (Six Sigma) can be a powerful one–two punch for improving your organization's IT processes.

Kaizen Events

Kaizen events are one of the hallmark activities in companies using Lean to improve their processes. *Kaizen* is a Japanese word meaning "continuous improvement." Kaizen events are short (a few hours to a week long), part-time (an hour or two per day) problem-solving team events designed to make an immediate improvement to a process area. Kaizen events are a hallmark part of the Lean philosophy that says that everyone should be constantly trying to improve what they do. That continual improvement philosophy includes the belief that improvements should start at the workplace and that it is better to create a culture of constant small improvements by the workers than a few giant improvements by management or specialists. Note that workplace continual improvement doesn't mean that we never make large infrastructure improvements, but that if that's all you do, you are missing out on most of the opportunities to make your business better. Furthermore, these constant, small workplace improvements add up quickly over time and often cost little or nothing to implement.

Before we describe a Kaizen event, let's make it clear that for this to work, management must be willing to let it work, meaning they must empower their employees to make changes in work processes and give them the time and minimal training needed to self-organize and do these events. Management must also agree to implement what the teams come up with. This means that a company where the managers think they have all the answers cannot possibly be a Lean business because they are unlikely to be willing to relinquish so much day-to-day operational power to their employees. Good management means creating an environment for success, setting realistic goals, empowering your employees to do their jobs, and removing obstacles to their progress. All of this is built into how Lean companies work.

Kaizen events are sometimes called Kaizen blitzes because they are designed to act like a wartime blitz, or rapid, overwhelming attack. In this context the attack is on impediments to effective business processes but the idea is the same—to assemble a team quickly, give them a localized target, let them do some quick planning, and then go after it with gusto. The team simply assumes that they will vanquish their foe in short order and are empowered by management to do it. You might be asking yourself, "How can a few people make any significant improvement in a few days to how we do business when it typically takes us six to twenty-four months to implement a new system?" The answer is simple. It is because infrastructure systems, despite our reliance on them, are not always the limiting factor to team performance. You might not like to hear this, but managers often point to "things" being the problem rather than "processes" being the problem because things are easier to identify and fix and frankly, if changing the thing doesn't fix the problem, you can blame the vendor, the thing itself, and so on. When a business process is flawed, it is the responsibility of the process owner—the manager. To fix it, the process owner has to accept responsibility (blame) and fix it by changing the process. That involves changing how work is done, how tasks are organized, how decisions are made, and so on. This seems to be a lost art in many businesses. Frankly, it's easier to blame the stuff and throw money at buying new stuff. That's why so many apparently successful IT projects fail in the eyes of the buyers. When all is said and done and the new software is in place, they discover that their organizational performance is really no better than it was with the old software. The sad thing is that because everybody worked so hard to get the new system in place, they have a party to reward all their staff's hard work. Rewards for doing the wrong thing well are all too common.

Here are a few examples of how Kaizen blitzes might be used in an IT organization:

1. Shorten an approval process.
2. Improve some aspect of software testing.
3. Reduce errors in the software module check-in process.
4. Streamline help desk processes.
5. Reduce code rework on a large software project.

Kaizen blitzes are not intended to identify or launch major projects, although that can happen; instead their focus is always on what an organization can do right now to fix this problem. Results are expected to be visible to everyone within a week of the blitz, or at most a few weeks later. With that in mind, proposing long-term or expensive projects is rarely in the scope of such teams. When an organization gets used to using Kaizen events for problem solving, the effect is contagious. Employees feel more empowered. Problems don't fester because there is a way to address them right away. The business gets steadily better and better as time goes on, without major upheavals. Changes are small but continuous, and the entire attitude of the employees and management becomes "can-do" because they have seen problems fixed with regularity.

A Typical Kaizen Event

Before the Event

Choose a facilitator, choose the team members (five to ten is typical), identify the problem(s) to be addressed, clear team members' schedules so they can participate, arrange for meeting spaces, establish goals, and set a rough budget for implementation. All Kaizen events are facilitated, and if this is a new kind of activity for the company, they will typically use a consultant to facilitate the events until they have the trained people on staff to do it.

Day 1

The team spends a few hours to a day learning specific Lean concepts, Kaizen rules, or other techniques determined by the facilitator to be useful for this event.

Day 2

The team studies the targeted process in detail. Whenever possible, they study it on-site by observing people doing the process in real time. They might make process flow diagrams, time and motion diagrams, or spaghetti diagrams as they see fit. They will also collect all relevant process measurements. Finally, the team creates a value stream map (VSM) and discusses the current process using the VSM.

Day 3

Brainstorm ways to improve the process. In some cases, implementation can begin immediately. Because the team is working at the workplace, often workplace experiments can be conducted while the team is present.

Day 4

The new process improvements have been implemented and a plan to ensure that the improvements "stick" (sometimes called a Continuous Improvement Plan) is created.

Day 5

Observe and fine-tune the process. The final result, along with the improvement plan, is presented to management by the team. If a consultant has been used to facilitate, it is important that the consultant not make the presentation. The employees must take ownership of everything they have done!

Kaizen events can be full-time events for some or all of the team members, or they can only require part-time participation from them. One of the hallmarks of regular Kaizen events is the first-day training. This kind of problem solving has regular, focused training built into it. Most people like to learn new skills. This constant exposure to new ideas, and refreshing of ideas that might have become stale, combined with regular successes from the Kaizen events, make for an energized workforce. If you do this right, it won't be long before people are volunteering to be on your Kaizen teams and because the teams will be making money for the company, the company will want to have all the events they can handle.

Muda, Muri, or Mura?

Muda, muri, and *mura* are Japanese words used to describe major categories of wasteful practices by Toyota when they created TPS.

Muda is wasteful activities. This is any activity that consumes a company resource and adds no value to the product or service in the objective eyes of the customers. As you get used to Lean concepts, keep remembering that it's not your eyes that matter, it's the customer's eyes. You don't find out about their response by applying an internal group think to it. You find out directly from the customer, or in the case of a consumer product or service, from someone who can objectively represent the customer. Muri is the condition where people or equipment are overly stressed. This is also a form of waste. Overburdening causes equipment breakdown, fatigue, and errors. You can consider it to be conditions where you ask people to do unreasonable or impossible things. Mura is unevenness in an operation, when workflow is erratic so that you have to alternately hurry up and wait. This is also a form of waste, as it leads to inefficiency in how your entire system works.

Muri is an insidious form of organizational waste. We can explain it best with an example. Let's say that one of your team's jobs is to produce a weekly report for the president. It's a very important task and being on time matters. You have made that clear. A team member tries to print the report but the printer is out of toner. There are no other printers available to him so he looks in the storage closet for a replacement toner cartridge. He doesn't really know where they are kept because this isn't his normal job, but the administrative person who normally handles it is out that day. Because the deadline is looming, he asks others, but nobody can help, so he drives to the local store to find a cartridge. They are out so he tries another store. Two hours later he is back at work, new cartridge installed, printing his report. You might never even know that this happened unless the employee is in a mood to boast about his heroic efforts. Chances are that an activity like this is worth complaining about to his co-workers but not boast-worthy to his boss. What is wrong other than being behind on other work as a result? By this, we mean behind on real work, which is certainly more important than the artificial deadline of the management report, which, if you ask your *customer* (remember them?) has no value. This team wasted a few hours and delayed a customer project. There is usually additional collateral waste as well, such as the time spent bothering other employees while looking for help. Maybe he even took the last toner cartridge from the office supply store and caused the next customer there to have his or her own disaster. This one episode might not seem that important to you now, but if there are thousands of employees in your company and unreasonable events like this happen once a week to every one of them (a reasonable assumption), over the course of a year, this one form of waste alone can result in huge costs. Inefficiencies like this happen when we expect our employees to "do what must be done" to service the business. That alone isn't the culprit; it is that attitude combined with a lack of appropriate methods of handling problems, combined with processes that are not properly designed, and combined with a culture where complaining is wrong—that causes muri to happen. In fact, the reason we called it insidious is that our employees are often proud to have wasted all of this NVA time to please you!

What about mura, unevenness in work flow? Why is that wasteful? There is a reason why high-volume manufacturing assembly lines are designed the way they are. When things flow at an even pace, both equipment and people can work at a pace that allows them to be efficient, not get tired, not make mistakes, or not waste effort. It might sound boring, and it sure can be, but it is efficient. In most kinds of businesses, lumpy demand causes great inefficiencies. Consider a restaurant. If a restaurant is open all day, they have three very rush hours of demand, at each mealtime. For those periods they need high staffing. They also need equipment that is sized to keep up with that demand. In between mealtimes, they tell many of their employees to go home. There is little steady work in the restaurant business if your job is directly related to the customer being there. What about the capacity of the equipment? It has to be sized to produce food at the maximum rate at which we serve it. What about the facility itself? Other than at the rush hour period, the facility is largely empty. Restaurants are the epitome of waste! In the IT business lumpy demand is common. Users use our systems at varying times of the day. It isn't unusual for an application to have a 10:1 range of user activity. When this happens you have to staff and size everything to handle the peak loads. Sometimes you can't control the demand, but at other times you can influence it, even if you might not think you can. Differential pricing, for instance, can be used to incentivize people to use off-peak times for load-leveling purposes. A bill payment process center can affect the lumpiness of their monthly flow of bills by when they send the bills out. Send them all out on the same day of the month and you'll get a high peak. Send one-thirtieth of them out on each day and your workload peak will be substantially smaller, allowing you to staff and size your operation more efficiently.

Muda—ordinary wasteful activities—is the simplest category of waste so we left it for last. Muri and mura are more sophisticated, so they are often tackled last unless they are in-your-face big! We wanted the last category you read about to be remembered the most because it is the most common and easiest to deal with.

Ordinary waste, as you will see, isn't so ordinary to those who are new at Lean thinking. Waste is any activity that does not contribute to turning the flow of inputs into the outputs specified by the customer once. Those activities that do contribute to turning inputs into outputs are called value-added activities. They are necessary for us to do our jobs. Everything else is NVA, or waste, or muda. Examples of value-added activities include the following:

- Necessary calculations
- Taking an order
- Processing an order
- Ordering necessary supplies
- Building what was ordered
- Delivering what you promised

Examples of NVA activities include the following:

- Checking your work
- Asking for clarification
- Fixing mistakes
- Contacting the customer again
- Doing a task over
- Transporting supplies or information
- Creating reports

Waste is often put into categories to make it easier to identify. The most common categories are as follows:

1. Defects
2. Overproduction
3. Waiting
4. Transportation
5. Inventory
6. Motion

7. Extra processing
8. Underutilized people

As we describe each of these next, let us remind you that it is impossible for you to become "perfect" at even one of these. Perfection is not the goal here. The goal is *improvement*. We try to make clear what is waste and what is not so that we can correctly identify when action might be needed and work on the right problems. In fact, people new to Lean thinking are often stunned by how inefficient their business processes really are. Rather than worry about that too much, our advice is to learn the principles, then apply them methodically to improve.

Defects

A defect is anything that you don't create perfectly the first time. The definition of perfect should come from your consumers. If it's good enough for them to unconditionally accept it, then it's perfect. It's not necessary to get better than that. Defects can occur at delivery to the customer or internally along your internal process. The customer for most people in most large firms is an internal one. If you do something that has to be redone, you created a defect and that is waste. Only perfect performance the first time is value-added. Examples of defects in an IT environment could be any of the following:

- Code that has to be rewritten
- Bugs in code
- Late delivery
- Code that doesn't work as specified
- Errors in data
- Performance that is too slow

Reducing defects in your daily operation is a great way of improving your process effectiveness. Six Sigma techniques are often used to identify and reduce defect levels. What causes defects?

- Inadequate control measures
- Poor-quality material
- Unbalanced staffing or inventory (not having something when it's needed is a defect)
- Inadequate training
- Bad process or product design
- Inadequate understanding of the customer's needs
- Poor maintenance

Overproduction

Doing more than necessary to meet the goal is a waste. In Lean thinking, it is bad to plan for the future. It is wasteful to create anything before it is needed. In the perfectly Lean organization, you will create things without defects as they are needed and nothing more. This is a good time to point out that if we were discussing this with you in person you could find fault with any of these waste definitions. You could make what seem like logical arguments to violate each one of them because of some characteristic of your business, customers, process, or whatever. If we ever have that discussion we'll listen to you quietly while you make your argument, then politely but firmly point out that (in this example) all overproduction is waste, period. If you are overproducing for some reason that you believe is justified then you have made a management decision to waste your company's resources, period. You are doing that because you believe a root cause exists that drives it. The correct action is not to naively accept the waste as inevitable, but to find out and eliminate the root causes in your process that caused those decisions to be made in the first place. Your ideal goal is no overproduction!

Waiting

Any time your outputs to the customer wait, you are creating waste. The Lean IT shop completes their deliverable instantly before they are required by the customer. The perfect fulfillment center packages items for delivery just as they are ordered. The perfect call center processes calls just as they come in, without holding. You get the idea. Any time your process stops, something is being wasted. If you are producing a product, the working capital in that product is accumulating cost for nothing while it sits around waiting. If you are servicing, then the customer sits around eating your goodwill while they wait. Of course you cannot drive all waiting to zero, but if you recognize that waiting is always bad then you train yourself to identify it as a wasteful activity when it occurs and to monitor parts of your process where it is likely to occur.

Transportation

All transportation except for final delivery to the customer is waste. Here we're talking about transportation of your output to your customer. This is easier to describe using a physical process. If you are making widgets, the perfect process has the raw materials show up at one place in your business, just when you need them, then every person and machine necessary to work on them come to them, perform their work flawlessly, and finish without defects just in time for delivery. Nice, huh? Notice that people are moving, and machinery might move, but the product doesn't. When products move, nothing is happening to them. Changing location isn't an improvement. Riding on a truck doesn't transform the product. Moving your data from here to there doesn't make it any better. If you sent your customer a bill for $20 for moving stuff from Building A to Building B would they be happy to pay it? Would you if you were the customer?

Inventory

All inventories are waste. In a product company this can seem like heresy. You need safety stock for emergencies, right? Remember what we said about the difference between reality and perfection? It's important to know what perfection is. Maybe you do need a certain amount of inventory right now because of some characteristic of your business, but by properly classifying all inventory as waste, you open your eyes to knowing that it's a legitimate target for improvement. In a service company, you might not think you have any inventory, but you do. You have parts and supplies. In some cases people are inventory. In all cases, having it hang around waiting to be used is a waste of resources. After all, if it is in inventory you had to pay for it, right? And you have to protect it and insure it. And are you 100 percent sure that it's perfect? Of course you aren't, so there are defects in that inventory that are undiscovered. The quicker that you discover defects, the better job you can do at identifying the root causes of them and eliminating them. So hanging around in inventory hinders the defect reduction improvement process, too.

Motion

All motion of people or equipment that does not add value to the product or service is waste. Note that transportation waste referred to the product or service that you are producing. Motion waste refers to everything else. This is the kind of waste where people run around in circles to get their work done. It is caused by bad work methods, poor layout, poor housekeeping, bad workplace organization, and the need for employees to feel like they are "busy" while waiting. In a traditional workplace environment, people and equipment work hard. The product or service moves at a pace that is dictated by the process flow and how well those people and equipment did their jobs. When efficiency measures were created, they focused on the workers and on the production equipment. How well are we utilizing our stuff and how well are we utilizing our people were primary operational measures of efficiency. In that environment people quickly figure out that they have to keep busy and keep moving all the time. In so doing, they create huge amounts of waste moving themselves and stuff around. In that environment, there is also an incentive to overproduce because that keeps equipment operating. Inventory wasn't considered waste then, it was considered an asset! In a Lean environment, the focus should be on how well the product or service delivery is moving toward the customer, not on how well the people or equipment are being utilized! The major reason for this is time to delivery and your businesses' throughput ability, both of which are improved when the output to the customer moves without stopping. By measuring the right thing, which is how long it takes to create and deliver your output, you will go a long way toward becoming Lean.

Extra Processing Waste

This is any effort that you spend on your output that adds no value from the customer's point of view. This is more common than you might think. Some examples might help.

- Doing something just in case it is needed
- Not understanding just what was needed
- Redundant steps in processing or approvals that add no value
- Sending information to people who don't need it or won't use it
- Working on the product because you have spare time

In all cases, always remember to think about sending those thousands of little bills to your customer as you consider what adds value:

- Bill for $5,400 to add Feature A because we felt it might come in handy
- Bill for $1,420 to have twelve people in a meeting where four would have done the job
- Bill for $145 to have three levels of supervisors approve a travel request

Underutilized People

This is the last, but not least major waste category. This one is insidious. We often think we are doing the right thing when we overhire skills for a job, but in fact we aren't. First, extra skills might make it harder to find and recruit the person. Second, we have to pay more for higher skilled people. Third, if we aren't challenging them, they are far more likely to leave us, causing turnover costs and disruption. Underhiring at low pay can have similar effects. If we hire at too low a skill level or too low a pay grade, we can also get high turnover because we are likely to be disappointed and fire these employees, or they will be overstressed and leave. Failing to invest in appropriate training is also a form of waste because it causes employees to lack skills necessary to do their ever-changing jobs. This is especially true in the IT field, which changes rapidly. Finally, perhaps not such a problem in the world of IT, is injuring people. An injured employee is waste. They cannot work at all or cannot work as effectively. We'll add sickness to injury. If we help to keep our employees healthy, they will be able to continue to work for us. Do you have high levels of eye or back strain? Repetitive motion injury? Stress-related illnesses? All of these can be undiagnosed wastes of resources. People have to feel useful to stay with you and be productive. Even if the items we mentioned aren't a systemic problem for you, perhaps you are wasting your people resources in chunks because of organizational efficiency or poor planning. One of us was recently conducting training at a large IT organization that was part of the U.S. Department of Defense. They had very tight security requirements. While there, the author observed two new hires who had reported for work and spent a full week being paid to sit in the cafeteria because their security clearances were not yet ready. They thought it was a joke but they willingly took the money to read novels and browse the Internet. It started off their new job with the wrong frame of mind—that inefficiency and wasting time are acceptable. In a more recent example, an embedded systems programmer recently went to a client's office to meet with three others from three different companies to do a system integration of the pieces that all four of them had separately done. One of the key players was not there. One of the three who was there turned out to be a non-U.S. citizen, and therefore was not allowed in the high-security facility without an escort, and the escort assigned to do it had that day off. The entire integration exercise was a waste because nothing was accomplished but lots of money was spent. This is underutilization of people in spades, but it is obvious to anyone who is paying attention and looking around. The more insidious and tougher to detect kind of waste is the employee who is dutifully doing her job but only with half of her brain engaged because the work isn't interesting or challenging enough for her, and in her spare time she is constantly looking for a better job. This variety of wasted people might not be as easily detectible unless you are regularly checking into how your people are doing and feeling about their jobs.

In summary, waste is all around you. This chapter was intended to open your eyes to some of the key forms of it. Like anything, if you become aware of a problem, then start to measure important process variables, you will be able to improve things. One of the hallmarks of looking for and eliminating waste is that it is simple to do, can have an immediate effect on your bottom line, and often costs little or nothing to fix.

Process Efficiency

We have been talking about waste in your processes. If there were no waste you would have a perfect process, at least by this measure. You still might be doing the wrong thing perfectly, but that is a different subject! So how do we measure how efficient a process is? There is a very simple efficiency measure that is used in Lean thinking and it has several names depending on the author. It can be called process efficiency, process cycle efficiency, or flow time efficiency. The concept is simple. First make a flowchart of our process steps and note every step that we actually perform, value-adding or not. Then identify those steps that are truly value-adding. Remember that for a step to be value-adding, it must transform the product or service in the direction of making it more valuable for the customer. Then examine each of those value-added (VA) steps and measure (an estimate is fine at first) how long it takes on average to actually perform the useful work. Add up all of the

VA times for the entire process and you will have the theoretical VA time for the process. If there are parallel paths in some parts of the process, choose the longest VA time of each parallel path. If your process handles different kinds of activities or products, you might want to do the analysis for each service category or product separately. Next, estimate how long it takes from when the request comes in until the output is delivered. This will always be longer than the theoretical VA time. In fact it will typically be much longer. It isn't unusual for this actual process time to be ten, twenty, or even one hundred times longer than the theoretical one! Why? The reason is simple: because there are many places in your process where the thing you are working on just waits. It just sits there with nothing useful being done. Remember when you analyze this that you aren't tracking how much sweat your people are putting out, you are tracking how much the product or service you are processing is being transformed. If it isn't being transformed, it is waiting, an NVA waste, despite how many circles your people might be running around.

What is a good VA ratio? This depends on your process and industry. Various industry consultants quote world-class ratios from 5 percent to 25 percent. Although you might get some satisfaction out of knowing what is world class, the fact is that for most businesses, most of the time, that is irrelevant. You have what you have and if you aren't happy with your performance you need to make it better. Making it better is what it's all about. The notion of a world-class goal is useful if you are going for the Malcolm Baldrige or similar state process excellence award, but short of that, if your VA ratio is 1 percent and you increase it to 2 percent, even if world-class performance for your kind of process is 10 percent, you will have doubled the effectiveness of your process and you and your owners will be pleased and you all might even be celebrating in Hawaii. One final note about VA ratios: Ratios for actual processes that we have measured have ranged from .1 percent to 20 percent. That's a huge range and it encompasses manufacturing, IT, and administrative processes.

Capacity Constraints

A discussion of process efficiency would not be complete without talking about capacity constraints. Every system has constraints. A constraint is simply the part of the system that limits its performance; it is the slowest element. You can have different constraints for different performance measures, so let's keep this simple and talk about your production ability, or throughput. If you are a software development shop, your throughput might be lines of code per day. If you are a tech support operation, it might be calls completed per day. If you are a data warehouse, it might be queries per hour. If you are a spam filtering service, it might be millions of e-mails scanned per hour.

Your business has multiple people and multiple physical things that are used in some way to accomplish its goal. Some of these are in series where one thing has to finish before the next thing can start. Some might be parallel, where both things can be done at the same time. In all likelihood, your system is a complex combination of these elementary constructs. If you make a flowchart of your process steps and plot the common paths that your inputs take as they are transformed into your outputs, and if you measure the capacity of each step in the path in the same units, the one with the smallest value will be the constraint. Your system's throughput will always be limited by this constraint. Figure 5.1 depicts six operations in series, each with a different capacity for handling business. No matter how large the capacities of operations A, B, D, E, and F are, the process cannot produce any more than the capacity of operation C. Operation C constrains the throughput of the entire system to six units per hour.

There is an entire methodology devoted to managing a business with constraints that we save for a later chapter. The reason we introduce it here is that when we are thinking about process efficiency, we will naturally want to know how to improve it. Can you even imagine presenting an efficiency analysis to your management without their first question being "How can we make this better?"

When striving to improve the throughput of a process your, natural inclination might be to find the constraint and make it go faster, and sometimes that works. However, we want you to think about your process in more holistic terms. That's why you are reading this book, to gain a broader perspective on how your processes work. If there is no dead time in your process, no places where things wait, no places where they accumulate, no places where you perform NVA and time-consuming tasks on them, then attacking a constraint is usually a good idea. All those things probably are in your processes, however. Recall the VA ratios we discussed earlier. Remember what we said were typical ratios? Let's be generous and assume that your VA ratio is around 10 percent; in effect, 90 percent of everything you are

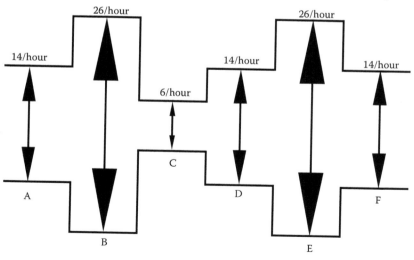

Figure 5.1   Process steps with different capacities.

doing in your transformation process adds no value in the eyes of the customer. It just wastes resources and time. Most important from their point of view, it wastes time. Time is not recoverable. We can't make up for taking an extra two days on something by adding a task that takes a negative two days so that in total, the task is done instantly! If you are concerned with the throughput of your operation, the right thing to attack in a process like this is not the constraining VA process step, but instead some of the NVA time. This is counterintuitive to most people. It has been engrained in most of us to focus on the places where work is being done and to make it more efficient. We focus on the operators in the call center to make them work faster. We focus on programmers to make them more efficient. We focus on computers to make them process faster. The fact is that for most processes, these are the wrong things to do! Instead of focusing on the productive parts of your business, focus instead on eliminating the wasteful, NVA steps. Focus instead on eliminating the inventory in your shop. Focus instead on eliminating layers of approvals. Let's be clear what "inventory" is. Inventory is any process input that is being converted to your sellable process outputs, or the outputs themselves. In some service businesses there is very little inventory. In a pure transaction environment inventory could conceivably be zero, but if you look, I'll bet you can find inventory in your process everyplace. All code that is in the process of being written or tested is inventory. All customers on hold or waiting for a response from you are inventory. All transactions in a queue waiting to be serviced are inventory. On the administrative side of your business you have lots of inventory, too. All orders waiting to be worked on are inventory. All e-mails in your in-box are inventory. You get the idea. It's hard to conceive of a real process with no inventory.

To understand mathematically why it is important to reduce inventory, we need to introduce one new concept and one simple process equation. The concept you want to know is that to minimize the lead time of any process, you should use the smallest possible lot size. The smallest theoretical size is one. A lot size of one results in the fastest possible throughput (given how your process steps currently work) and a lot size of one minimizes lead time. Lead time is the time from when you get an order to when you deliver. Although this concept is theoretically true, you might never be able to achieve it and it applies to production operations where there is a regular flow of items or services through the process. Still, this book is about process improvement, so it's good to know the principles. If your business can be thought of as a production operation, then think about what a single item is that travels through your business and think about how many of them are grouped together as lots today. To the extent that you can reduce the size of your typical lot closer and closer to one, your ability to deliver quickly (lead time) and the volume per month that you can produce (throughput) are both improved. An administrative example might help to make this clear. Let's say that you process five different types of paperwork in a typical week. You previously decided that to be "efficient" you would devote one day to each type. On Mondays you process purchase orders, on Tuesdays you do travel requests, and so on. Although you feel that you have made yourself efficient by doing this, you have created two bad things for your customers and your company. One is that your lead time is now up to a week because if a purchase order comes in on Tuesday, you won't touch it until the following Monday. Second, the rate at which you can process items has been throttled. This isn't as clear to demonstrate and because this is an introduction to the subject we won't attempt it. Do you see what you have done? You feel better and perhaps in some ways you have made yourself more efficient, but you have ruined the business process. You weren't focusing on what is important, delivering value to the customer; you were focusing on how to maximize your own productivity. Customers don't care how productive you are, they only care about how much you can do for them, how quickly you can do it, and how good the quality is.

The equation you want to know that relates this concept is called Little's law:

$$WIP = Lead\ Time \times Throughput\ Rate$$

This is written in a way to calculate how much inventory you will end up with in your process given a lead time and throughput rate. To put this law in a form more suitable to the IT world, we can express it as $N = \lambda * T$ where N is the average number of items in the process, λ (Greek letter lambda) is average arrival rate, and T is the average time an item stays in the process (lead time). This applies to how many calls are in your calling queue, how many people are in a store, how many lines of code are in your development shop, how many purchase orders are waiting to be processed, and so on. Whether we call it work in process (WIP) or N, it is inventory, or items hanging around in your business taking up space. In the case of inventory, it is taking up capital as well. A financially efficient company would operate with minimum WIP because any money you have tied up in WIP must be obtained (via loans or capital), must be paid for (interest or dividend), must be housed, must be insured, and so on. One more bad thing about WIP is that it often harms the quality process. It does this by delaying the discovery of errors. If we don't quality test something until it gets to the end of our process, then the longer that something is in our process, the more time has passed from the time a defect was created until the time it is detected. This makes quality improvement more difficult because the evidence related to how it was created might be gone. On top of that, the error that resulted in the defect might be in all the items in WIP! If there are one hundred items in WIP, then all one hundred of them could be infected with the quality defect. But if we have a very Lean process with only one item in WIP at a time, the error will be discovered before it can infect other production items. In summary, to a Lean thinking company, all WIP is bad and we strive to minimize it. Little's Law tells us how to do that. Because WIP = Lead Time × Throughput Rate, then to reduce WIP you need to reduce lead time, reduce throughput rate, or both.

We titled this section "Capacity Constraints." As you can see, we covered a lot of concepts here. Our goal is to open your eyes to many of the characteristics of your business process that constrain your ability to produce quickly and efficiently so you can focus on the right ones. Sometimes it really is the obviously slow VA process step, but often it is not that at all; it is the fact that you process in batches, or the fact that you accumulate too many things before working on them. If somebody isn't constantly taking a systems-level view of your business, then you will be bombarded with requests to improve pieces of the business that will all seem perfectly logical to the requestor, and might seem perfectly logical to you as well, but that will result in no overall business improvement because the improvement is not being done on a system constraint. If we are both working in series and you are the bottleneck, no amount of improvement in what we do is justified, despite its local appeal to us or the people around us. This is one of the major reasons why companies spend vast amount of money on projects that have apparent financial payouts yet never affect the bottom line. Nobody is looking at the entire system when the decision to improve a piece of it is made. Don't you get caught in this trap yourself!

The Five Ss (Your Mother on Steroids)

Although this is the last topic in this chapter, it is usually the first thing that a company does when they adopt Lean thinking. We call it "Your Mother on Steroids" and you'll soon see why. One of the principles of Lean thinking is that you can't be efficient in what you do if you live in a state of disorder. Disorderliness causes inefficiencies in lots of ways. The person with a messy desk who claims that it's efficient for her because she knows exactly where everything is located is not the person we should be modeling our businesses after. That person might be right if she is a hermit, or a solitary writer, or some other creative person who works by themselves. In a company where people work in teams, however, messiness is an efficiency disaster. Although Lean started in Japan, it has spread around the world and nobody that we know of has elected to skip this phase of Lean, although different companies implement it to different levels of detail. So what are the Five Ss?

1. Sort
2. Set in Order
3. Shine
4. Standardize
5. Sustain

In the United States, we normally add a sixth S to this list, especially in manufacturing environments, and that is safety. The entire Five S concept is simple. Let's walk through them in a story.

Most workplaces have the things needed to do the job someplace in the vicinity. They also have many things that are not needed to do the job! Maybe some of that latter category was needed at one time but it isn't needed now. Maybe it is needed occasionally but not normally. Maybe it never was needed at this location but is simply being stored for someone else. Whatever the reason, there is excess stuff in every place in every environment. In the Sort phase, we identify everything that is needed to do our tasks at each workstation, keep it there, and remove everything else! Get rid of the stuff you don't normally need. It's that simple. The Sort phase of this Five S cleanup effort seems pretty simple, but there are many issues to deal with. First, how do we decide what is needed? What if you need something once a month? Should that stay? Once a quarter? What will you do with the stuff you take away? Where will it go? What if you need something that someone else is throwing away? In this phase, your company goes through a huge junkyard exercise. Anybody who has not been through this will be amazed at the huge volume of stuff that can be removed from a workplace. There are logistics to consider that often go like this. First, designate a central location for all of the removed items. Then designate a tagging system so we can track where it came from, who put it there, and why. Next, designate places for stuff you decide to keep for occasional use. Then allow people to look through this huge pending junkyard for stuff they might need, being careful not to let them take anything that isn't essential for their work. Finally, sell, junk, or give away everything else.

This Sort phase is a fairly simple exercise that involves simple training, no complex concepts, and the entire organization. Not only does it succeed in clearing lots of stuff from the workplace, stuff that was in the way of productivity, but it also serves as a simple way to start teaching people about Lean and efficiency concepts. As a side benefit, it's a good way to give simple leadership tasks to people who might be looking to grow in that area. The clever manager will take advantage of all of this.

After you have done your sorting, next comes the Set in Order phase. This is another simple concept. Once you have only what you need at your workplace, arrange it so that it is in the most convenient places for you to use. Put frequently used items closest to you. If you do repetitive work, arrange things so that you don't have to turn around or walk or move something to get to it. Think about the little details of your workplace and arrange your "stuff" so that you can do your job with as little movement as possible. Also make things easy to put away. Having to open a drawer to put something away might not seem like a big deal, but if you do it five times a day, that's 1,250 drawer openings and closings a year. Can't you do something more useful than that with your time? Part of this phase is storing similar items together for logical consistency. Some places color code things to make them easier to identify and pick up. Label items and storage locations so you know where everything is at a glance. If you use specialized tools or equipment, you might consider making special carts or tables for them if it will help. For instance, if an item is heavy and needs to be moved to and from a workplace regularly, storing it on a work surface that is the same height means it can be slid rather than picked up. Sliding is faster and safer. Putting things on wheeled carts can make it easier to share common equipment. Arranging for quick disconnect cabling or standardizing the cables used can make sharing items more convenient. Beyond lists of common things like this, there are really no formal rules for this stage. Just think about where things are and how they move in each work area and organize it for convenience. Like the Sort phase, this phase is done mostly by each individual in the company, so it's a widespread activity and all will have it in common. As part of your employee training for this phase, be sure to explain the difference between VA and NVA activities. While they are organizing their workplace, have them look for ways of eliminating or reducing all NVA steps. This phase isn't only for individuals. This is a good time to have teams look at bigger picture workflow and consider rearranging work teams, perhaps putting people closer together who need to communicate often or who use common equipment, and so on. In other words, this is an opportunity to implement standard old industrial engineering workplace organization steps. Do you think that because you are a knowledge worker that this doesn't apply to you? Think again! What kinds of resources do your employees need? How many hoops do they have to jump through to use them? This phase is about eliminating those hoops to make their everyday life easier. Are they constantly switching between applications? Can you make that easier to do? Do they need to work on multiple things at once? Would multiple monitors help? Is it easy for them to have meetings? What about virtual meetings? How often do they have to move things around to do something? Would duplicate items reduce that movement? Remember all such movement is NVA. You might think this doesn't add up, but it does. When you clear the clutter out of a person's work space and make it efficient for that person to do what he or she does most of the time, he or she is not distracted with the minutia of constantly having to divert creative thought processes to mundane tasks like finding paper for the printer.

The next Five S stage is the Shine stage. In this stage we expand the old adage that cleanliness is next to godliness into cleanliness is mandatory for efficiency. Once unnecessary things are out of the way and everything has its place, clean up the workspace—all of it. If you have ever been in a company that practices Lean, everything is clean! There are two reasons to do this. The first is practical: Clutter is inefficient and dirt hides problems. The second reason is emotional: People feel better about living in a clean environment. It makes them proud. Although nobody likes to do the cleaning, everyone likes to live in a clean place. A Lean environment is kept that way by discipline. The entire Five S program, besides the physical benefits it offers, is a way to start building a level of discipline into your workplace. Some of the more complex Lean changes require a disciplined approach to work. If you are unable to get your employees to clean up their own workspaces, what makes you think you can get them to do more complex things? The argument that cleaning isn't necessary has to be dispelled. Part of what we do when we insist on a clean workplace is to instill a habit of discipline in our employees, which is a good habit to have. There will be grumbling as they transition from sloppy to neat, but you can be sure that several months later when all this has become natural, all else equal, they will be happier to be at work every day, and happy employees are creative employees!

The next Five S phase, Standardize, can be thought of as an extension of the Shine stage. Here we make cleaning and organizing routine. We establish preventive maintenance on important equipment. We clean regularly. Everyone has cleaning-related tasks to do either daily or weekly, depending on the nature of your business. Traditional Lean books refer to physical cleaning and moving equipment maintenance. In an IT world, physical cleaning is just as important, but we aren't as likely to encounter oil and product spills. Instead, we find disk drives that need defragging or checking, databases that need compacting, printers that need cleaning, communication lines that need testing, and so on. Instead of waiting for things to break or grind to a halt, we establish reasonable schedules for maintenance and do them on a schedule, just like we have meals every day. One of the principles here is to push this kind of work to the people closest to the workplace and keep maintenance specialists away unless they are really needed. Standardize can also mean to establish what normal means in a workplace with respect to where everything is, and to be able to quickly identify abnormal conditions. In a department that has a production orientation, like a data center or a call center, this is easy to do. In a department that does unique projects, this might not make much sense to do. Lean is flexible. We adopt those facets of it that add value to our business process and minimize or eliminate those facets that don't help or are impractical.

In the final phase, Sustain, we build systems into our work practices that help us to maintain the order we have established. Do this with periodic audits, with Five S checklists posted at key locations, with regular awards for good Five S performance, and so on. To sustain this Five S state, several things have to be true:

1. Employees have to be aware of the program. You have to train them!
2. Employees have to have time in their schedule to do the required tasks.
3. Management has to have a structure in place for Five S (goals, standards, etc.).
4. Management has to visibly support the effort by following it themselves, providing leadership, providing resources, and providing recognition.

If your company has a formal safety program, you might want to consider making this a Six S program with Safety as the extra phase. Safety in an office environment doesn't normally have the focus that it has on a shop floor, but there is a definite role for it because there are definite dangers. Here are some dangers that office workers face:

1. Tripping over cords
2. Electrical and fire hazards from improper use of extension cords
3. Back injuries from improper lifting or poor storage shelving practices
4. Cuts from paper, scissors, sharp edges of cases, and so on

5. Electrocution from unsafe practices of working around electrical equipment
6. Eye strain from improper lighting and monitor placement
7. Repetitive motion injury (carpal tunnel syndrome)
8. Broken noses and bones from running into opening doors or while rounding corners
9. Scalds from hot beverages in the break area or while carrying them to the workplace

Should you feel inclined to dismiss this as trivial, here are some facts on carpal tunnel syndrome from the U.S. Department of Labor:

- The U.S. Department of Labor has concluded that carpal tunnel syndrome is the "chief occupational hazard of the 1990s," disabling workers in epidemic proportions.
- Currently, carpal tunnel syndrome affects more than 8 million Americans.
- Carpal tunnel syndrome is the top reported medical problem, accounting for about 50 percent of all work-related injuries.
- Only 23 percent of all carpal tunnel syndrome patients were able to return to their previous professions following surgery.
- Up to 36 percent of all carpal tunnel syndrome patients require unlimited medical treatment.

Every Lean company that we've ever seen has had a Five S or Six S program, and they implemented this program as their first step toward a Lean business. How big an effort this will be depends on your current state of cleanliness and workplace organization. Starting here allows you a chance to introduce beginner-level Lean concept training with something tangible and simple to do. It allows you to get in control of the program. It also allows you to identify employees who will embrace it and those who might fight it. All this will be useful as you proceed on your Lean journey.

Chapter 6

Understanding Six Sigma

We started Chapter 4 off by briefly introducing Six Sigma as a fairly rigorous methodology for solving business process problems. Six Sigma tools are oriented to repetitive business processes, those that regularly produce outputs. It is data-based problem solving; it requires that we have very specific measures of performance and that we be able to quantify current performance with measurements—enough measurements to matter. Once we have quantitatively assessed current performance, we rigorously determine what the root causes are for unacceptable behavior, these are also confirmed with data, and then we systematically attack those roots until our system performs as desired as demonstrated by more data. There is nothing magic in this. It is the straightforward application of measurements, statistics, and scientific problem solving. A scientist might look at Six Sigma and say "What is all the fuss about? We've been doing this for a hundred years." And she would be right! However, businesses have not always been run with scientific methods. Businesses are created by entrepreneurs, people who have visions and leadership skills, people who have passion and endurance and sometimes great luck. As these businesses expand, the leader has less and less direct impact on the business and the processes that make it up so the company begins to rely more and more on the experience of their employees. Passion and vision are important but are not particularly useful at letting others know what to do in large groups. Also, passion and vision don't normally help create repeatable processes. Repeatable processes are necessary to have a reliable business operation. Six Sigma problem solving is oriented around the creation and improvement of repeatable processes. It is a methodology that allows businesses to solve problems in a scientific way rather than relying on hunches, "experience," or the way we've always done it. What is "experience" anyway? You know exactly what experience is: Experience is what is left after mistakes. Sometimes experience kills people but those who survive are considered valuable to many businesses. Why should that be? Does experience make me a good problem solver? Does it make me a good leader? A good trainer? Maybe, but maybe not. Relying on employees with experience is dangerous when you need reliability and predictability and high performance unless you are happy with your systems running just the way they have in the past, because experience tends to make people want to repeat what worked for them in the past. Six Sigma gives us a way to use employees with normal experience and knowledge but harness what they know to solve problems and improve your business in ways that are predictable and better than normal. The Six Sigma system will make your process improvement efforts successful, not whether you happened to pick the right person for the job. You never have enough right people anyway, right?

What Is a Standard Deviation?

We have been talking about things being predictable and repeatable. Why is that important and how do we measure it? These terms are closely connected. If something is repeatable, it means that it will tend to do the same thing over and over. If you are shooting a rifle at a target, and you were very repeatable, you could perhaps fire every round into the same hole. Even if the hole is nowhere near where you are aiming, if they all go to the same place, you have a repeatable process. If what you really want is to hit the bull's-eye and your process is repeatable, it's easy to adjust what you are doing to hit it. Simply adjust the sights on the rifle so that the position of the round lands closer to where you want. As long as you continue to fire the rifle the same as you did before, a successful adjustment will now have you hit the target every time. If you are familiar with guns, you will recognize this as a very simple adjustment to make. But what if when you look at your initial pattern, the rounds landed all over the place? What if there was no pattern to them at all? If sometimes they were high, sometimes were low, sometimes missed it completely, and sometimes hit the target next to you? Besides the fact that nobody would want to be anywhere near you, this would be a much more difficult process to fix. Your process is not repeatable. Because of that, it isn't predictable. Repeatable processes are predictable. We can estimate reliably what they will do in the future. Unrepeatable or erratic processes are not predictable. We have no idea what will happen next. That's why the smart shooter will get far out of the way when the unrepeatable shooter comes to the range! Let's describe one other situation here. Let's say that after firing a group of rounds, you see that not all the bullets go into the same hole, but there is a grouping of them that has a discernable shape. It will probably be round. Figure 6.1 shows these patterns.

If every time you fire a group of shots, you get a random but discernable shape, you also have a predictable process! Your process is just as predictable as the person who puts them all into the same hole, but the two of you have different amounts of variation. If three shooters are all predictable (i.e., they all have circular patterns of

Figure 6.1 Random shot pattern.

holes in their targets), but each has a different size pattern, the one with the smallest pattern has the least amount of variation and the one with the largest pattern has the most variation.

How do we measure how much variation a process has? The most ubiquitous metric for this is the standard deviation (stdev). The stdev is a statistical measure of how much variation there is. In the case of the shooter, this would be how much the shots vary around the center of the circle of shots. It does not measure how close to the center of the target we are, just how big that circle of holes is. Figure 6.2 shows two shot patterns. The one with the smallest diameter (least variation) has the smallest standard deviation.

Part of the Six Sigma technique is simply for everyone to know the proper way to describe things and knowing what a standard deviation is and how to calculate it is the first step for a team to have a common language to describe variability. If we want to make data-based decisions, we cannot rely on statements like you might hear on the firing range such as "That's really good," or "You have really improved." We have to be able to quantify variability and express it in the right terms and the standard deviation is what we use. Much better statements are "Last week the standard deviation of your shots was 2.3 and this week it's 1.5. Good job!" The bigger the standard deviation, the more variation there is, so normally we are trying to make it smaller. A smaller stdev would mean a tighter grouping of shots. Now we have a precise language that we can use to describe variability to each other. This is important because people do not have a natural way of distinguishing between two groups of things, one of which is slightly more or less variable than the other. Our minds and brains just don't think that way. We need to calculate the stdev to really

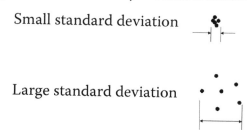

Figure 6.2 Two different random shot patterns.

know. Table 6.1 is an example. The data represent how long a standard query from two different databases takes in milliseconds.

Table 6.1 Query Time Example

	Query Times (milliseconds)	
	Database A	Database B
	17.7	26.8
	20.2	22.8
	20.3	25.1
	18.9	16.4
	20.4	12.9
	17.4	29.1
	20.4	14.3
	20.9	17.2
	19.8	11.1
	22.0	16.4
	20.4	18.7
	18.6	26.4
	21.3	15.6
	18.7	13.6
	20.4	26.0
	20.1	18.2
	20.6	20.4
	21.4	19.9
	19.9	25.0
	17.9	22.5
Mean	19.9	19.9
Stdev	˜1.3	˜5.3

Both databases have the same mean (average) query times but B has a much larger stdev than A, meaning it is a lot more variable and users of that database will see more variation in query time performance. One of the first things that Six Sigma practitioners learn is that although it is common business practice to compare two things by comparing their averages, it is a really bad idea to do that. Averages do not tell you much about a process. When you add the standard deviation information, you know a lot more. In this case, the averages are the same but the two databases have widely different performance and users will notice it. If there is a specification on response time, Database B will fail it much more frequently than Database A.

DMAIC

DMAIC is an acronym for the most commonly used Six Sigma methodology. About 95 percent of all Six Sigma projects follow the DMAIC methodology. The acronym is the first letters of the stages of a Six Sigma performance improvement project: Define, Measure, Analyze, Improve, and Control. This methodology was developed to provide an organized way to solve problems. Using a standard structure for problem solving, all the process improvement teams go through the same steps and nothing is forgotten. The methodology also provides standard places for management review. In addition, the methodology provides a standard terminology for everybody to use. This helps both management and employees know where everybody is on each project. If I say that I'm in the Analyze phase, then you will know what I mean.

The Define stage is where we start each project. It's helpful to think of the outputs of each stage to know what the stage does. In this stage we establish the goal of the project. We should know who our customer is, which process we will be working on, which part of the process we will work on, which of the process variables are important, what the goal is for those process variables, how much money we expect to save or other benefits we will get, when the project will be finished, who the project team is, and who the stakeholders are. It is in the defined stage where we first see evidence of Six Sigma thinking. The goal of a project always has to be stated as a measurement, the value of which will be improved. It might be stated as several measurements and goals for each of them. Each of these measurements is an important process output that matters to the customer. All six similar projects must identify who the customer is for each process. The customer sets the acceptable parameters for each of the key process outputs. These are usually expressed as specifications, but might take other forms. The key is that no project can proceed unless a quantifiable goal is stated. At the end of the define stage you will have a well-defined project with well-defined and quantifiable goals.

The next stage is the Measure stage. At the output of this stage we should have a thorough understanding of how the process is behaving right now. By understanding we mean a quantitative description. This description will include current process variable averages, standard deviations, behavior over time, and histograms. In addition, we will know whether the process is stable or not. Another thing we will know at the end of this stage is whether or not the process has a capability and what the value is. We discuss what capability is in more detail later, but it is basically the measured ability of the process to meet customer demands. The *sigma level*, for which Six Sigma is named, is an example of a capability measure.

To do all of this we have to collect data, and to know what data to collect, we need to know which characteristics are critical. Sometimes this is determined in the Define stage, but sometimes what we are given in the Define stage is not sufficient for us to collect data. The first thing we would then do is determine the precise measurements necessary to determine process capability. For example, let's assume that your project is to improve the turnaround time for software support requests. How are we going to measure this turnaround time? Does it start when the initiators first think about it? When they create their request form? When they submit the form? When you receive the form? What if there are approvals necessary for the request to be submitted? Do all of those approvals have to be finished before the request is considered started? In a similar vein, when is this request complete? Does it end when the programmer thinks he or she is finished? Does it end when the end user says that it is finished? Is it complete after the end user has tested it? Although this is a simple example, it illustrates the precise nature of the measurement definition that is necessary to collect data. This might seem a little picky, but it's not. Defining precisely when the start and finish points of the project are helps everybody to agree on a common definition of the critical variable, and it allows us to actually collect data unambiguously.

Let's talk about data for a moment. You run the IT organization. You're swimming in data. Any database project should be a snap for you, right? We have some bad news. The chances that the data that you will need are the data that you have might be quite small. Of course, in some cases you'll find you have just what you need in your databases. In other cases the agreed-on definition will result in the discovery that you don't quite have what is necessary. In addition, for certain aspects of data-based decision making, we need very specific kinds of data, frequently the kinds of data that are not collected by businesses. Businesses collect data for different reasons and problem solving. They collect data to assess financial results. They might collect data to determine which of their functions are performing best. The most common data collected are averages; everybody collects averages. However, as we have already seen, data averages do not tell the whole story. In fact, they tell only about a quarter of the story. We merely point this out to make you aware in advance that many Six Sigma process improvement projects will require that you collect new data. You might consider this bad news, but it is not necessarily bad at all. If you are not collecting data that will help you to determine process performance right now, you will be after each project. In addition, it frequently does not take very many data to make meaningful decisions about process performance. Very often only about one hundred data points are needed to make intelligent decisions. This is so few data that they can often be collected manually if necessary. In fact, one of the problems with IT organizations and process improvement is that more time is spent trying to find ways to collect data automatically when it would be cheaper and faster to do it manually.

The third stage in a DMAIC process is the Analyze phase. The overall approach in Six Sigma problem solving is to carefully define a problem, find the root causes for the problem, and then attack the root causes. The purpose of the Analyze phase is to correctly identify what those root causes are and prove it with data. In this disciplined problem-solving method, your opinions are not worth much. In fact, nobody's opinions are worth much. It is not that they are valueless, in fact we use the opinions of the team to come up with ideas for what the root causes are and that is normally the very first thing we do via a brainstorming session. Then we proceed to gather evidence to prove what matters and what doesn't. This could be a simple exercise or it could be most of the project, depending on how difficult the problem is and how complex the process is. This is where the similarity to the traditional scientific method comes in. Your opinions as to what the root causes are constitute your hypotheses. No scientist would act on a hypothesis because it's just a guess. They conduct experiments to prove whether the hypothesis is likely to be true or false. We do the same thing. We might be lucky and have historical data that we can analyze using some basic statistics that will help to convince us which of our "guesses" are true and which are not, or we might have to conduct some experiments and collect some new data. Again, this could be a simple exercise or a very long and expensive one. How much we are willing to do depends on the value that we would gain to solve the problem. Nobody would spend two effort-months to prove or disprove a root cause hypothesis that would save the company $10,000. They sure would, however, if it had the potential to save $1 million. Sometimes the cost of implementing solutions is cheap and fast, so we could abandon our scientific method and simply try various solutions. Although this approach might be repulsive to many rigorous Six Sigma people, we are realists, and sometimes trial and error is just plain effective. The difference between random trial and error, however, and a managed decision to do it for a few carefully selected potential root causes that were arrived at in an organized fashion, is huge. As long as we know what we are doing and why and can defend our decision, we see nothing wrong with avoiding experiments. More often than not, though, the analysis of historical data or the collection of new data because we had not been collecting the right data before to answer these questions, or constructing controlled experiments to determine cause and effects are necessary. Figure 6.3 shows a generalized process with inputs, process variables, environment variables, and outputs.

Every output has multiple characteristics. Our project is always defined as improving one or more characteristics of one or more outputs of a process. For example, reduce the number of times that incoming support calls take more than three minutes to complete. The output is the call. The characteristic we care about is the call length. The process itself has many variables, of course. Some of them might be how many people we have, what their training level is, characteristics of

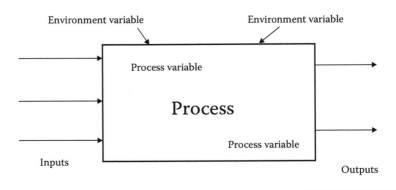

Figure 6.3   A simple process diagram.

our phone system, and so on. The inputs in this case are also calls. Some characteristics are the topic of the call, the education or experience of the caller, and so on. The environment might include things like the time of day, the temperature of the call center, whether it is a nice day outside, the level of noise in the room, the number of disruptions that are present, and so on. One thing we'd like to point out here is the folly of experience. People are good at a lot of things, but people are not very good at determining patterns within complexity. In other words, they are not very good at determining root causes in complex processes. In fact we'll make the statement that the more experienced someone is, the less likely he or she is to come to the right answer of what true root causes are in complex situations. The only exceptions to this are physical processes that are very standardized, such as an oil refinery. The reason we say this is because people feel compelled to give their opinions. In fact, you as a business manager put them into this position every day. You demand that they make decisions, even when it's scientifically impossible for them to know they have made the right one, because you have no formal decision-making process in place, yet you still demand decisions so your employees make them. They make hundreds of them every week, and many of them are, in the eyes of the formal problem solver, simply random decisions, half of which are right and half of which are wrong. The objective of a formal process such as the DMAIC process is to ensure that important decisions are usually right and to not allow experience to make those 50-50 calls for us. Experience can kill a business. In summary, when we finish the analyze phase of a DMAIC problem-solving process, we know what is causing our problem and we have evidence to back that knowledge up.

Perhaps it seems like a long time coming if you are the impatient sort, but in the Improve stage, we come up with solutions. Finally! This stage also often starts with a brainstorming session. But now we know what the root causes are. Let's reflect a minute on just what we mean by a root cause. A root cause is something that is controllable and has a direct effect on the characteristic we are trying to improve. If we could have controlled the characteristic itself, if it had a big knob on it we could turn that made it bigger or smaller, we would have turned it, but it doesn't. So we find root causes that do have knobs on them, things we can change that will improve the process characteristic we care about. This problem-solving session again can be short and simple or long and complex, depending on your process. Frankly, at this point most teams have pretty good ideas of what to do, so solutions often flow easily. The hard part, after all, was finding out what the real root causes are. Now that we know them for sure, we can attack them with gusto. In fact, we often have multiple solutions offered so one of the things we do in this phase is choose the best one. That might be a technology exercise, a financial one, an environmental one, or a combination of factors. Sometimes the solution is not obvious and we might have to conduct some other experiments and collect some new data to figure out what to change. Sometimes solution ideas are easy to come by, but analyzing which are the best ones can be very expensive or complex. If your problem is where to locate a new data center to increase response time, some of the solutions might involve relocation of data centers, combining them, or adding new ones in various places. How would you choose between them? This kind of problem doesn't lend itself to a calculation answer, but it can be easily simulated. In fact, dynamic computer simulation is often used to help choose from competing solution options when the effects cannot be calculated and trial and error is too expensive. Simulation concepts are taught in most Six Sigma Black Belt programs, but actually doing the simulation is a specialty and normally requires that you use a consultant who knows how because your own people would normally never do this or would do it so infrequently that it isn't cost effective to train them. One of the services that our firm provides is simulation for project teams.

Not only do we figure out what the best solution is in the improve stage, but we also implement it! At the end of this stage, the process improvement is installed and the process is now running per our goals. Some Six Sigma programs split this stage into two, where the improve stage involves figuring out what the solution is and the implement stage actually implements the solution. This is because there are different skills needed to problem solve (improve) and to build (implement) so it seems like a logical break. Although that is true, most programs only have one I in DMAIC and it's the team's job to get the solution done, even if they subcontract it to another group.

The final DMAIC stage is Control. This is unique to the Six Sigma approach. Most managers have heard of the Hawthorne effect. The Hawthorne effect is a temporary change of behavior or performance in response to a change in the environmental conditions, with the response being typically an improvement. The term was coined in 1955 by Henry A. Landsberger when analyzing older experiments from 1924 to 1932 at the Hawthorne Works (outside Chicago). Landsberger defined the Hawthorne effect as *a short-term improvement caused by observing worker performance.* In other words, it's not what you did that improved performance, it's the fact that you paid attention to it that caused everyone around you to behave better than normal. As soon as you leave, things will go back to where they were. Even if the Hawthorne effect isn't operating on your project, because your problems are more technical and equipment oriented and less reliant on people's behavior, there is still a tendency for systems that have undergone an improvement to degrade back to where they were. This happens for a lot of reasons, including the habits of people, but regardless of the reasons, if you want your improvement to stay there forever without you watching it, you need to build something into the process that will ensure it. That's what the Control stage is in Six Sigma. In this stage the team makes sure that appropriate things are done so that the process will continue to perform at its new level. This can include administrative things like making sure that training materials or written procedures are modified, making sure that new specifications are transmitted and understood by everyone who needs them, including suppliers, and making sure that critical control points are monitored and that procedures exist to react quickly when something goes out of balance. The Control phase isn't as exciting as the other phases because it tends to involve administrative and wrap-up activities, but the wise business owner will not let Six Sigma teams call their project finished until the Control phase is done. In Value-Train's Black Belt program, student project reports are not accepted unless they include a Control phase plan.

So there you have it, Six Sigma in five letters—DMAIC. Six Sigma is called a tools-based methodology because the DMAIC framework itself is fairly simple, and most of the work is done using a variety of tools such as flowcharts, various statistics, control charts, brainstorming exercises, and so on. Most of the specific tools and techniques used in all of these phases might already be familiar to you. In fact, very little was actually invented by the creators of Six Sigma. Their two most obvious inventions were the DMAIC process itself and the notion of a capability index called the Sigma Level, for which the methodology was named. It is for this reason that people with a background in quality, process improvement, or scientific approaches might already know many of the specific tools that they need to participate on a Six Sigma project team. Unfortunately, many business decisions, even very important ones, are made by the seat of our pants, so a formal methodology like this is very useful to make sure that some rigor is used in your process improvement decision making. As with anything, efforts like this depend heavily on management. If you train your people on how to do the Six Sigma approach and don't use it yourself or don't allow them the time to make good decisions, or demand fast answers that can't be justified, you will be your own worst enemy. From our experience, about half of all the corporations trained in Six Sigma approaches fail to use it effectively because senior management really doesn't believe in it. They don't enforce decision-making rigor and don't use it themselves. Your people will emulate your behaviors, regardless of what you send them to training for.

Because Six Sigma uses data so much, let's talk about some more characteristics of data. Earlier in the book we talked about continuous and attribute data types and data collection plans. Now we will talk a little about what to do with it once you have it.

Data Displays

Displaying data is important. It isn't the first thing we do, but let's start with displays because they are the most visible representation of data, certainly in management presentations. This isn't a statistics book or technical manual, but we need to emphasize this because every project will have to deal with it.

The most fundamental way of displaying data is to simply list it: Put it in a table. That's how you will probably get it, after all. However, it is often a poor way to display data because everybody's eyes will quickly glaze over looking at hundreds or thousands of numbers. An improvement over simply showing the data is to sort it. By sorting it, at least we start to put some order to it. We can display it several times, each sorted differently. This is a little help, but not a big one unless you are looking for very simple things. The next general category of data display is to display summaries. Now we have lots of options. If the data have categories we can summarize by category, and so on. What kinds of summaries are useful? We've already mentioned averages and will talk about them later, along with other summary statistics that describe your data.

The data displays you are probably most used to seeing are graphs. Graphs are ubiquitous in business, and they are also often badly used. Certain forms of graphs are better for conveying certain characteristics of data, so learn to choose your graphs with thought. Here are a few ideas.

Bar graphs can be displayed vertically or horizontally and are best when trying to show differences between values or groups of values. Figure 6.4 is an example of a vertical bar graph and Figure 6.5 shows a horizontal bar graph. Each has some

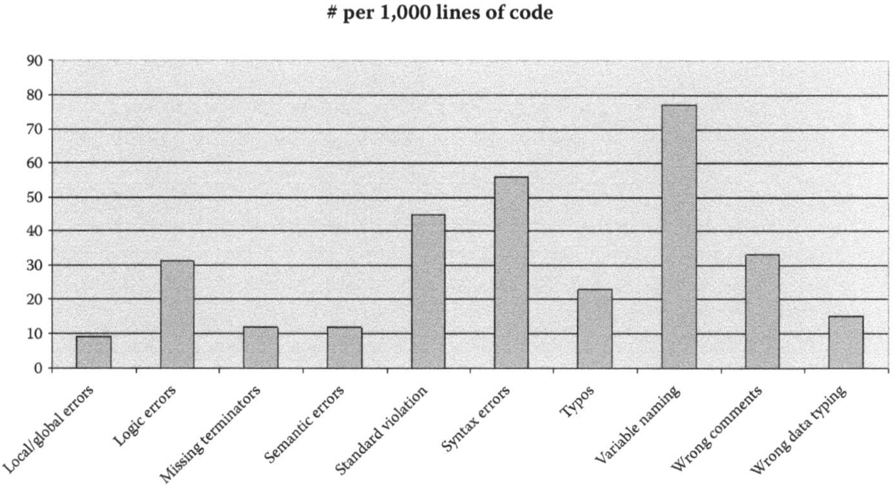

 # per 1,000 lines of code

Figure 6.4   Vertical bar graph.

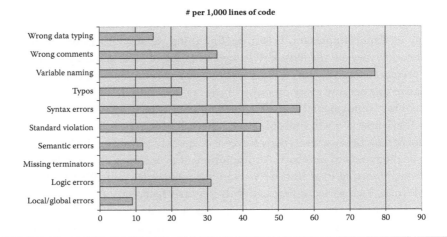

Figure 6.5   Horizontal bar graph.

subtle advantages, but both do basically the same thing. In each case the length of the bar is proportional to the value you are displaying.

Figure 6.6 shows an example of a *dot plot*. Dot plots can show lots of data in an uncluttered way and can show data trends.

Figure 6.7 shows a *pie chart* of operating system usage in a company. Pie charts are simple to visualize and are best used when you want to show proportions of things that make up a whole. One of their disadvantages is that when values are similar, it is hard to see the difference. Another disadvantage is that they aren't very useful for lots of categories; about five categories plus or minus a few is fine.

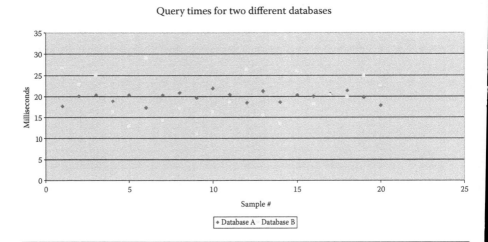

Figure 6.6   Dot plot.

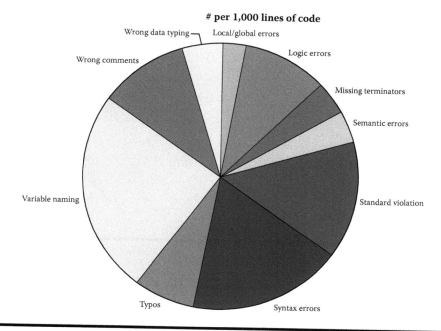

Figure 6.7   Pie chart.

Figure 6.8 shows a *line graph.* This is the most common way of showing how something varies over time. Time is by convention on the horizontal axis. A line graph can also show how two variables behave with respect to each other to look for potential relationships.

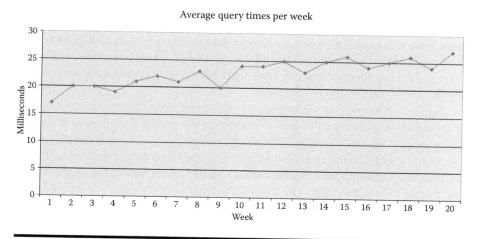

Figure 6.8   Line graph.

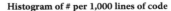
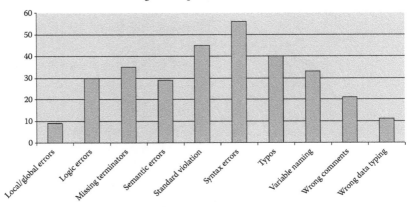

Figure 6.9   Histogram.

Figure 6.9 shows an example of a *histogram*. Physically, it's a vertical bar graph with the categories on the horizontal axis arranged in a fixed order. If the data represent measurements, the categories are the center points of the range of values that are counted. If the data represent reasons why something happens, the categories are those reasons in no particular order. The histogram's primary purpose is to show the distribution of data values in a sample or population. In a bar graph, the frequency of occurrence is represented by the height of each bar. In a histogram, the frequency of occurrence is represented by the area of each bar. Because the width of the bars is all the same by convention, this results in the height being proportional to frequency in most cases. Choosing the appropriate width of the bars is very important. We won't bother you with formulas for that, but instead suggest that you use the Microsoft Excel histogram tool to make your histograms, just like I expect you will use Excel to make most of your other graphs. The histogram tool is found in the Data Analysis ToolPak, which comes with Excel, but is not installed in the standard installation. Use the Tools/Add-Ins menu to install it before you can use the additional functions it provides.

Figure 6.10 shows two *scatter plots* on the same graph. One shows the number of seconds it takes to cut a board as a function of the width of the board. The other shows cutting time as a function of the thickness of the board. Each dot represents the time to cut one board, and its width or thickness is represented by the dot. This is simply a dot plot where each dot represents a pair of values, one scaled on the X axis and one scaled on the Y axis. The result is a picture of the relationship between the variables. This kind of plot is useful if you are looking to see whether X and Y might be related to each other. If you see a random mess of dots, they are probably not related. If you see a clear relationship line, they very well might be related. Notice that we're hedging our bets here by saying "might be." The fact that a scatter plot

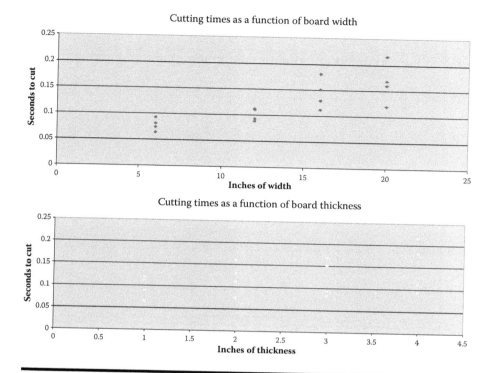

Figure 6.10 Scatter plots.

produces a discernable shape is not proof, but it is a great smoking gun. Figure 6.11 shows programmer errors per one hundred lines of code versus the hours of sleep that person got the previous night. Although there is a lot of scatter, there seems to be a relationship between the two. If you had enough data and could rule out other things being the cause, it might lead you to institute a program to encourage your employees to get enough sleep at night to improve software quality.

Be careful how you select the scale of your graphs. A poorly chosen scale can make a dramatic change seem insignificant or vice versa. In fact, unethical people do this on purpose all the time. Biased news media are famous for sensationalizing things to sell papers and manipulating graph scales is an easy thing to do. As long as they are reporting accurate data they cannot be accused of making up facts, but consider the two graphs in Figure 6.12.

Both are accurate plots of the same data. One makes it look like the financial sky is falling in and the other makes it look like it a minor variation in business as usual and no big deal. If I want to present the information dispassionately I would choose the latter. If I have an agenda and only want to sell more papers I'd choose the first one, perhaps with a dramatic headline. Corporate presentations are not beyond this kind of manipulation either. In most cases it is probably done out of

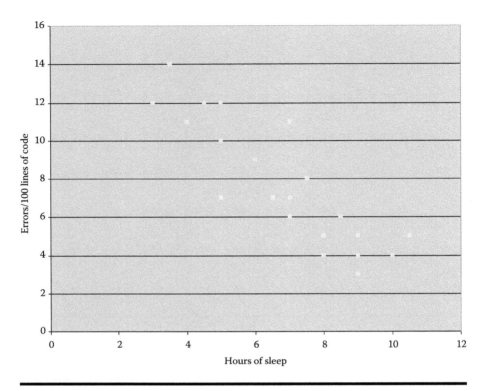

Figure 6.11   Scatter plot of code errors vs. hours of sleep.

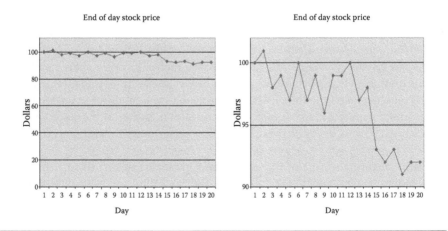

Figure 6.12   Two different scatter plots of the same data.

ignorance, but we've known managers to bias their proposals with carefully selected data sets and graphs knowing that their audience was not likely to challenge data because of their own unfamiliarity with methods.

Descriptive Statistics

There are two basic categories of statistics to know about: descriptive statistics, which is what we overview here, and inferential statistics, which we do not explore in detail but might mention from time to time. Descriptive statistics are simply a group of data summaries. They are ways of summarizing, or describing data that you have. It's time consuming, confusing, and boring to list 1,000 data points, but if you do that you are describing exactly what the data are. Instead, why not describe the data in ways that are easier for people to understand? That's all that descriptive statistics are. We'll cover the most common descriptive statistics used in process improvement here.

Measures of Central Tendency: What Do You Mean?

Measures of central tendency are summary statistics that tell you what the values tend to be. The most commonly used one is the average. The word *average* really isn't specific enough to use, however, if you want to be precise in your discussion of data. *Average* is really a general description of central tendency. We are going to be a lot more precise than that and hopefully you'll see why. The most common measures of central tendency are arithmetic means, geometric means, medians, and modes. There are others, but this will cover most things you are likely to encounter. In fact, arithmetic means and medians often suffice. The arithmetic mean is what you probably think of as the average. We'll just call it the mean from now on. The AVERAGE() function in Excel calculates it. They probably should have called this the AMEAN() function or something similar, but in a nod to the common but incorrect use of the word, they called it AVERAGE. It's simply the sum of a list of values divided by the number of them. The formula is shown in Figure 6.13. The median is calculated very differently. To find the median, sort all the numbers from low to high, then line them up; the median is the value in the middle of the list. Half of the numbers will be larger and half will be smaller. The MEDIAN() function in Excel calculates this statistic. The mode is yet another measure of central tendency. The mode is calculated in Excel by the MODE() function. The mode is the value or range of values that occurs most frequently. If you make a histogram (to be explained shortly), the tallest bar is the mode.

All three of these—the mean, median, and mode—represent central tendencies, or the value that the data tend to have, but as you can see, all are different. Here is a simple explanation of how their meanings differ. The mean is used when

$$Mean = \frac{\sum X}{n}$$

X = a single data value

n = number of values (X's)

Σ = symbol for summation

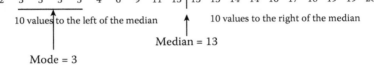

Data Values as They Were Collected

20 13 11 4 2 13 9 19 14 17 16 19 3 6 3 3 18 14 3 13

Mean = 11

Data Values After Sorting

2 3 3 3 3 4 6 9 11 13 | 13 13 14 14 16 17 18 19 19 20

10 values to the left of the median   10 values to the right of the median

Median = 13

Mode = 3

Figure 6.13 Central tendencies.

you want an answer that has the smallest average difference (smallest error) from each of the real data points. Use the median when you want your chances of being too high to equal your chances of being too low. Use the mode when you want to be correct as often as possible, without regard for how, or to what degree, your wrong choices are wrong.

An even simpler way of deciding for some people is to simply use the mean when your data are symmetrically distributed. Although lots of process data are symmetrically distributed, a lot of them are not, too. When data are not symmetrically distributed you should normally use the median to represent the typical value. Don't use the mode at all unless you have an experienced Black Belt or statistician around to tell you when. We won't go into why, but we're willing to bet that you have blindly used the arithmetic mean to compare important things in your company when you should have used the median. The difference can be so striking that it reverses the decision of which is bigger than the other. Some typical statistics that are from unsymmetrical population distributions and that therefore should have their central tendency be described with the median are as follows:

■ Housing prices (there aren't the same number of cheap houses as expensive ones).
■ Salaries (there aren't the same number of CEOs as clerks).
■ Number of people arriving by hour at your restaurant (you don't get the same number of early lunchgoers as late lunchgoers).

It's easy enough to tell which one you should use. Check the shape of the distribution with a histogram. We'll show you how to do that shortly. Once you know what it is, it isn't likely to change. Next time you see housing price statistics in a report check what they report. They will report median housing prices because housing prices are not symmetrically distributed. Now you know why. The next time you see central tendencies reported to you, ask your staff if that is the right central tendency measure to use.

Measures of Spread

Measures of spread tell us how much variability there is in our data. Like central tendencies, there are several different measures we can use. Measures of central tendency tell us what our process variable tends to do, but as we have already seen, that isn't enough. It really isn't even close to enough. We should also know how much variation there is in the data. You have already seen an example where the means are similar but the amount of variability is very different. In many process, you will care a lot about that, yet it is seldom reported. If you learn only one thing from this book, learning to always ask to see the measures of spread along with the central tendencies will make you a more effective decision maker.

The simplest spread measure is the range. The range is simply the difference between the largest and smallest number, or if you remember number lines from school, the distance between them. Spreads are almost trivially simple to calculate. Find the largest number, find the smallest one, and then subtract the two. Ranges are always positive numbers. If someone gives you a negative range, he has made an error. Larger ranges mean there is a lot of variability, and smaller ranges mean less variability. Ranges are often used to use to calculate variability measures for small samples often used to create control charts, which we describe later in this book. However, they were chosen before computers became common on every desk and in every cell phone in almost every pocket because even without computers, everybody with an education could subtract. There is no Excel function for the range, but Excel does have functions to find the maximum and minimum of a set of data—MAX() and MIN()—so you can use those to create this simple formula to find the range =MAX()-MIN().

The problem with using ranges to measure variability is that as the number of values you are considering gets larger, the range gets less and less representative. Think of it as a calculation democracy. We want to know how much variation there is in a set of numbers so we will choose just two numbers to represent the group, the biggest and the smallest, and from their properties, will claim that we know how much variation we have. Well, if we only have two numbers, it is perfect. What if we have three numbers? We are using two out of three of the values for our calculation. The third number doesn't get a vote. That's still better than most democratic elections. What if we have five numbers? We would use two out of five numbers to calculate the range and the other three numbers do not get a vote. Off-peak elections have similar population representations. What if we have ten numbers? Now 80 percent of our values are not involved at all. What if we have 1,000 values? Of those, 998 are not involved in the variability calculation. That doesn't seem fair and it certainly isn't representative. To solve this problem, it is standard form to use the standard deviation to represent how variable your measurements are in most cases. In fact it is used by convention whenever you have more than ten values. The standard deviation uses all of the values in your data set to calculate a measure of variability, so it is very robust. Forget about calculating it by hand unless you are really bored. Use the STDEV() function in Excel instead. Although there are other measures of variability, these two will suffice for the vast majority of business process improvement work.

Do you think it's possible to have two different sets of numbers, both of which have the same range, but that are very different in their variability? Sure it is, and the bigger the set of numbers, the more likely that is. Table 6.2 shows an example of two sets of measurements that have very different amounts of variation as measured by the standard deviation, yet the minimums and maximums are the same.

Table 6.2   Same Min and Max, Different Standard Deviations

	99	92
	77	79
	110	89
	100	78
	100	108
	98	106
	97	110
	100	77
	99	110
	102	78
Minimum	77	77
Maximum	110	110
Stdev	8	14

Distributions (Not Those from Your IRA)

We've mentioned histograms and data distributions a few times, so it's time to explain them. All processes have random variation to them, period. Do you want your business process to produce exactly the same thing every time? Then get another job—it can't happen. Everything in life varies. If you don't think so, you just aren't measuring it closely enough. One big aspect of process improvement is reducing variability. If you can do that, therefore making your business more consistent, then you can predict results. If your process is consistent but not quite what you want, as a rule, it's easier to adjust a consistent process than it is to adjust one that is flopping all over the place. For one thing, you can tell immediately when you have made a change! Look at Table 6.3. These are two sets of values from two different processes. Both of them average 100. Process A was adjusted so that its average value went from 100 to 105. Process B was adjusted in the same way. Do you think you could tell which process actually increased in value just by looking at the numbers? Most people can tell from the Process A values because there is little variability in that process, so a shift in the mean is easy to detect. Most people cannot tell about Process B because there is so much variability that the shift in mean is not easy to see. If you calculate the means for each of these columns of numbers you'll

Table 6.3 Same Means, Different Standard Deviations

	A100	A105	B100	B105
	101	104	122	120
	98	103	120	106
	100	105	103	95
	99	106	111	66
	100	107	66	126
	103	105	99	109
	99	106	92	100
	99	103	78	115
	99	107	110	88
	102	103	99	122
Mean	100	105	100	105
Stdev	1.6	1.6	18	18

see that the 105 columns all have a mean of 105 and the 100 columns all have a mean of 100. Variability masks it just like it masks performance in your processes.

One tool that lets us see the central tendency and variability all at once and graphically is the histogram. We introduced this as a form of data display earlier but now want to talk about it in more detail. If processes vary, is that variation random? The answer is that all processes have random variation in them. There can also be other, nonrandom variation there, but we discuss that later. For now, just consider a process with only random variation. Perhaps we are measuring the time it takes to do a query to a database. A hundred queries will produce a hundred different time measurements depending on a lot of factors. If you make a picture of this randomness, will it have a shape to it? Is there a pattern to random events? Oddly, in very many cases there is. If you study a particular process from the point of view of a physicist you will see probabilistic patterns in what it does and those patterns will manifest themselves in the form of a shape when you make a histogram of the data. A good example is the act of throwing dice. Let's say that you enjoy a friendly game of craps after work with your buddies. It's a simple game. Throw two dice and count the number of spots that are showing when they stop. How many different possible values are there in that case? Think about how dice are made and you'll agree that the only values that can appear are the integers from two through twelve. If you throw the dice several hundred times and count how many of each number you get, assuming the dice are not loaded, and you make a bar chart of the values, you will have a histogram. What shape will it be? If you said flat you would be wrong. If you have ever played craps you know that seven is the most likely number to appear and two and twelve are the least likely, and the others are in between that. In fact, the theoretical shape of the histogram for two dice is a triangle with a peak at seven. See Figure 6.14.

So throw your dice 199 times and make a histogram like our perfect one. Figure 6.15 shows several of them, from different sets of 200 throws. They are

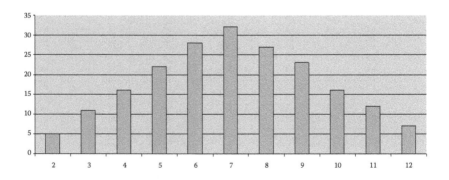

Theoretical # of times each value should be seen in 200 throws of 2 dice

Figure 6.14   Histogram of 200 dice throws.

# of times each value was actually seen in 200 throws of 2 dice – 1st Trial

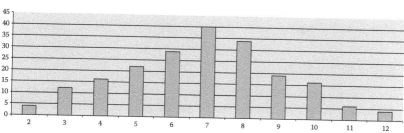

# of times each value was actually seen in 200 throws of 2 dice – 2nd Trial

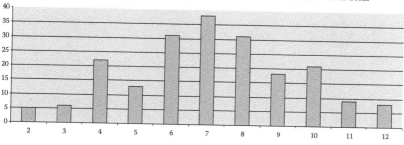

Figure 6.15   Histograms of 200 throws of 2 dice, first and second trials.

sort of triangular shaped, aren't they? But why aren't they exactly the shape of a triangle if the dice behave like we claim they do? Because of the randomness of the experiment.

There is no way to predict what the next throw will be, but the pattern of many throws is predictable. Every time we run an experiment like this, we'll probably get different answers, but also every time we do it the patterns will all be similar. This is an example of a process having a characteristic distribution shape. All of our processes have such a characteristic shape. You probably don't know what those expected shapes are. A company that practices Six Sigma problem solving does know what they are because they are an indication of how healthy your process is. All of us who use Six Sigma make histograms. They are the third element out of the four things that you have to know to characterize how your process is behaving. These four things are as follows:

- Central tendency
- Variability
- Histogram shape
- Variation over time

Unless you know all of these, you don't really know what your process is doing. Most of you think you know just because you know the averages. Now you know how little you really know.

Normal Distributions

The histogram shape that most of us have seen and fondly remember if we ever had a statistics class is the "normal" distribution. It looks like a bell so it is often called a bell-shaped curve. The statistical name for it is the Gaussian distribution. Figure 6.16 shows a few typical histogram shapes encountered in business process analysis from the National Institute of Standards and Technology online handbook at www.itl.nist.gov.

For all histograms, the horizontal axis has the units of the measurement you are characterizing and the height of the histogram at each value of X indicates the relative frequency that the X value will occur. Two parameters define the normal histogram, the mean and the standard deviation. The mean tells you where the central tendency point is. For a perfectly shaped curve, that will be at the peak. The standard deviation tells you how much variation there is, which in this form is represented by how wide it is. You can think of the standard deviation as the width. Wide curves depict processes with more variability than narrow curves, so just like in Hollywood, skinny is beautiful when it comes to business process histograms. The reason this distribution is so well known is that it is characteristic of many processes. Remember, in our context randomness has a shape and the shape of the randomness of many processes looks like this bell-shaped curve. Consider some of the characteristics of this shape. First, it's symmetrical about the mean. There is an equal chance that the process will generate values higher or lower than the mean. Second, the most likely value to come out of the process is the mean. Third, as

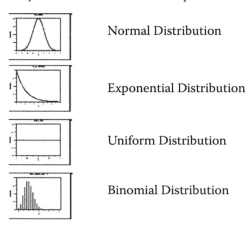

Normal Distribution

Exponential Distribution

Uniform Distribution

Binomial Distribution

Figure 6.16 Several typical histogram shapes.

you get further and further from the mean, the likelihood that a value will occur drops off rapidly. So what are some examples of some real processes that might have shapes like this?

- Grades on an exam
- Depths of holes that you drill
- Length of phone calls to your call center
- Query times for a database call
- Length of a sales call
- Size of orders you receive

The area under a histogram is always equal to probability. Let us give you a few examples starting with all of the area being equal to 100 percent. We can describe what these probability numbers mean in two different ways. Given a range of X values on the horizontal axis, one interpretation is the probability that the next output from the process will be someplace between those two values. So the probability that it will be someplace between negative infinity and positive infinity is 100 percent. The probability that it will be to the right of the mean is 50 percent (half of the area is to the right of the mean). The probability that it will be between ±1 standard deviation is 68 percent. The probability that it will be between ±2 standard deviations is 95 percent. The normal distribution is so well known and has such useful properties that it is the most commonly used distribution in applied business statistics. For instance, for all normal distributions:

- About 68 percent of the area under the curve falls within one standard deviation of the mean.
- About 95 percent of the area under the curve falls within two standard deviations of the mean.
- About 99.7 percent of the area under the curve falls within three standard deviations of the mean.

Collectively, these points are helpful to give you a fast estimate of where the data should lie given only the mean and standard deviation. For instance, there are only 3 out of 1,000 chances that a process will generate a value more than three standard deviations away from its mean (100% − 99.7% = 0.3% = .003 = 3/1,000). In fact this knowledge is used in control chart theory to test whether something is unusual or not.

Before we leave the normal distribution, we want you to know about one special one of them, the standard normal distribution. That is one with a mean of zero and a standard deviation of one. What is useful about this is that the properties of the standard normal distribution are put into tables to make it easy for people to look up and are then used in other statistical calculations. An example of a standard normal curve table is in Appendix C. The horizontal axis of the distribution is given the letter *z* for reasons that only math majors know. The numbers to the right of the *z* values are fractions that represent the area under the normal curve to the right of that value. When multiplied by 100 these become probability percentages. These *z* values are sometimes called *z* scores. A *z* of zero means it is at the mean. By convention, the table goes from $z = 0$ to $z = 7.5$. If you look at the fractions at large *z* values you will see that the probability of anything showing up there in a real operating process is extremely remote indeed.

Excel has a function for the normal distribution called NORMDIST (x, μ, σ, cumulative). *x* is the value of the measured variable at which you want to know a probability. This function returns the area from minus infinity up to the value of *x*. μ is the Greek letter mu and is always used to denote population means in statistics. σ is the Greek letter sigma and is used to denote the population standard deviation in statistics. The last parameter in the function is the cumulative flag, which should always be set to TRUE or 1 if you want the function to output the area under the curve, which is what we want. This function returns the area to the left of the texted value (*x*), which means the fraction of your population that your process will have a value at or less than *x*. Table 6.4 includes some examples.

Excel also has a function for the standard normal distribution, NORMSDIST(z). In this case, we already know what the mean and stdev are (0 and 1) and this function does not have a cumulative flag, it is set to one by default, so all you need to give it is the *z* value and it gives you back a fraction. In fact the *z* table in the back of this book was generated by a matrix with this Excel function in each of the probability cells referring to its respective *z* value.

Table 6.4   Examples Using the Microsoft Excel NORMSDIST Function

Example >>	A	B	C	D
Process mean (μ)	12	12	12	12
Process standard deviation (σ)	2	2	2	2
Value to check (x)	12	10	8	6
Fraction of times process will be less than the check value (x) Uses NORMSDIST()	0.5000	0.1587	0.0228	0.0013
Fraction of times process will be greater than the check value (x) Uses 1-NORMSDIST()	0.5000	0.8413	0.9772	0.9987

Non-Normal Distributions

We hope that last section wasn't too technical. Once you get the idea of the normal distribution it becomes second nature. And once it becomes second nature to you, you discover a horrible thing: Many of your processes are not normally distributed! We're only going to say a few things about non-normal distributions because we don't want this to be a statistics book. The first is don't try to learn about non-normal distributions by searching the Internet! There are actually hundreds of different theoretical distributions, each with its own characteristics, and math graduate students and professors seem to love writing about them on the Internet. If you insist on doing this, do it just before bedtime some evening when you are having trouble getting to sleep and save money on sleeping pills. Practicing Six Sigma Black Belts only need to be able to use about eight of these distributions. One of the reasons that distributions don't always matter is that there is a characteristic in statistics called the central limit theorem (CLT). The CLT says in effect that if you take samples from a population that is not normal, the sample averages will tend to be normal anyway. This allows us to play a little trick on the laws of probability. If, instead of looking at all of our data, we instead do regular sampling of it, we in effect convert the results to a normally distributed population and can therefore use the same tools to analyze every situation. Although this isn't always true and is only an approximation anyway, it's good enough for us. Our goal isn't to be mathematically precise, it's to find useful tools to solve business problems quickly and simply and get on to the next problem. This is especially true in the use of control charts to analyze stability, which we deal with in the Control Charts section of this chapter.

What are some common non-normal distributions you might encounter? Here is a simple but useful list. This isn't intended to teach you, but simply to familiarize you with a few of the common ones and their names so you won't feel ignorant should you hear them mentioned.

Normal distribution: We've already covered this in some detail.

Binomial distribution: This is a discrete distribution (all the measurements are true–false) and it is commonly used to find probability of finding defects in samples. It describes things like the probability that you will find errors in a code module.

Poisson distribution. This is another discrete distribution useful for very small probabilities. It is most commonly used to model the number of events found in an interval of time. It could describe, for instance, the number of certain kinds of people hitting your Web site per hour.

Uniform distribution. This is a continuous distribution where the probability of all values is the same. The histogram of a single six-sided game die is a uniform distribution.

Exponential distribution. This is a continuous distribution that is characteristic of how long it takes to do something, often called repair times. This might describe how long it takes to solve a customer problem or how long it takes to find bugs in a software module, and so on.

Student's t *distribution.* This is another continuous distribution that looks a lot like the normal distribution. It is used for certain calculations and is one of our favorites because it was developed by a graduate student working for a beer company.

F *distribution.* This is another continuous distribution that is used to analyze standard deviations.

Chi-square distribution. This is yet another continuous distribution that is used to examine the likelihood that histograms are a certain shape.

Six Sigma problem solvers use knowledge of these distributions in several ways:

■ To see whether data from a process under study has the correct distribution. If it doesn't, it might be unstable and this knowledge gives us a clue to what to work on.
■ To find out how key inputs are distributed so they can be correctly modeled in a simulation (we discuss simulations later).
■ To make certain calculations, most notably testing whether populations are different or not or calculating confidence intervals (also discussed later).

To someone who is new at Six Sigma, probability distributions and histograms might seem a bit like math voodoo, but they are used simply in the applied world of Six Sigma and there is normally no need to get too wrapped up in them. If you find two of your Six Sigma people spending valuable time arguing over which distribution to use and losing everyone else on the team, sit them down and tell them to do a sensitivity study—one in which they calculate what the effect of using the wrong tool would be for this decision. In many cases they will find that it won't matter. Don't let them get wrapped up in details that don't matter!

Process Monitoring

Recall that we've said several times that before you can thoroughly understand your process you need to know four things about it:

1. Central tendency
2. Variability
3. Histogram shape
4. Variation over time

We've covered all of these but the last, which we will do now. Process monitoring is simply the ongoing measurement of important process variables to tell how it is performing. Any good business does some form of process monitoring all the time in the form of reports, dashboards, and so on. In the world of Six Sigma, we use a specific type of process monitoring to assess whether our key processes are performing up to snuff. We also have a very specific definition of what "up to snuff" means. All processes are dynamic, so monthly or weekly reports are simply inadequate to give a useful measure of your process health. They are only useful for historical accounting purposes, which isn't to say they aren't important, but to "improve" a process you need to know a lot more about it than some accounting data; you need to know all four of the things on the preceding list and especially, the last one, how your process is behaving dynamically with respect to time. To do that we need time series data on your key variables, something that is rarely done by unenlightened businesses, and that is quite often done wrong when it is tried. We'll show you how to do it right here, at least at a high level.

Variation Analysis: What's So Special about It?

Why do we monitor the dynamic behavior of processes? The most important reason is to find out whether they are stable or not and if they are not, why not and what we can do about it. That is to say, how consistent are they and are they behaving the way we need them to be, and if they went awry, when did that happen and what sort of problems affected it? Variation analysis provides useful clues for problem solving, the kinds of clues that help us to make our process better. To understand how process monitoring works, you first need to understand a little bit about variation. Recall that we've said that everything varies, even your best company processes. There are two fundamental types of process variation. We call them common cause variation and special cause variation. *Common cause variation* is the inherent, random variability that exists in all processes. The better the process, the less there is of that random variation, but it will never be zero. *Special cause variation* is variation that is there for specific reasons; that is to say, something identifiable interrupted your process flow and caused the change to happen. We call that "something" a special cause event, or an assignable cause event because we can assign blame. If we look hard enough and have the data to track it down, we can find out why it happened. We can find the root cause for the problem. Once we do that, we can eliminate it so it won't happen again. As an example, imagine that you decide to analyze how long it takes you to get to work every day so you collect data on trip times. If you collect data from one hundred days you'll have one hundred times. Most of them will be different. There is lots of variation in that process of driving to work. If you make a histogram of the times, you'll see that they are normally distributed. You can calculate the mean time, the minimum time, the maximum time, the standard deviation of the times, and so on, and summarize your trip to work times statistically. If you think about the root cause factors that affect your trip times, you could easily come up with a list of them. Some of them might be under your control and some might not be. Here is what that list might look like:

- The time you started
- The speed that you drive
- The route that you took
- How many lights you caught green or red
- The weather conditions
- Whether you paid attention or not and made any mistakes
- How many other cars were on the road
- Whether you stopped for gas or other reasons

You get the idea: These are things that change every day. You don't notice them because they are always there and you certainly don't collect data on them. If you did you would probably discover that they appear to be random. That's why your resulting trip times appear to vary randomly. The things in that list are examples of process variables that are responsible for the random variations in your process. If you plotted those one hundred trip times they would appear to be random, perhaps with that normal distribution shape we discussed, but on a time plot they would look like random driving times to work. All processes behave like this. Suppose your mean trip time to work is forty minutes and your standard deviation is five minutes. Because normally distributed processes have 99.7 percent of all of their values within three standard deviations of the mean, your trip times are highly likely to be between twenty-five and fifty-five minutes. That is the mean plus and minus three standard deviations (40 ± 3*5 minutes). In fact there are only 3 chances out of 1,000 that a single trip would be outside of that range. One day it took you ninety minutes to get to work. Traffic was terrible. It took you four or five cycles to get through every light. That was a very unusual day. Something happened that day that was outside of the random variation that you normally experience. That something would be termed a special cause event. It was not part of the normal, random variation you were used to experiencing. All processes can have special cause events. Process improvement people like discovering that process variation is due to a special cause event because that means that something unusual happened and when something unusual happens we can, if we investigate correctly and soon enough, find out what it was. Once we know what it was we can make a judgment about whether it is likely to reoccur and if it will and we don't like the consequences, we can do something to either eliminate the chance that that cause will happen or adjust our process so that it is immune to it now that we know what it is. What could the special cause event be that caused that ninety-minute drive to work? It might have been an accident, a police blockade of a road to let a long funeral or a visiting king's motorcade pass, or an ice storm. Some of these potential reasons might have been obvious to you, like the ice storm, but others you would have no way of discovering without some investigation. Even if you investigated, there is no guarantee that you would find the reason, but you certainly would never find it unless you do investigate! Had you discovered that the root cause was a visiting dignitary and that it had been announced in the paper, if getting to work within your normal time means a lot to you, that could suggest a process improvement, namely to check the paper for local visiting dignitaries and alter your starting time or route if they are in town. Perhaps you could even use a Google alert to do that for you automatically. What if the data weren't so obvious? It takes a lot of time to investigate why the traffic was snarled and you don't want to bother doing that all the time. The control chart, which we explain shortly, is a tool that allows us to separate the special cause data from the common cause data so that we can know when to launch into a witch hunt for suspects. There is no sense fighting the normal everyday traffic variability, right? But when our analysis makes it clear that the time was not part of the normal, random life we live in, then we can be sure that it is worth our trouble to investigate.

Process Stability

We have made a few references to process stability, so now we'd like to expound on it. Why do we care? For the simple reason that to improve a process we have to fix it in stages. It's like raising children: You can't get them into college until they have first made it through high school and can't do that until grade school, and can't do that until kindergarten, and can't do that until they are potty trained. Here are the stages that your process will have to go through. Think of them as steps on a ladder. Your legs aren't big enough to skip a step. Our first task in a process improvement effort is to assess where the process is to start, and that tells us what to fix first.

■ Chaos: Everyone pretty much does what they think is right.
■ Order: Processes and procedures are in place that ensure some measure of regularity.
■ Stable: The performance of your process only has common cause variation.
■ Refined: Your process is optimized to meet your customer's goals.

If the processes under your control are not chaotic you need to get some order and discipline into them first or you are wasting your time with other improvement efforts. Business process improvement consultants love doing this mainly because it is labor intensive and they can use cheap labor and charge you a lot. They can create work processes and procedures, make big manuals, impress you with how many flow sheets they have created, and so on. It looks in the end like they have done a lot of work, and it is the best process improvement value in terms of dollars spent per pound of paper created. But have you ever seen an orderly process that does not perform well? Of course you have. We doubt that anyone reading this book has not run into countless examples of groups that seem to have all the trappings of well-organized processes, yet are nothing but frustrating to work with. What causes the sort of frustration we are concerned with here? There are two things. One is how stable the operation is, or how consistent it is. This is the equivalent of the ability to predict what will happen in advance. The second frustration is quality—the knowledge that the performance meets your expectations. When you have written processes and procedures in place with controls to ensure that they are followed, you are at the second step on the ladder. When your process is stable it is at the third step of the improvement ladder. When it meets customer expectations, it is at the fourth step of the ladder. It is a law of physics that you can't skip a step. That is why we spend time quantifying where we are before we start to address improvement methods.

Control Charts

Control charts are one of the main Six Sigma tools. They are the tools that enable us to detect whether there is any special cause variation present in a process or not. If there is none, and if the histogram looks correct, then we know we have a stable process. If the process is stable we know we are on step three of the improvement ladder and that all of the variability in our process is random, or common cause. That means that the process variation we see is inherent in how the process works so to make any improvements, we have to redesign the process. As a rule, this is harder to do than tracking down and eliminating the causes of instability but it's doable or we wouldn't have high performance systems at all.

Control charts are graphs of how a process variable behaves over time. This provides the fourth dimension of the four things we need to know to completely characterize our process—central tendency, variability, shape, and variation over time. Control charts are not simple time plots. Just because you have a graph of how something behaves over time, it isn't a control chart. Control charts are very specific graphs designed to show the presence of special cause behavior. They are the primary tool we use to determine process stability. When control charts were invented, about eighty years ago, they were done by hand so some of the standard ways of doing them now reflect that historical start, but nobody in their right mind would make more than one or two control charts by hand now. There are plenty of software packages that make control charting easy. If you visit http://www.value-train.com/CIOsecrets you can see a list of software packages which we use for control charting as well as others that are available. Excel add-on packages are simple to install and use, and there are dozens of them available.

Types of Control Charts

Earlier we mentioned that there are two major categories of measurement types, continuous variables and yes–no attributes. There are also two types of control charts to correspond with these measurement types. Control charts for continuous variables have two graphs. Although it's called a control chart, it is really two different graphs. One graph is a plot of how the characteristic's central tendency varies over time. The other is a plot of how the variability of the characteristic varies over time. Everything varies, remember? So these charts will never be straight lines. That variation that we see is hard for human brains to make sense of. Control charts are simply tools that allow us to see patterns in what is otherwise a confusing mess of variability. The control chart was invented by Walter A. Shewhart while working for Bell Labs in the 1920s, so it is not a new tool. In the early days of control charting, people went to school for weeks to learn how to spot these patterns. We now have the luxury of computer software to do it for us in an instant so control chart interpretation schools are obsolete and interpretation is close to instantaneous. Control charts for attributes (yes–no data) have only one graph. Attribute data have less information in them when you think about it. If someone tells you that she is taller than her car, you know a lot less about her height than if she tells you how tall she is. Table 6.5 is a list of control chart types listed by variable type. It is beyond the scope of this book to go into the characteristics of each type and when they should be used, but there are plenty of materials to help make that decision and a good Six Sigma course will also teach you and give you practice.

Although this might look like a lot of options, the fact is that the chart you need to use is normally a function of the kind of data you have available. Most good control chart software packages have wizards in them that guide you to the correct chart. There are also decision flowcharts that can help you do that, like the one in Figure 6.17.

Figure 6.18 is an example of an Xbar, R chart. The top graph shows process central tendency over time. The central tendency in this control chart is the mean of a randomly selected group of five measurements, all taken at one time. The number of measurements taken at once is called the sample size, or sometimes the subgroup size. In this case the sample size is five. The points are at equally spaced times apart

Table 6.5 Types of Control Charts	
Control Charts for Continuous Data	*Control Charts for Attribute Data*
Xbar, R	P chart
Xbar, S	NP chart
Median, R	C chart
I&MR	U chart
EWMA	
CUSUM	

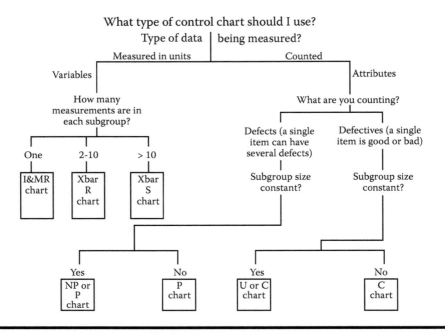

Figure 6.17 **Flow chart to determine type of control chart to use.**

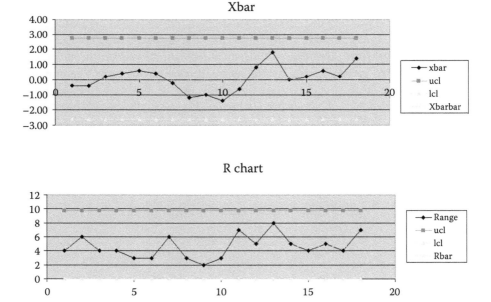

Figure 6.18 **Sample Xbar, R control chart.**

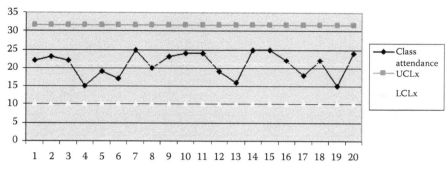

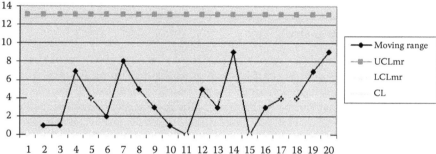

Figure 6.19   Example of I&MR chart.

and they must be for the chart to be valid. The second graph in the Xbar, R chart is the plot of process variability versus time. The process variability is measured by the range of the sample in this case. The time between points is determined by the analyst based on the natural frequency of the process. The sample size is determined by the likelihood that outliers will occur and is a decision made by the control chart analyst in advance. We won't go into details of how to choose those here.

Figure 6.19 shows an individual and moving range (I&MR) control chart. We use this type when there is only one variable measurement that exists at each sample time. This is common in many service applications. Examples might be to plot how many database queries we have each hour or how many customer orders we have each day or how many hits on the Web site we have each minute, and so on. In each case there is only one value that exists, so this is the proper kind of chart for it.

This last control chart shown in Figure 6.20 is an example of an attribute control chart. It is a p-chart, and the p stands for proportion. It measures the proportion of samples that are true (or false). It is often used for defects. This one shows the proportion of Web pages that failed to load in under three seconds, which was the specification.

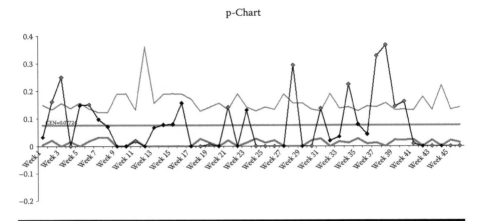

Figure 6.20 Sample p-chart.

In addition to the plotted data, which on these charts are all represented by lines with dots on them, a control chart has two other distinguishing features. The first are the two control limit lines. Control limits are straight, horizontal lines on a variable control chart that can be horizontal or crooked like the one shown earlier on an attribute chart. The control limit lines are calculated from the data and represent the 99.7 percent probability limit for the variable being plotted. It's related to the three standard deviation probability for a normal distribution curve. This stuff is all related once you get into it, like a big, incestuous family of tools. The other feature on all control charts is the central tendency line, which will always be a horizontal straight line that is the average of all of the plotted data points. The combination of the plotted data, the central tendency line, and the two control limits are all that are needed to determine if a process is stable. That is done by interpreting the chart after it is built. One last comment about making these charts: Someone who is reasonably proficient with Excel can create a control chart plot. The Xbar, R charts shown in this chapter were drawn with Excel. The p-chart was done with a statistics package. What cannot be done in Excel without special add-in software, unless you are a very good VBA programmer, is the interpretation that we cover next.

Interpreting Control Charts

Recall the purpose of making a control chart—to determine whether there are any special cause variations present in your process. We do that by interpreting the graphs we have just made. Stable processes have variation, too, but the variation in a stable process is random. Recall that randomness has a shape to it, so when we have enough points plotted (one hundred or more process values is the accepted value for "enough"), we can examine the shape characteristics of the control chart and see whether it looks random or not. Any nonrandom features are designated special cause variations. They are smoking gun places where something unusual broke your otherwise stable process. Those are the first places where we look for root causes to improve things. Because humans are not good at recognizing patterns in messy data, we need a system to identify them. This system is the combination of the creation of specific format control charts and a set of rules to interpret them. The rules are called the Western Electric (WE) rules and there are about a dozen of them. We aren't going to go through a list of them here because this isn't a technical tutorial, but we do want to give you the idea so we describe a few of the rules to illustrate how they work. Good control chart software will automatically apply these rules and highlight where in your process data a rule is violated and which rule it is. Those two pieces of information are a detective's dream! Finding and solving process problems is similar to finding out who committed a crime and arresting them. Knowing which control chart rules were violated and when they were violated is the equivalent of having a video camera record the scene of the crime, an increasingly common occurrence, much to the dismay of the dumber criminals. It is also an increasingly common occurrence in companies that employ Six Sigma because it augments our natural talents and focuses our actions to activities that are likely to be productive.

One of the most well known of the WE rules is that if a plotted point is outside of the control limits, either above the upper one or below the lower one, then that point represents a time when the process was experiencing special causes variation; that is, behavior that is outside of the normal, random process experience. Because it wasn't likely to happen in normal process operation, there is probably an identifiable reason for it, so it is worth investigating should we want to reduce incidents like that and make the process better. Without the control chart and that control limit to give us a marker that separates normal behavior from abnormal behavior, we would be limited to our minds' interpretation and everyone would tend to see different things and chase different potential suspects. The control chart gives us a rational way to decide to spend time and energy on problem solving where it is likely to pay off. If you look at any messy data plot for long enough you are sure to find suspicious patterns. The WE rules take our human minds out of the pattern recognition business, where we don't tend to be so good. By the way, we've mentioned before that there is a statistical rationale for declaring a point outside of a control limit to be special. That is because it has been calculated to have only a 3 out of 1,000 chance of occurring in a normal, random, stable process. This is an arbitrary limit that the inventors of this technique chose for making this decision. Think of it this way: If all you ever did your whole life is look at control charts and chase down root cause problems for special causes using this rule, then you would be successful at finding the problem 997 times out of 1,000 attempts and the other three times you would be chasing a phantom that didn't exist. If this makes you uncomfortable, get over it. Can you name one other repetitive activity in your life where you have that good a track record? Probably not!

Another common WE rule is that if seven points in a row in your control chart plot are all above each other or below each other (i.e., they make a "run" up or down), that qualifies as a special cause event because in a normal, random process that is highly unlikely to happen. In fact, although it certainly could happen rarely, the odds are only about 3 out of 1,000 that it would. The WE rules are chosen so that they all have the same probability of occurring naturally in a stable process. Think of it this way: Let's say someone is in front of you flipping a coin and calling out the answers and you are writing them down. You know a coin has two sides. The person in front of you makes the following calls: "Head, head, head, head, head, head, head." Right about now you are very likely to want to see that coin. You are going to start believing that the caller is either cheating you and not telling the truth or has a two-headed coin. That's the principle that WE rules use. When very unlikely patterns occur, we identify them as places to go hunting for process improvements. Sounds simple, doesn't it? It is, with the right software package! We've mentioned these magical software packages a number of times. If you are dedicated enough to be reading this far into the book, go to www.Value-Train.com/CIOSecrets. If you want to know about WE rules, there are links on www.Value-Train.com/CIOSecrets to several reference sources. Remember, as useful as control charts are, making them is not the point. The point is interpreting them, finding out where they signal process problems, and investigating and fixing those problems. The control charts are simply a sophisticated tool wrapped in a fairly simple presentation that allows you to separate the wheat from the chaff, or in this case the special cause from the common cause variation. In the DMAIC cycle, control charts are used primarily in three different stages. They are often used first in the measure stage to assess the process to help guide us on how to start our process improvement journey. They are sometimes used next in the analyze phase to examine the stability of some of our suspected root causes to do the same thing—give us a data-based rationale for how to start fixing those. Finally, they are often used in the control phase, often on an ongoing basis, as a regular health checkup for our important process variables so we can identify and catch problems when they first occur while they are special cause problems and before they become systematized into common cause problems. Control charts are one of the most useful tools in the Six Sigma process improvement tool kit.

Process Capability

So you have improved your process to the point where it is stable. Now what? Just because it is stable doesn't mean it meets your customer's needs. Doing something wrong every time is stable, but that won't do much for your bottom line. You won't be that bad or you probably didn't have the money to buy this book, but one thing you need to be able to do is state the performance of your process in terms that are common to you and your customer. Six Sigma uses several performance measures to do this. They are called process capability measures because they describe the ability of your process to meet customer requirements. Students often ask me why this is necessary. They say something like, "I know what my process does, I can count the defects it made last week." Here is why that's a bad idea: Remember that everything varies, so last week's performance is simply a random sample. Not all weeks are the same. If you take several weeks of data and average them, that might be better, but it's still a random sample. There is no guarantee that the next few weeks will do the same. Remember that we said that making decisions based on means alone is a really bad idea. To top it off, those data are historical and things change all the time. Is it right to use historical data to predict future performance? The answer is that in some cases it is fine to do that, as long as you use the right measures. If your process is stable, if it has no special cause variation in it, then past performance can be used to predict the future, but it still isn't right to use a small sample average to do it. Fortunately, we can use the magic of statistics to allow us to calculate fairly simple future predictions of process performance when we use the right historical data. Recall our mantra about the four things you need to know to really understand your process: central tendency, variability, histogram shape, and behavior over time. Using all of these we can create some simple ways to calculate performance measures that tell you, and your customers, what your process is capable of doing right now and what it is likely to do in the future unless you change it. These benchmarks have become industry standards for specifying process performance in contracts between companies. Although there are several of them, we describe three of them in a little detail and give you a chart to compare them and others. Much has been written about these, so you can easily learn more by Web searching, although like some of the other topics, be forewarned that Web searching can result in conflicting descriptions and confusion as well.

Specification Limits

To determine how well we are performing, we need to measure our performance against a standard. Because we are making quantitative assessments here, we are evaluating specific process parameters, all of which are measureable, so we can collect hard data on them. If our process parameters are measureable, it is possible to have quantitative goals. In fact, Six Sigma methodology "requires" that we have these goals. After all, what is the point of constantly moving if you never know when you've arrived? In fact, the DMAIC methodology requires that we get our goals from our customers, not invent them ourselves. An important part of the entire DMAIC approach is that customer demands should drive our performance. As you will recognize, although our primary business processes all have as their ultimate customer the entities that purchase our goods or services, we have many internal subprocesses that have as their customer other internal company processes. In either case, the customers of our process are the entities that receive our outputs and those entities are where we must get our specifications.

We have used two words as synonyms in this section so far, goals and specifications. These are industry-specific words that mean the same thing. They might also be called promises, limits, or SLAs, or customer requirements, or perhaps something else in your world. The important things are that (1) they exist and that both you and your customer know about them and agree to them, and (2) they are measureable with methods with which you both agree. We'll use the word specification in this book. When business-to-business (B2B) partners do business with technical products these specifications are often explicitly defined by the customer and are often part of contracts. When you have a business-to-consumer (B2C) process your customers are many, perhaps millions, so how do you tell what the specifications are? Good question. Unfortunately that's beyond the scope of this book because it is a complex topic. However, we can give you a few places to start. First, you can "assume" a customer specification, or you can survey customers in various ways, perform focus group interviews, and so on. You can statistically test the market's acceptance of various product specs by test marketing and good data collection. You can also assume the market's specifications by looking at the data from competitive products. Competitors' specs can then become your specs. Should yours be better? That's a marketing question, isn't it? Will producing to better specs result in more sales or let you charge higher prices? That is beyond the scope of what we are discussing here, but we wanted to mention it because these topics all intersect. There is no need for operations and marketing to fight with each over it. What needs to be clear is that operations needs hard customer specs to measure their performance, and if it is marketing's job to get them, then they should do it. If operations has to assume one until the "real one" is determined, so be it. They can proceed with their process improvement decisions independently and update their view if the customer specs ever change. At that point updating your capability calculations will be trivial. What is important for our purposes is that you have a specification, one way or another. Once you do have one, you can assess the capability of your process to meet that specification.

Internal Specification Limits

If your customer is internal, we need to go through the same process. However, to be effective, all performance specs need to be related to the end customer specifications. Internal limits shouldn't be arbitrarily assigned or used because they have been historically. Figure 6.21 shows a diagram of a chain of internal specifications that lead to an end-user specification.

When you aren't focused on end-user specs while creating internal process specs, one of two things will happen. Either you will set your internal process specs tighter than they need to be so you will cost the company more than is necessary to do the job, or you will set the internal specs looser than they should be, making it impossible to meet the customer specs. Conducting this assessment of internal specifications isn't always done formally, but if you are doing a formal process improvement

Internal specifications			
Overall process:	**Service call to fix cable internet problems**		
Step # / **Process inputs**	**Process step**	**Process outputs**	**Measures**
1 — Calls, call center operator	Collect customer info	Service ticket	Ticket errors, ticket completion, customer info accurate
2 — Service ticket	Schedule house call	Schedule time, date, service tech assigned	Schedule satisfactory to customer, scheduling errors
3 — Service tech, customer equipment data	Assemble parts and tools needed	Parts and tools assembled	Error rate
4 — Part and tools and service tech	Conduct house call	Repaired system, customer satisfied, reports	Error rate, customer satisfaction rating, schedule performance, cost

Figure 6.21   A specification chain.

project and your customer is internal, a valid question to ask at the chartering stage is to ask if the internal customer can verify that their specs are necessary to meet end-user customer specs. Simply asking that question might produce very interesting and useful conversations. Managers operating in a process-oriented company will not have any problem with that question. Managers operating in a functionally oriented company will have a great deal of problem with this question. Functional mentality has to be eliminated in favor of process mentality for company-wide process improvement to work.

Measuring Process Capability

The first measure you should know about is the one that was invented as part of the original Six Sigma program developed at Motorola, the Sigma Level. The Sigma Level is a number from zero to anything that is a relative measure of performance. In practical terms, we can say that the Sigma Level goes from zero to seven because we don't believe there has ever been a process that is any better than a Sigma Level of seven. This rating system is like the number of stars in a restaurant rating: The more stars the better. The higher the Sigma Level is, the better the process is relative to customer expectations, meaning the fewer defects it will make. A 3.7 Sigma Level process is better than a 3.2 Sigma Level process. This methodology was named Six Sigma to reflect a very challenging but achievable goal for the best processes in the world. Recall the Zero Defects program of the 1970s and 1980s? One of the things that program suffered from was its name, as simple as that sounds. Although management and the consultants that coached them preached "zero defects" all the time, everybody else in the company knew that zero defects could never happen, so people's mindset started out with "Here we go again with another unrealistic management theme of the year." Despite its name, the goal of a Six Sigma program is *not* to reach a Sigma Level of six on all of your processes, or even on any of them;

it is more like the U.S. Army slogan: "Be all that you can be." The actual goal is to get your process as good as the economics of your business require. A Sigma Level of six represents world-class performance, which few processes do achieve. It is sort of like calling it the Michael Jordan methodology. We know that 'we' are unlikely to ever be that good but Michael "is" that good and so have a few others been, so we know it's possible, and furthermore if we emulate his methods we are bound to be better than we currently are.

The most descriptive process capability measure is the defects per million opportunities (DPMO) measurement. Every time your process produces an output, you have an opportunity to make it right or wrong. If it is wrong per the customer specs, it is a defect, whether you sell it or not. This calculation is a prediction of what your process will do, assuming it doesn't change (i.e., a stable process). Sample DPMO numbers might be 10 DPMO for a world-class process to 20,000 DPMO for a much worse one. These values can also be expressed as fractions or percentages. 10 DPMO is a fraction defective of .00001 or .001 percent defective. Does 20,000 defects per million sound like a lot? That's a fraction defective of .02, or 2 percent defective. Many service processes cannot achieve this level of performance; their defect rates are far more than 2 percent. Most manufacturing processes have defect rates much lower than that to be competitive. Typical defect rates in service processes are as a rule at least ten times worse than typical defect rates in manufacturing processes, but all of the same principles apply. One of the reasons that relative measures have become popular is simply because so many people have problems dealing with very small or very large numbers. They make mistakes with them and cannot remember them. The Sigma Level Index solves that problem by limiting the values to a simple range from zero to seven where our minds are more comfortable. Using a relative performance measure also makes it easier for us to compare processes and that range represents a huge range in performance improvement. Most companies are lucky to improve a critical process performance by one point on the Sigma Level scale. One point on the Sigma Level scale can represent a hundred-fold reduction in process defects so it is a really, really big jump.

Note that if you have two customers for a process output and if those customers have different requirements, then the Sigma Level measures for the two customers are different, even though your process in both cases is the same. All process capability measures are dependent both on the process performance and the customer requirement. We like to point this out because it is often overlooked. We can always tell whether a company or person claims to understand this when they make statements like "All of our process have a Sigma Level of X." This is simply impossible, except in the case of a very simple company with only one process output and only one class of uniform customers.

We would not be doing this topic justice if we didn't point out its flaws. This is a good time to point out one of them. Sigma (σ) represents the standard deviation of a process. Sigma Level is a relative performance measure for a process as we have just discussed. The standard deviation is used in the calculation of the Sigma Level but the two are very different things. In fact, because people like to take shortcuts, they often call the Sigma Level the process sigma. You can see where we are going with this, right? If we tell you the process sigma is 1.8, are we quoting the Sigma Level or the standard deviation? You really don't know. To avoid this confusion, the use of another process capability measure has become almost universally accepted and that is the CpK. The CpK is basically the Sigma Level divided by three. Giving it a new name avoids confusion between the capability measure and the standard deviation. In addition, a sort of universally accepted standard for a "pretty good process" is a Sigma Level of three. A CpK of one seems like a more natural place for that pretty good point to be.

Appendix D includes the key formulas and calculation procedures for the calculations we have mentioned.

Identifying and Verifying Root Causes

We have discussed the DMAIC approach for organizing process improvement projects and discussed the collection and presentation of data and how to determine stability and assess performance. How do we improve performance, though? After all, that's why we are doing all of this. We improve performance simply by finding out what the root causes are for our problems. Recall our earlier description about things we can change, things with "change knobs" on them. Root causes are things that are changeable and that matter. When you change the root causes, the characteristic you care about changes and you can prove it. The histogram and control chart we made gave us valuable clues to identifying when and what kind of special cause variation occurred so if we have those kinds of problems we attempt to find the root causes for them and eliminate those causes. Those are often single root causes. If the process is already stable, we are usually trying to find a suite of root causes. There is likely to be several of them. It's our job to find out what the candidates are, then to determine which ones are real and which ones aren't, and alter the real ones so our process gets better.

What is a root cause? There is no absolute definition, but for our purposes it's where we find something that is a real, verifiable cause, that is not itself caused by something else, and to which we can make changes. The principle that we are assuming when we go looking for root causes is that it's better to treat them than to treat the symptom that they cause. All process problems can be dealt with in ineffective ways. We are making an assumption when we do root cause analysis that finding and fixing those causes are the most effective way of solving the problem and having it not reoccur. We are also making the assumption that it is the cheapest way. This might not always be true, so in all business-oriented problem solving we should have our financial hats on. If you can solve the problem effectively by masking it or counteracting it a lot cheaper than by finding and fixing the root causes, there is no reason why you shouldn't. As a practical engineer, one of the authors has implemented many solutions where he knew the root causes but chose to leave them alone because they were too expensive to deal with. A good example of this is when outdoor temperature is the root cause. We cannot control it without a huge expense, so it is cheaper to add a heat exchanger or insulation when the outdoor temperature swings are affecting our process.

Cause-and-Effect Diagrams

The first step in root cause problem solving is to find candidates for the root causes. We typically do this with a brainstorming technique. There are many of them, but one of the most common is the cause-and-effect diagram, or C-E diagram, or Ishikawa diagram (the inventor), or fishbone diagram (named because of how it looks). These are all the same thing. The technique is simple: Assemble a group of people in a room. The people need to be subject matter experts (SME) about the process, its outputs and inputs, and the environment and people involved in it. No one person is likely to have all that knowledge, so we assemble a group. Included in this group should be at least one or two people who know little or nothing about it to avoid myopia. This is a facilitator-led, team brainstorming activity. The facilitator starts with a clear description of the problem we are trying to fix. There should only be one problem. If you have multiple problems, repeat the process for each one, most likely with at least some different team members.

The facilitator draws a box on the right of a whiteboard with the problem statement, and a horizontal line out of the left of that box to the left end of the paper. From that horizontal line, draw a diagonal line sloped away from the problem box for each major category of potential root causes. It is the facilitator's job to establish these categories ahead of time and they depend on the kind of problem you have. Typical categories include people, equipment, material, methods, and environment. Feel free to add any categories that make sense for your problem, but keep them very broad. Feel free to leave any out if they don't apply. Be sure to explain the categories to the group. They might suggest others that you can then add. Once you have this framework established, the rest is routine, although it can be tiring. Simply choose one area at random and ask the group to suggest something in that area that might be a cause of the problem. When someone does make a suggestion, draw a line off the area and write it down. Then ask that person what causes the thing he or she mentioned and write down those answers on new lines off the most recent one. Others can offer suggestions, too. Keep repeating this process until nobody has any further detailed suggestions for that first cause. Then back up to the slanted area line you were working on and do it again, looking for yet other causes of the problem in that category. Once you have exhausted a category, move to another and continue until you are done.

Follow the rules of brainstorming. There should be no critiquing of ideas by others. Only clarification questions can be asked. Any idea, however silly it might seem, is okay. You don't have to offer any proof or defend your idea. There should be no snickering or laughing at other's ideas and no suggesting solutions (in this session). The object is to get ideas flowing and to stay in idea-generating mode and avoid trying to solve the problem. Because this can be tiring, we like to have everyone stand up and do one subcategory standing about every ten categories. This gets the blood flowing, keeps participants more active, and people think differently standing up than sitting down, we believe. Another thing we sometimes do is have everyone move one chair to the left every few categories. This again introduces some physical movement into the process and it changes everyone's point of view—literally. Again, we offer no proof that these ideas will improve the quality of the output, but it does help keep the meeting more interesting. Figure 6.22 shows a completed fishbone diagram.

There is one last step we haven't mentioned yet. You will be looking at a board full of ideas, some of which are probably very good and others of which might be useless. Recall what the purpose of this meeting is: to generate candidate root causes for your problem solving. Everything on your diagram is an unproven opinion. We don't make process changes based on opinions; we make them based on proof. There is no proof on this diagram, but there might well be enough work to keep you busy for longer than the project schedule should you bother to collect evidence on every idea. Before the team disbands, take some kind of a vote and choose the two, three, or four most likely root causes. There are several ways to do that. We like to give each person one to three votes, depending how big the final diagram is and let them come to the board and place a check next to the root cause they think is most likely. We've never failed to see this result in a fairly clear consensus of just a few things. Circle those things and you now have your task for the next phase of the problem solving—to gather evidence that proves or disproves that each of them causes your problem.

You can find templates in various software packages that can serve as a starting point for making pretty fishbone diagrams, but frankly, we haven't found any of them to be useful. We do them on large pieces of paper on the wall or whiteboards. When done, take a photo of it and transcribe it into the graphics package of your choice for presenting later. With so many people having camera phones today, there is bound to be someone in the room who can snap a few readable pictures with his cell phone if you didn't bring a scribe or a camera with you. Have two people do it in case one's battery dies before he can get it into a computer. If you have a tablet computer that can display using an LCD projector on a large screen, you can draw on that and then save the diagram and send it to everyone's Blackberry or iPhone immediately. You might be surprised how many potential root causes come out of a meeting like this. We have fifty to one hundred routinely.

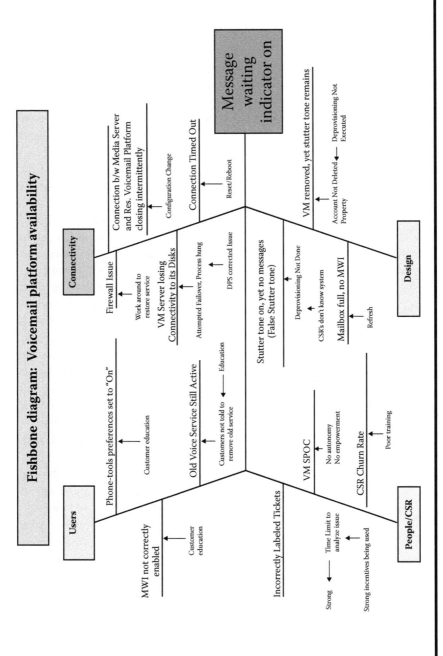

Figure 6.22 An example of a Cause and Effect diagram.

Five Whys

You might have heard of the Five Why approach to finding root causes. This is an approach that was reportedly developed at Toyota as part of their Toyota Production System (TPS). You can integrate it into a fishbone session or try it as a stand-alone process for isolated issues. The principle is to simply act like a three-year-old. Ask someone with process knowledge what they think the cause of the problem is. When they answer, ask them why they think that, and when they answer that ask them why again. Continue until you've asked why at least five times or until you've been punched, whichever comes first. There is a widespread belief that doing this is more likely to lead to an understanding of the true root cause than simply asking once. It forces people to examine their motives for each answer and forces them to get increasingly detailed. A good example is this: The report is late (the problem).

1. Why? I wasn't able to get to work on time today.
2. Why? My car battery died.
3. Why? I left the interior lights on last night.
4. Why? I had dropped my keys and turned the lights on to look. I was in a rush to get inside and didn't think about the light.
5. Why? My dog had just died and I had to bury it.

So it is the dog's fault that the report is late? You can certainly imagine all the different answers that could have been offered to each of these why questions, many leading to different final root causes. One of the problems with this approach is the lack of structure. Asking this open-ended why question alone isn't enough to guarantee that you will get someplace useful. Still, this is a popular and often useful habit for many people and it helps to avoid accepting the first cause that someone throws out when asked why something happened. One of the problems with this approach is that if you ask the same five whys multiple times, you are likely to end up with different answers. If you ask different people you might get different answers. It's a fine habit to get into, but not a good way of identifying root causes for serious problems. The fishbone method essentially combines the five whys method with some structure and is far more likely to lead to likely root causes, at the cost of more time.

Pareto Charts

Pareto charts are one of the most commonly used tools among quantitative problem solvers. A Pareto chart is simply a bar chart sorted so that the largest bar is on the left and the smallest is on the right. Each bar is a count of how often something is observed so the height of the bar is equivalent to the relative frequency of occurrence. In fact, a Pareto chart is simply a histogram that has been sorted. One other

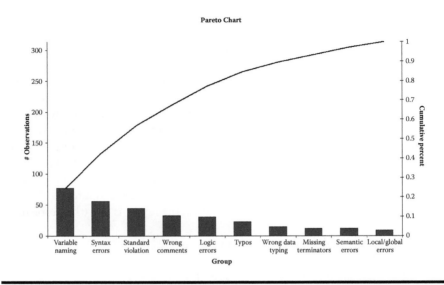

Figure 6.23   A Pareto chart with qualitative categories made with SPCXL.

thing is added to the bar chart: a line that adds up the cumulative total of all category bars up to that point. The scale for the individual bars is usually shown on the left and the scale for the cumulative line is shown on the right. The cumulative line is used to quickly determine how many of the categories you would have to eliminate to solve a given percentage of the problems. For people who like the 80–20 rule, we would find 80 percent on the cumulative scale and see how many bars from left to right, and which ones they are, we would have to address to fix that much of the problem.

The histogram tool can be used to make Pareto charts in Excel when all the data are numeric. There is a check box when you run that function where you select whether you want a standard histogram or one in Pareto form. The chart can be used to help us decide which of many problems to work on or which of many possible root causes to attack. If the bars represent named categories instead of data ranges, you can still use Excel but need to do more work. You can download a category Pareto chart example to use as a template from http://www.value-train.com/CIOSecrets. Figures 6.23 and 6.24 show examples of both types of Pareto charts.

C&E Matrix

Another popular and easy-to-use root cause tool is the cause-and-effect (C&E) matrix. Do not confuse this with the cause-and-effect diagram, often referred to as a C&E diagram. The C&E matrix is different. To avoid confusion, some people

Histogram

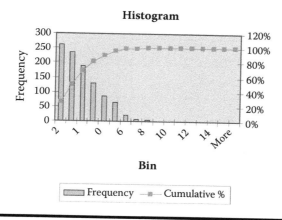

Figure 6.24   A Pareto chart with numeric categories (made with Excel).

call it the XY matrix. The matrix can be used for a variety of purposes, including helping you to determine root causes. Figure 6.25 shows an example.

The C&E matrix can be used after a C&E diagram exercise to help decide which of the suspected root causes should be addressed first when there are many of them. This tool is useful as a general-purpose decision-making aid any time there are multiple characteristics with varying degrees of importance and varying solutions; for instance, the decision on what kind of car to buy for your family.

Importance to problem >		10	8	4	8	
Process characteristics >>>>		Reliability	Usability	Speed	Cost	
Suspected root causes or inputs ▼						Total
1	Variable naming	5	1	3	8	134
2	Syntax errors	10	2	1	3	144
3	Standards violation	2	2	2	6	92
4	Wrong comments	1	1	1	8	86
5	Logic errors	9	6	5	7	214
6	Typos	3	3	1	1	66
7	Wrong data typing	8	3	1	3	132
8	Missing terminators	7	4	1	4	138
9	Semantic errors	2	2	2	7	100
10	Local/global errors	7	5	2	8	182

Figure 6.25   C&E Matrix for software errors.

Importance to problem >		10	8	4	8	
Process Characteristics >>>>		Price	Reliability	Size	MPG	
Car being considered ▼						Total
1	Lexus	6	10	8	8	236
2	Ford Explorer	8	7	9	5	212
3	Cadillac	7	8	9	6	218
4	Volvo	6	9	7	7	216

Figure 6.26   C&E Matrix for car purchase.

Figure 6.26 shows a matrix for deciding what car to buy for your family. The family would brainstorm and agree on the characteristics that matter to them and put weights on them, then list the available cars and rank them by how well they meet each characteristic. The total column is simply the sum of each input score times the importance value at the top of its column.

It is important to remember that this, like all such tools, is just a helpful guide. Don't spend too much time on it because the relative importance numbers are usually somebody's opinion and the ranking numbers are also somebody's opinion, so we are summing the products of two opinions. This is not data. The more you can quantify the elements of this matrix, the more useful it will be. For instance, in the car decision example, if your characteristics are miles per gallon and trunk size in cubic feet and number of passengers it will hold, those are unambiguous values. If your characteristics are color and styling, they are very ambiguous. Be aware that if your team is presenting you with an XY matrix, it has been known to be used to manipulate management into agreeing with the opinions of the team by presenting what appears to be data because it is full of numbers and equations. Just remember, it's not data!

Chapter 7

The Customer and the Workplace: Putting IT All Together

Analysis tools and methods are necessary and good, but they need to be used in the proper context to be useful. In this chapter we discuss the context from a broader point of view: the customer and the workplace. Improvement methodologies are designed to make the workplace produce outputs that the customer wants. It is the intersection of those two entities where performance is defined and where business is a success or failure.

Managing Your Customers

If you are a business with one product and one customer, managing your customer might appear to be pretty simple. In a real business with many customers, where you have many departments, locations, and employees, however, how do you do that and what does it even mean? Each customer sees your business through multiple touch points. Perhaps at first they were exposed to marketing activities, so they saw your marketing group. Then they are exposed to your sales force and see sales staff. They might call you and see your call center or interact with your Web site and see your Web interface. If they buy something, they see your fulfillment people. If your products require installation or service, they see your service group. When things go wrong they see your support group. For financial transactions they see your accounting group. Every time your customers encounter your company, do they see a consistent business? Do they see similar values? Do your employees see the same customer, meaning do they know what the customer expects and do they know the history of their involvement with you? Customer relationship management (CRM) software is an IT application category designed to make the answers to some of these questions good ones, but it is only as good as how you use it. It is not our purpose to discuss CRM software applications here, but instead to focus on the fact that to please customers many parts of your company have to know what the customer requires and the various parts of your company have to know how you are doing. Blindly punching data into a CRM system won't accomplish this. You need a company culture of service to customers to do this. Your CRM system, or an informal version of it, will only serve as tools to enable your good people to fulfill your company's best intentions to satisfy your customers.

There are many voices that are all talking at the same time in business. There is the voice of the customers telling us what they want. Our processes have voices, too, telling us what they are doing. The business has a voice as well, telling us what the owners need. Our employees also have a voice, telling us what they are capable of. Often all these voices are speaking at the same time and it can easily sound like a dysfunctional family reunion. It is helpful for us to think about the various stakeholders involved in business transactions and to clearly hear their voices and keep it straight who is saying what. Only then can we all come to reasonable decisions about what to do. Because this book is about process improvement, we need to know about all these voices so we can do our job of knowing what process to improve, what to improve on them, what the goals are, and so on. Hearing all these various voices clearly makes it possible for us to do this with confidence.

Voice of the Business

You wouldn't have a job if you didn't work for a company, and that company is owned by someone. That someone for most of you is likely to be many people in the form of stockholders. They are the owners and they get a voice. Their voice is simple: They want a return on their money within a certain time. The owners are represented by the executive management of the company, whose job it is to understand the owners' needs and translate them into a clear voice of the business (VOB) for everyone else. The VOB can take several forms, but the form that is most often needed by process improvement teams is the required ROI. This will drive what improvements are worth making and will provide a yardstick with which to compare multiple projects all vying for money to implement them. Although strategic, cultural, or other reasons sometimes affect project decisions, financial reasons always affect them. Lean- and Six Sigma–oriented process improvement efforts always need to be closely connected to the VOB, perhaps as represented by the finance department. Process improvement teams can get excited about what they are doing and easily lose track of the financial impact of what they are proposing. Good managers make sure that they don't get too far without a financial reality check. This can come in the form of required ROIs, minimum payback periods, capital budget limits, and cost of defect among other things. When implementing Lean initiatives especially, we have a special problem to deal with, often referred to as Lean accounting. Depending on how your company's accounting system is designed, it might actually penalize you for improving business processes by making great improvements look financially bad for someone. Standard cost accounting often fails to recognize processes and as we eliminate inventory, which are counted as assets in standard financial reports, it can appear in the short term that the company is going financially downhill when, in fact, our processes are getting more and more efficient. Accounting systems are seldom set up to measure process performance; they are set up to measure functional performance. Functional performance is irrelevant when process performance is poor, but you cannot always tell that from the monthly financial reports with all of their allocations and arbitrary decisions taken to make things balance into neat functional buckets. We don't have time in this book to go into this, but if you are an executive considering embarking on major process improvement efforts, especially when you will be using Lean approaches, please familiarize yourself with Lean accounting before you get too far and make sure that your financial and accounting groups know how to accurately measure the performance improvements your teams will be making. You don't want an obsolete VOB system quashing good improvement ideas.

Voice of the Customer

We know what the owners provide via the VOB; now let's see what the customers provide. We call that the voice of the customer (VOC). We've used the term *customer specifications* and *customer requirements* in this book, and those are VOCs. Because we want to be logical and quantitative in our approaches and decision making, we need numbers for the VOC just like we have numbers for the VOB. Ideally all process outputs that go to customers have quantifiable criteria that define whether it is acceptable or not. Let's rate a service process that one of us just experienced, a delivery from a well-known delivery firm. The criteria were as follows:

1. Should arrive within three days: OK
2. Should arrive with no visible damage: OK
3. Should arrive dry: Fail (It was raining out and they didn't protect it)
4. Customer should be notified of arrival: Fail (No ring, no knock, no e-mail, and no call)
5. Cost should be under $12: OK (My son sent it, but I paid for it)

Of these five criteria, some are easy to quantify and others are harder. Arrival time and cost are both easy to assess. Notification seems easy, as it is a series of yes–no questions and answers to questions like "Did they ring the bell?" or "Did they send an e-mail?" They are difficult to measure, however. There might be no way to prove some of it, and what if the driver and the customer don't agree? How do we handle that? What if their process is to call or e-mail the customer, but the call or e-mail didn't get through? Do those count as yes or no answers? What about the no visible damage requirement? How should we assess that? How wet is wet? It was actually raining when they dropped the package off, but it was not covered in plastic. The box got quite wet before the customer found it, but what was inside wasn't affected by the water. Do they get credit for this or not? Is it useful for a package delivery firm to think about all these details in advance and have procedures to ensure the quality of each one, as well as detailed metrics for how to measure them? The answer to that lies in what the customer really needs.

Critical to Quality

There are often a huge number of potential quality measures we could deal with, but the ones that we must deal with are those that are critical to the customer's perception of quality. We call those the critical to quality (CTQ) parameters. In a sophisticated B2B transaction, the customer might have a well-defined and communicated list of their CTQs to measure your performance against, but in other cases you might have to figure them out. Certainly in a B2C business you'll have to figure them out because you might have thousands or millions of customers. Although they don't speak with a single voice, they do all speak with a single statistical voice, so if you listen carefully enough and study the data you can get, you can "hear" it. We can determine our CTQ variables by surveying customers, with focus group interviews, by studying customer complaints and praises, from warranty claims, and by conducting controlled market studies varying product characteristics and studying the resulting customer purchasing changes. The latter is perhaps the most expensive thing to do and is most often used by high-volume consumer product companies, but it can be practical for high-volume service or transaction processes as well. Other companies do it by accident when they change a characteristic of their product and it changes sales. If only they were paying attention when they did it, they might learn a useful conclusion.

CTQ measurements really are those measurements that will cause the customer to take positive or negative action, such as do more business with you, pay a higher price, or stop buying from you and use a competitor. There are many measurements, but on which ones will the customer take action and change their business with you? In the delivery company example, delivery time and cost are CTQs. Where the driver left the package might make the customer happy or irritated, but the customer can accommodate whatever they do, so unless they throw it in a fish pond, that probably is not a CTQ for the customer. Likewise, the package being wet is observable, but unless the customer sustains a loss, he or she is unlikely to take action. The customer might complain to others, but won't change suppliers or call them up to complain. Perhaps the delivery company knows this. Packages are often delivered in large plastic bags when it was raining or rain was threatening. Perhaps they are using some probability knowledge of their own. Perhaps they know that it takes a lot of rain to damage the contents, that most contents aren't affected anyway, and that the package is likely to be seen and picked up before it is likely to rain enough to make a difference. Perhaps they have calculated the cost of the bag and extra time it takes to wrap the package and the probability of a loss if they don't do that and have arrived at a rule for when to bag it and when not to bag it to minimize customer complaints and cost at the same time. That's what we would do.

A useful tool for figuring out what the CTQs are for a process where you don't have precise ones given to you by the customer is a CTQ tree. This is a simple chart that starts with a general statement of the problem as given to you by the customers, or perhaps as defined on behalf of the customers, perhaps by a marketing department. Once you have this statement, your team does some brainstorming and comes up with some more specific components that make up the CTQ. As an example, let's say that you develop software and your customers all want high-quality software. That is nice, but it is too general and not measureable. It is their statement, however, so you start with that. The team might then devolve that into some observable characteristics of high-quality software. Perhaps they come up with three things: It looks good, it works fast, and it has very few bugs. That's better, but still too general to hold anyone accountable, so the next level of the tree assumes some measureable parameters that we propose be used to define each one of those. The first category gets devolved into no grammatical errors, consistent fonts and colors, and no more than four fonts on a page. Figure 7.1 is an example that shows a completed CTQ tree. On the right side we have specific and measurable parameters that we will use to tell how we are doing and that will be the basis for our improvement projects.

By the way, the CTQ tree isn't done just because you make it. The final tree outputs need to be shown to the customers or their representatives to be sure that your interpretation of their high-quality software statement is reasonable to them. Until they accept it, you aren't done. Just remember that general, hard-to-measure statements are on the left, and specific, easy-to-measure statements are on the right.

Kano Analysis

When you end up with a lot of CTQs for a process, it is natural to ask if all of them are really equally important, especially if you don't have a single, sophisticated customer telling you what they are. Even when you do, what we are about to tell you might help with a big customer who hasn't thought about the relative importance of their specifications. You can usually tell this if you think the specifications are

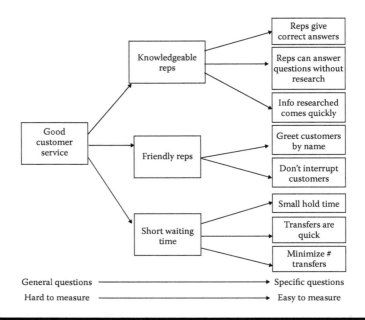

Figure 7.1   A critical to quality tree.

difficult to satisfy all at the same time and when you ask the customer to prioritize them you hear back, "They are *all* number one!" This is often a giveaway that the customer hasn't thought enough about what they really need. One way of helping to properly categorize the importance of multiple specifications is by using Kano analysis. Kano analysis was developed by Professor Noriaki Kano in the 1980s to explain how various product or service attributes differ in their influence on customer perception of quality. In other words, not all attributes have an equal effect. In the Kano model, some attributes are necessary at a minimum level and if you don't have them, the customer will be dissatisfied. On the other hand, if you have more than a minimum amount, you won't get any credit for it. These are referred to as basic needs. They are the characteristics that customers expect to be there; without these present at the minimum level, the customer reacts negatively. This description is shown on the bottom of the three Kano curves. If you are in the market for a candy bar, perhaps a basic attribute is safety. You expect that it will not harm you. Once the "do no harm" threshold has been met, however, perhaps as measured by amount of contaminants, having any fewer contaminants doesn't impress you. If you don't get sick when you eat it, you are happy.

Next come what are called performance attributes, characteristics of your service that fall into the "more is better" category. These are represented by the middle, straight line curve on the model. If your metric is a performance attribute, then the better you can make it, the happier your customers will be. When Dr. Kano developed this, he didn't equate happy with warm and fuzzy, but rather with being willing to pay more or buy more. This is a business model, not a love story. For your candy bar, a performance attribute might be the weight of the bar. All else equal, you prefer more candy to less, so bigger bars for the same money get your attention, and when you find the really big bars on sale, you likely can't resist at all.

The top curve represents "delight and excite" attributes. These characteristics, when present, make your customer pleasantly surprised to have done business with you and can create great loyalty. The thing about these attributes is that it often doesn't require much of them to do it. Perhaps a delighter in the candy bar example would be an unexpectedly pleasing color, taste, or gift inside. We are not talking about the kind of gift that is advertised all over the label and that invariably disappoints, but the kind that is not advertised and delights you to find it. We have yet to find one of these in a candy bar, but we have found delighters in hotels and restaurants and recently from a regional Internet service provider, who delighted one of us by answering the phone happily on a major holiday and helping the author through a problem he was having. We have found delighters at a local car repair facility and from two Web software services that we started using this year. A Web site hosting company consistently delights one of us by responding to questions in minutes when their guarantee is hours, and they are always helpful. Their fast, helpful answers, although they caused this customer to become loyal, are now expected, so are now basic needs. We would be dissatisfied if they stopped doing it. Delighters don't have to be expensive, and they produce such strongly positive reactions that they can drive business to you. Of course, over time, what was a delighter yesterday might become a basic need tomorrow as industry capability changes and customer expectations shift. The point is that thinking about the Kano model with your product or service offering characteristics can help you to identify which of your CTQ variables might fall into which of those three categories and as such help guide your improvement projects. It can point out inexpensive ways to create excitement, regular improvement opportunities that pay for themselves, and places where it is possible to overimprove where you might get no additional return for making things better.

Voice of the Employee

Traditional Six Sigma methodology uses employee input implicitly in how problems are solved. For instance, when we find that there are special causes of process variation, we are told that the first thing to do to find a solution is to ask the employees who are close to the process because they are most likely to have observed cause-and-effect behavior. Likewise, as we go through the DMAIC process, direct involvement by the employees in and around the process is required at several stages, once when we brainstorm potential root causes, and again when we brainstorm potential solutions once we have proven what the root causes really are. In traditional Lean-only approaches, the employee is front and center in the action, starting with widespread training on 5S and Lean principles, and improvement projects tend to be much smaller, more frequent, and led by employees. When the two methodologies are combined into a Lean Six Sigma approach, it makes sense to explicitly recognize the employee contribution to performance. Processes in all cases have employees in them, so employees are always part of the process, too. One of the difficult lines to walk when making process improvements is to recognize this and to educate the employees who are involved in the process to be studied that they aren't to blame for an underperforming process. In fact, management is always to blame for processes that don't perform! The employees are an important part of the process, but in most companies, management sets the process steps, the metrics, the decision-making methodology, the schedules, the staffing levels, and everything else that has a fundamental effect on performance. Management also chose the employees and the jobs they will do and decided what training and incentives they will get! How can management not bear all of the responsibility for performance? Employees can do their best, but if they are in a poorly designed process, their best will not produce a competitive output. It is management who is always to blame for poor performing processes. One of the best things that a management team can do is to admit this and state it explicitly early in their process improvement efforts. If you do this and encourage a measurement-based culture, you will help to eliminate fear and encourage cooperation among your employees. Process improvement is always exciting and rewarding, both emotionally and financially, when done right, but if it is done by unenlightened management who seeks to shift blame to employees or suppliers or defective equipment or anything else, then it will fail. Just listen to Dilbert and realize that it is always your fault! Keep your employees front and center, informed, and participating, and you'll have fun and have a high-performing business.

Voice of the Process

Process performance is a measurement of how well the process meets customer expectations. Now that we have a handle on the VOC, let's examine the voice of the process. There are three areas of interest to us:

- Which of our processes are most important?
- How are these processes behaving?
- Where is our critical process information located?

In the next sections we discuss each of these.

Processes That Matter

Which processes matter the most to our customers? After all we have a lot of them and they cannot all be equally important. Quantitative decision-making companies make it a periodic exercise to categorize their processes into high, medium, and low impact on their customers. This helps them to prioritize project selection and to focus on those process improvements that are likely to bring the greatest value to their customers. There are many dozens of software tools that help companies sort out their multiple projects and processes and organize and prioritize them in various ways. It is far beyond the scope of this book to go into them, but they are easy to find by simple Web searching. We have even recently seen a complex, multiple-page spreadsheet designed to evaluate project evaluation tools! We won't quote the source, because it made our heads hurt to look at it. Anyone who takes the time to learn enough about dozens and dozens of software tools for prioritizing projects and knows them all well enough to fill out that spreadsheet has to be a consultant who is avoiding getting anything useful done while piling up the billable hours. It is unlikely he or she would do that on his or her own time. We prefer simple tools for this. The C&E matrix discussed earlier can certainly be used for this and is well suited to help with complex decisions. Even simpler than that is the four-quadrant decision grid. Two examples are shown in Figure 7.2.

This grid is used when you only have two major parameters you are considering. If you have a few more, you can use several four-quadrant grids and the best

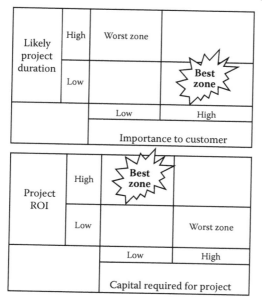

Figure 7.2   Four quadrant decision grid.

projects are the ones that end up in the most desirable quadrants of the most grids. To use the grid you first establish what the two criteria are and put one on each axis, labeling the two choices for that axis low and high, or equivalent terms. Then take each of the projects you are considering and evaluate it on both scales and decide which of the four boxes in which it goes. You can get fancier and put a scale on it, too, if you have enough data to make that useful. The worst and best quadrants will be obvious. How good the other two are relative to each other depends on other factors. You might be able to number the quadrants in order of increasing attractiveness based on other criteria. One of the examples in Figure 7.2 has the capital required for the project on one axis and the calculated ROI on the other. This is commonly used when money is all you care about. It is often a bad idea to make all decisions based only on these two factors, but it is fairly common. The best quadrant here contains projects that require the least capital and have the highest ROI. Based on this, you would do all of those projects before you would do any in other grid quadrants. The other grid example is a more customer-focused one where one axis is importance to the customer and the other is the likely project duration. The best quadrant here would contain projects that we can do the fastest and mean a lot to the customer. If you use the Balanced Scorecard approach in your business, those combination of metrics might also provide a useful framework for choosing the best projects to work on. Since you have already taken the time to establish Financial, Customer, Growth and Business Process metrics, you could rate potential projects against those metrics and see which projects would result in the best addition to the scorecard metrics.

The Three Reals

The Lean methodology doctrine is based on a few simple ideas. One of them is that management has to get their butts out of their comfy chairs and get them to the workplace to see and know what is going on. Only then will they be able to make decisions that are useful and even then, it is seldom management alone that should make those decisions; they need serious input from the workers and the workplace. We are not talking about company directions and other strategic issues; we are talking about how to make the internal process work better. What good is a brilliant strategy if we execute it like a drunken sailor?

The Japanese developed the concept of the three reals as part of the TPS. They call them Gemba, Gembutsu, and Genjitsu. We call them respectively the real place, the real product, and the realistic action. Simply put, we should not come to any conclusions about what our processes are doing until we observe those processes. This does not mean just observing the second- and third-hand data and reports that our managers hand us, but seeing the work being done by the actual people in the actual workplace and get a feeling for how it is done and what the practical difficulties are. If the numbers don't evoke vivid images of work, then we have lost touch with our business and will make bad decisions. Although we are at the workplace, we need to carefully observe the real products, whatever they are. If they are physical, pick them up, feel them, look at them, and use them. If they are services, experience them. We should know what our process outputs really are, not just a carefully managed description of them on a Microsoft PowerPoint presentation so that we only see what our employees want us to see, with all the warts and imperfections carefully concealed. Only when we are familiar with the actual product will the data that we have about it make sense. When one of us worked for Frito-Lay, one of the first things we noticed was that they provided free company products to every employee everyday in the break rooms. For a snack food company, that makes sense, and you might think it is just a cheap employee perk, but the fact is that by doing that, they regularly exposed every employee to the company's products in a very real way. We saw them, opened the bags, felt them, smelled then, ate them, and had to deal with the aftereffects of consumption, some of which were good and some of which were not so good. Frito-Lay has a commanding market share of salty snack foods in the United States. At the time, Frito-Lay was also one of the most profitable businesses in the United States. Their employees were very involved in their work, no matter what they did. We believe that this regular exposure to the real product helped, and not just in a psychological way. Because of this job, the author also traveled to the manufacturing plants regularly. Most manufacturing plants are a miracle of cleverness, and as an engineer he saw miracles of cleverness and ingenuity everywhere. Because of his constant exposure to the real product and the real process, he and his co-workers could make good decisions about how to improve things, and did some impressive things. The same author also ran both engineering and software businesses, and their outputs are very different. Both are service businesses, but both produce physical products, which in the case of the engineering firm were often drawings and specifications and in the case of the software company were software packages that in turn produced analyses and reports of different types. Both also delivered services. The engineering firm delivered advice, guidance, project management, and various other kinds of management services. The software business produced software installation, configuration services, training services, and customer support of various types. In both companies, he saw and experienced every physical and service output we had in one way or another. If he couldn't experience it himself, he spoke with customers who did, not only with his own employees, but with customers. It's amazing how direct customers are. They will tell you everything about your company's performance that they have seen. They don't hold back. In fact the word *direct* is too soft a word to describe them. Blunt is probably a better word to use. In some cases when we had really been doing poorly, gruff, impolite, inconsiderate, and rude would be better words still. Your employees simply won't tell you like your customers will, yet many managers are afraid of customers. In fact, we've worked in places where most people were prohibited from speaking with customers. That's the complete opposite of the three reals. The last real is realistic action. When real people work with real customers while observing real problems, and when they are tasked with fixing problems and provided the resources to do it, then realistic solutions will arise. This is a theory, but speaking as one who has spent more than three decades in all kinds of businesses, it is as good a theory as has been seen. We don't need equations to make us believe it.

Processes Capability Revisited

A part of the third real is to make decisions based only on data: no hunches, no decisions based on your years of wisdom, and no consensus decisions by the management team, unless that is part of a data-based process. The Six Sigma term process capability is simply measuring how well the process is performing as it relates to the voice of the customer. By paying attention to the voice of the process, process owners can identify parts of their operations that are performing poorly and use that information to identify and prioritize potential projects. As we have seen, to be objective, we take pains to quantify all three voices, the business, the customer, and the process. Once we have done that, the process capability calculations that we discussed earlier in the book are an easy way to provide a simple measure of compliance. They conveniently combine customer and process voices into a single metric and make it simple to compare different processes in the company, all of which have different customers and needs.

Process Flow Tools

To improve processes you have to describe and understand them. There are a variety of tools that are useful for this purpose that we want to introduce you to. Some of these are useful for all processes and others are specific to IT systems. This section provides a brief overview of some of the important ones, along with some ideas for when to use them.

SIPOC

When we teach a Black Belt course, every student must complete a real-world project to complete the program and become certified. One of the things we require that they all include in their analysis is a SIPOC diagram. The letters in the acronym stand for

- Suppliers
- Inputs
- Process
- Outputs
- Customers

Although it is called a diagram, it is often simply a list for each category. The idea is simple: Start by describing your process in the P box or section. Nothing need be too detailed here, just a simple statement so that it's clear which process you are trying to fix. Then list the outputs of the process. All processes produce outputs; if they don't, they aren't processes. Often there are more than one. List them all. In the customer section, list all of the customers. Every output has to have a customer. You don't always have to list them by name; by category is often enough. Every output has to have a customer. If you find an output with no customer, one of your new project goals should be to delete all activity unique to producing that output because it is probably an unnecessary leftover from the past. Once you've done this part of the SIPOC, go back and list all of the inputs. There is usually more than one input. The job of a process is to turn inputs into outputs, so it must have inputs. For every input there must be a supplier. Inputs have to come from someplace; they don't just materialize out of thin air. Find out where they come from when it isn't obvious, and list them. The result of this is a high-level understanding of the basic process flow. You will then know who is supplying what to which process, what it produces, and for whom. If you cannot do this, you probably don't understand your process well enough to launch into any serious process improvement efforts. The act of doing a SIPOC helps to define the scope of the project to management and others. All of the SIPOC elements are useful. To start with, we now know the process on which we are focused. Most project scopes are defined as improving a characteristic of an output of a process. How do we assess how well the process is doing? We do it by comparing what it produces to the customer specifications. You know where to get those specifications from because you now know the customer. Once you find problems, how do you fix them? Generally speaking you fix a process problem by fixing some characteristic of the process itself—but not always. The process might have problems producing the outputs the customer requires because the inputs are flawed. If the inputs are flawed, how do we fix that? We do it in one of two ways: Either modify the process so it can handle what we now understand are inputs we didn't previously understand, or go back to the supplier and have them correct their outputs, which are our inputs. You can do that collaboratively with a joint project, or you can simply demand better performance, or you now know how to specify better input performance in a way that allows you to shop for a better supplier. The SIPOC is therefore a wonderful overview of the entire system. In most cases you should be able to create one in an hour or two. If it takes more time than that, you probably needed to spend that time anyway, and there is no better time than right at the start of the project. Figure 7.3 is an example of a completed SIPOC diagram.

Use Case Diagrams

A use case diagram is a tool normally used for software system design but can be useful in analyzing and improving system performance as well. Figure 7.4 is a simple example.

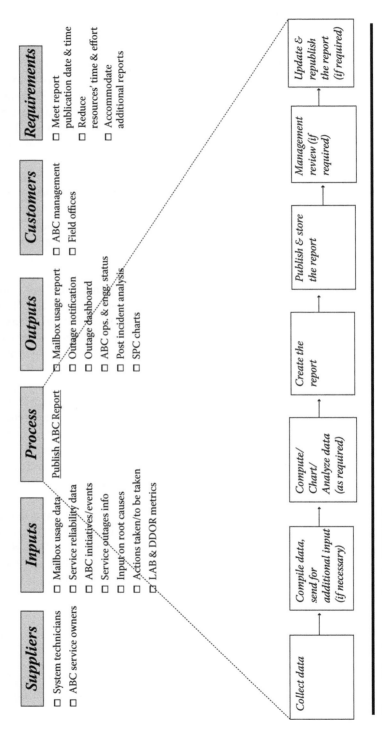

Figure 7.3 An example of a SIPOC diagram.

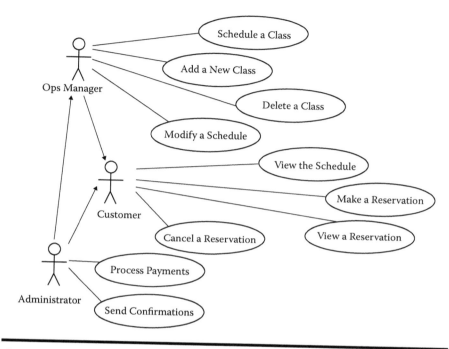

Figure 7.4   A sample use case diagram.

When focused on IT process improvement, these can be used to help see what is going on because they are familiar tools to the IT audience. Because we are generally interested in improving an aspect of system performance, we can extend the design use cases with metrics that indicate how each function is to be assessed. Although a process flow diagram might be a tool that describes a physical process well, a use case diagram is a common way of describing especially the relationship between users and system functionality. Because your improvement project is almost always described as a process output characteristic that doesn't meet customer specs, you can show that as metrics on a use case for the particular class of customers that are the source of complaint, generally your customer. Some measures that can be applied to IT system performance are things like the following:

- Percentage of time that an action is completed by a function
- Cycle time that it takes to perform an action
- Percentage of time that errors occur that are recoverable
- Percentage of time that errors occur that are not recoverable
- Presence or absence of a condition (yes–no)

One thing to be careful about when doing this is to not confuse software system performance with your business performance in the eyes of the customer. Your customer could often care less that you are using software to perform part of your business. They care about your performance in much broader terms than that, so unless software is your business, do not allow yourself to limit your description of system performance to the software that might be at the heart of it. If you do your SIPOC model first you are not likely to make this mistake.

Spaghetti Diagrams

For anyone who loves spaghetti as much as we do, this topic is disappointing because there is no actual spaghetti involved. This tool was developed to simply map the path that a worker takes during the course of performing her daily job. It was developed as a manufacturing systems improvement tool and is used by Lean practitioners. We don't normally pay attention to the path we take every day, but if we were to see a time-lapse photo of ourselves during the day with our path drawn on the photo, it would look like a bowl of spaghetti, hence the name. In a physical operation where the actions of people are an important part of efficiency, this is a very simple, hand-drawn, useful tool. The same tool can be used to trace the path the documents take through an organization, however, or the path that a file or data element takes as it travels through a complex set of software modules. One of the Lean thinking principles is to learn to see waste. Movement of any sort is considered waste. This simple tool can make movement visible, expose inefficient travel paths, give us a chance to see it in action, and give us ideas for streamlining and improving our process flows. Efficient process flows are usually easier to troubleshoot and easier to repair when something goes wrong as well. Figure 7.5 is a spaghetti diagram for a password approval process for a military base that handles logistics IT support. The diagram shows the contorted path that a typical approval process takes. This tool only shows paths, not times or other attributes. In this case the time is about two weeks and this process has to be followed by a separate piece of paper for every software application that the new employee needs access for. If the employee has been newly hired, he usually spends weeks getting paid and doing nothing while this process happens.

Swim Lane Diagrams

You are all familiar with flowcharts, but I do find that many people don't know what a swim lane diagram is. They are simply modified flowcharts. Imagine making a flowchart like you normally would. Then imagine that each element in the flowchart has an attribute such as what building it is done in, or which department is responsible for it, or what software application it is handled in. This extra attribute is like another dimension. Let's take what building it is done in because physical things are so easy to visualize, and let's say that there are four different buildings involved. We then create four horizontal lanes, one for each building, and rearrange the same flowchart, leaving all the connections as they were, so that

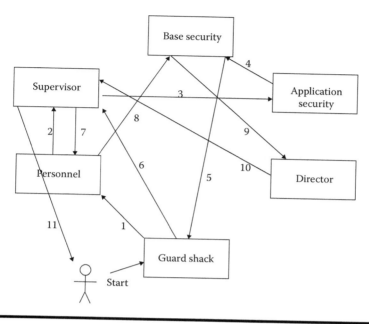

Figure 7.5   A spaghetti diagram.

each element is in the lane associated with the building in which that function is done. It is a simple modification that adds a useful extra dimension of knowledge to your understanding of process flows. Common lane types are company departments, building locations, and software applications. One of the reasons this is so useful is that process problems are often associated with hand-offs between departments, applications, or locations, so you can see in a crystal-clear manner where those hand-off points are. Swim lane diagrams often cause you to ask process performance questions you cannot answer and can help you identify points in the process where additional data collection might be illuminating. Swim lane diagrams can also be vertical if you prefer. Many flowcharting programs allow you to create them, but they might call them different things. IGrafx calls them departments. Visio calls them cross functional flow charts. IBM calls them line of visibility charts. Figure 7.6 is a simple example.

As an aside on names, most of the tools we discuss here have multiple names, depending which industry or company you are in, so it is often hard to tell what someone means when he or she mentions a tool name. Be sure you are both talking about the same thing if you are working with someone new and you discuss a tool like this for the first time. If you both look at an example it will usually be clear. We looked up one of the tools in this book in a Web search and found sixty different names for it! We'll spare you the list.

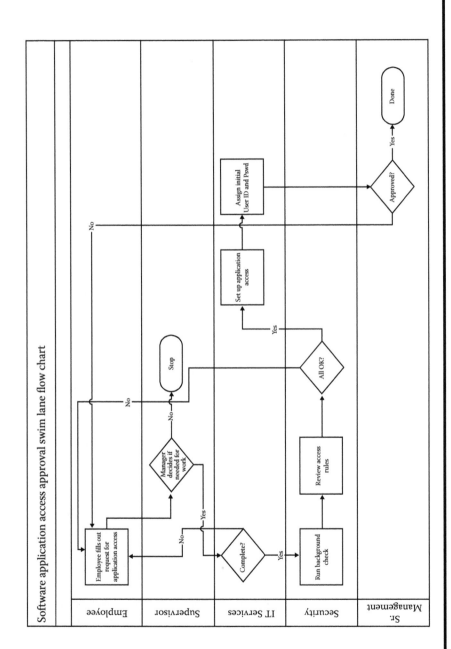

Figure 7.6 A swim lane diagram.

Value Stream Mapping

One of the primary tools of the Lean methodology is the value stream map, a tool designed to analyze your process from the point of view of how efficient it is, meaning in this case, how much waste there is in your operation. VSMs are used when you need to become more efficient in what you do. They are also used when you need to be more responsive to customer needs; that is, to be able to deliver in a more timely fashion and reduce the lead time between order and delivery. They are also used when you need to reduce inventory, which isn't generally an issue for most IT operations. They are not particularly useful for defect or quality improvement. Control charts and capability calculations are more suited to that. VSMs are only generally defined, leaving lots of room to modify them to suit individual needs, but simple to use and easy to interpret. There are plenty of good sources of information for how to design and use VSMs, so like the other topics in this book, we concentrate on giving you a broad view of them. Figure 7.7 is a simple example of a VSM.

The key elements of a value stream map are as follows:

- The customers, shown in the upper right hand corner as a box with a jagged top.
- The suppliers, shown in the upper left hand corner as a box with a jagged top.
- The process steps that add value, shown as a line of boxes.
- Process step information boxes shown below the process steps.
- Places where the product waits (inventory locations) shown as triangles.
- Arrows of various types that show how product flows.
- Boxes and lines that show generally how information flows from the customer to each operation to tell the operation what to do and when.
- A value stream line at the bottom that shows approximately how much time value is being added to the product and how much time no value is being added.

The total of all the times should add up to how lotng the product is in your business—from the time you acquire the resources to create it until the time you deliver it. At the end of the value stream line is a ratio of VA to NVA time. This is often a shockingly low number. The map in Figure 7.7 is of a simple software development operation. Customers send orders to a central planning and scheduling group, who in turn send them to the software group. Orders wait for an average of one day prior to being processed by a job entry clerk. That clerk takes thirty minutes on average to process an order but because he is doing lots of things, it takes eight hours on average for the order to get through him, so the VA time is thirty minutes and the lead time is eight hours. From there it goes to a software designer who lays out the design. That designer has a queue of projects and projects wait an average of three days in that queue. Inventory queues are shown as triangles on the map. The software designer spends four hours laying out the software design but because she has lots of other

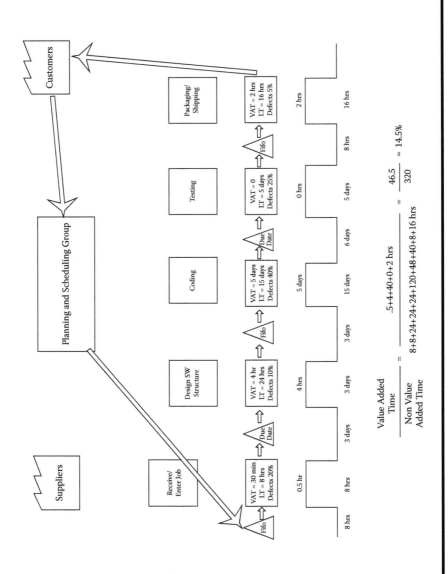

Figure 7.7   A sample value stream map.

things going on as well, it takes three days for her to complete it, so the VA time for that operation is a half-day and the NVA time or lead time is three days. The rest of the operations shown on the map are coding, testing, and packing and shipping. We showed the testing time as all NVA because in a pure sense, all testing is wasted effort. If the upstream process were done error free the first time there would be no need for it. You can make your own decisions about whether testing time should be all or part VA time or none at all. The point of the map is to give a picture of just which operations really do add value, where the product waits, and where you spend time that adds no value. By looking at the process in this manner, we can get a high-level view of where we have opportunities to reduce waste and decrease lead time. Another thing that can be learned by using this tool is to confirm or bust management myths about where time is really being spent. We tend to focus on the places where "work" is being done when we want to become more efficient. To create a VSM, we need to collect data on what is actually happening so the map represents reality, not management's guesses. This alone can be revealing. Rather than focusing only on the coders, for instance, in this operation, most of the lead time is not actual coding time; it is due to multitasking (batching of work) and queues between operations. Coding only contributes 40 hours of lead time to a process that has 320 hours of lead time. Think about that. Without an analysis like this, it is easy to focus on the wrong things when trying to get faster turnaround time.

Value-Added and Non-Value-Added

To understand VSMs, you first need to better understand the concept of VA work that we touched on earlier in this book. It is simply the work that is required to produce your output. All other work is NVA. There is a third category that is relevant for some businesses: NVA work that you are required to do. How could that be? It is normally because of regulations, laws, or sometimes contractual requirements. If this kind of work is meaningful, you can track it separately, but it is still NVA work! It doesn't add anything to the transformation of inputs into outputs. Earlier in the book we mentioned sending a bill to your customer for each element of work that you do and if the work is VA then the customer should be willing to pay for it. Although that is a cute way to think about it and can sometimes be helpful, let's be more precise by reviewing what the major categories of NVA, or waste, are.

Let's start with an obvious one: All defects are waste. If you made it and then threw it away, it is obvious waste. If the customer found it and threw it away, it is an even bigger waste!

Waste occurs in service businesses also. When the cable guy comes to your house to fix something and doesn't succeed, he has created waste. Errors on bills or forms or letters are all waste. Mistakes in coding or anything else that requires correction and rework is waste. Employee turnover is a type of defect and is waste because you made a hiring error. Engineering change orders are waste because the project wasn't specified correctly the first time. You get the idea. Think of perfection: Everything other than doing it right the first time is wasted activity, material, products, or all of these.

All overproduction is waste. In a Lean organization, we make exactly what we sell, when we sell it. Making things in advance is waste. Forget the reasons you might have for wanting to do that. They might be legitimate for your business today, but it is still waste in Lean terms and should be recognized as such. Product overproduction includes making things early and producing to stock. Administrative overproduction examples include creating code, drawings, or documents before the next step in the process needs them and making too many copies of things.

In Lean, all inventory is waste. Yes, that's right: All inventory is waste. That includes the supplies and raw materials you need coming in, the work in process while you are creating your outputs, and all finished goods in the inventory. You don't want any of it. If any accountants are reading this book, we suggest that before you have a stroke, you get a book on Lean accounting. Inventory is generally considered an asset, but in Lean terms, it is waste. In an inventory-intensive business, the journey to Lean will make your traditional financial statements look like you are going out of business for the first few months or years as you continue to improve your operation, because your assets will be declining as you eliminate inventory and WIP. Equipment utilization might also decline, but that's another topic and it is also just fine as long as we keep focused on the goal, to minimize the time from order to cash. Look around your operation and observe the things that are piled up; that's inventory. Start in the supply room and look at the office supplies. What if you provide equipment to your customers like computers, modems, and cables? Do you have stocks of them in inventory? If so, it is all waste. When you process data in batches, you have waste in the batches. Everything beyond single-unit processing is a form of inventory. Your piles of sales literature are waste and should you provide contract services, your service employees who are waiting to be used are wasted "people inventory." In a perfect Lean world, you obtain what you need as you need it and process it as quickly as you can one at a time and with no waiting. As you read this, you might be tempted to shut the book now and claim that this whole idea is ridiculous, but before you do, remember why we are being obsessive about this. It is not to eliminate all waste—that is clearly impractical; rather it is to clearly identify what is waste and what is not so that when we look for areas of our operation to improve, we are working on the right stuff! Be patient and read about the rest of the wastes.

All excess motion of people is waste. In a perfect Lean operation, all people stay in one spot and the work moves to you when it's needed and away from you when you are finished with your part of it. You should do so little moving that you need to keep stretching to avoid getting blood clots. It hardly seems practical, right? Do you have to walk to a copier? Walk to meetings? Travel to other offices for various part of your work? Perhaps you've just moved into a new facility and you've organized your offices so that people are closer to each other than they used to be and there is less of that. Whatever walking and moving you still do is all waste and is a fair target for an improvement project. Don't get too hung up on each of these wastes. Your VSM is a tool that can help you identify where system waste is the worst. Once you know that, you can think about the waste definitions here and consider what is causing it and how to improve it. We won't let the sometimes picky sounding definitions get in the way of making good process improvement decisions; instead they will help guide us.

Another waste is waiting. In this case it means when the things you are producing wait. If you are delivering a service it is when your customers wait. Customers don't want to wait. If they want a car and you make cars, they want it right now. If they need a service and you provide that service, they want that right now as well. Anyone who can design their business process to reduce waiting has a competitive advantage. You cannot send the customer a bill for $250 for two weeks of waiting to get the vice president's signature.

When your systems go down, things wait, people wait, and customers wait. When your system response time is slow, people wait also. When you need approvals, things often wait, and when you need information, things wait. Design your processes so that you have what you need when you need it and waiting will be minimized. It is interesting that the medical service industry has started to embrace Lean in a big way. It is also interesting that waiting is one of the biggest wastes in it. When is the last time you had any medical work done where most of your time was spent waiting? Hospitals and doctors have been horribly inefficient for decades and they simply didn't care because they were a monopoly and have been protected by government regulations. Is the government efficient? Any regulation designed by a government agency is bound to make your processes worse. Medical facilities have been organized to make it efficient for the doctors at the expense of the customer. A Lean operation focuses on eliminating customer waiting. The U.S. health care system is in a time of rapid change. One of the good things that is likely to come out of the changes is more transparency and competition as people become more and more responsible for their own health care; this in turn forces doctors, clinics, and hospitals to be of higher quality and more responsive simply to survive. They won't like it, but they will have no choice. We've done process improvements for companies that make consumer products and for hospitals among others. It is incredibly ironic that more effort is spent making potato chips just right than is spent making sure that people get efficient and low-defect treatment in a hospital or doctor's office. That's another story, however. Don't let your process outputs wait at any point along the production stream if you want to be world class.

All transportation of material or information is waste. We called transportation of people *motion*. Material has to be moved if you are creating products and people have to move around to deliver service, but that movement should be minimized. All excess transportation is waste, period. If you have a group of people working on a project and they are in different buildings in town, or in different cities, there will be waste as you move people around for meetings and things. If you are producing a product and have to move it from building to building for various operations, you are creating transportation waste. I know what you are thinking now: It is cheaper to put up with that waste than to colocate the equipment or to move the people. Maybe it is, but that isn't the point. The point is to not rest on your laurels and think it is efficient because it isn't. If the VSM shows that part of your operation to be the worst in terms of NVA time, perhaps it is worth doing the relocation. Often economic decisions like that are not soundly made. They are made to minimize local budget expenses, and so on, not to improve the entire process flow of the company. If improving the process flow allows you to produce 33 percent more with the same resources and space by eliminating a transportation waste, that economic benefit is likely to swamp the local cost–benefit analysis that drives most relocation decisions. All of the tools we discuss here, including how to identify waste, are simply there to be used to make the *system* better based on a high-level system analysis.

All extra processing is also a form of waste. What is extra processing? It is anything you do that could be considered a process step but isn't really necessary in the eyes of the customer. Examples include doing things just in case they are needed, spending more time on something because you have the time, redundant approvals, generating extra copies, sending e-mails and documents to people who really don't need them, and doing things because you "thought" the customer required it but they really didn't (caused by poor communication). Extra processing can also happen when you reenter data or collect data or reports that aren't really used to improve the operation (travel expense reporting comes under this category, as does cost accounting and monthly auditing or financial reports). You have to do some of those things, or at least you think you do. They do nothing for your customer, however, so they should always be on the table as a target for reduction when they do anything to impede the flow of your products or services. Extra processing is sometimes in your process because it is the way it was always done or because you emulated a market leader with a benchmark study, or because you did it that way when you were prototyping it but now that you are in full production you could do without it but unconsciously leave it in, not challenging the necessity of that step. A food company one of us worked for had a process step that nobody understood. Commercial food production is often simply a scaled-up version of how you first made a recipe in a kitchen. Steps that were done during kitchen trials might not really be needed, but they aren't challenged or there isn't time for additional experimentation as you are rushing to market, so big process inefficiencies stay in the process. Similarly, in a software business one of us took over, he found a lot of administrative processes that crossed department lines where everyone in the process had a job to do but everyone had long since forgotten why they did it or how their step was useful for the next step. In one outrageous case he had been presented with a monthly report showing a backlog of work. This accumulated work backlog amounted to about $1 million when he came to the business. The owners, a venture capital group, and the author decided to ignore stuff like that at first because we were in crisis and had to survive first, but once we had dispatched most of the alligators, we started looking at internal processes. We had always been uncomfortable with this million-dollar backlog and didn't have an intuitive feel for it. One day we put everyone in a room who was involved and we flowcharted the process. What we found were redundant entries, data that were not understood, and an accumulation process that was a mistake. Our million-dollar business backlog was essentially zero and nobody knew it for years. The company was small enough that this was a very big deal to us. To make matters worse, the venture capital firm that purchased the company paid for that backlog as an asset and the books had been audited by one of the biggest audit firms in the country. The auditing firm clearly had no idea what they were looking at either, and the complexity of the process was hard to follow. They made a few assumptions that were all wrong and blessed it as correct.

The last waste is underutilized people. This is an insidious waste because it is hard to quantify in some cases, but it is real. Examples include hiring people without the right skills, including overqualified people, employee injuries, and employees who get sick. Your people cannot produce for you when they are sick or injured. Safety programs are very strong in the United States and they are popular, not only because the law says they have to be present or for altruistic reasons, but they make good financial sense. Wellness programs have taken longer to take hold but are being done for the same self-serving reasons. Employees who are fit and healthy are more productive. Another way to underutilize people is to give them too little authority to be effective in their roles. This causes them, and your business outputs, to wait while they find an approver. Similarly, not giving employees adequate tools to do their jobs can slow things down or force a variety of situations, all negative in terms of business efficiency. A highly centralized command-and-control type of organizational structure tends to be quite inefficient because of this. People constantly have to wait for approvals, and while they wait, the customer waits. How many times have you had a trivial problem at a store checkout counter, perhaps a return over a certain amount or something that was priced wrong and needed to be corrected? You are surely familiar with what that means in most stores. You will wait … and wait … and wait while the frustrated cashier tries to find someone with enough authority to refund your $1.29. That underutilized person in the job causes waiting, and that is waste. It also caused a supervisor to travel, and his or her motion was wasted motion. When you transact a store where the front line employees have appropriate authority and tools and you need a refund, they simply press the right key, give you your refund, smile, and you are out the door quickly. It's so rare that it makes you happy for the rest of the day. You might even mention it at dinner that night!

In summary, knowing what waste is helps you to see what your process is really doing and helps you to correctly identify potential areas of opportunities. Perhaps in your particular business some of these definitions aren't quite right, but you can use them as concepts and a starting point. Happy waste hunting!

Complexity Analysis

When products or processes are overly complex, waste and defects are an inevitable result, so often people strive to simplify their processes, not because of any scientific proof that complexity causes problems, at least not that we know of, but from a commonsense human understanding that it does. When one of us was designing automation systems early in his career he had some rule-of-thumb formulas for estimating how long it would take to design a control system and how long it would take to program the associated software for it. The estimating method was simple: He counted the inputs and outputs (I/O) and multiplied the total times an hour per I/O factor. He then estimated the complexity of the system and adjusted that first number for that. A simple system has a multiplier of 1.0, moderately complex 1.5, and very complex 2.0. How did he judge complexity? He developed logic diagrams and counted calculation modules and the number of logic diagrams and calculation modules were used to determine his complexity factor. A very simple system with 200 I/O might take five pages of logic to describe it. A complex system with the same number of I/O might take twenty pages to describe it. His system was quite easy to use and was not theoretically based, but was an experiential model. He kept track of projects he did and their complexities and time needed after the fact and used his historical data to adjust his estimating model going forward. Although it was far from perfect it was an order of magnitude better than pulling a number out of your knapsack. Why not simply ask the "old pros," you might ask? If he was lucky enough to have a suitable old pro handy, he certainly did that but in general there aren't enough old pros to go around and they are never around when you need them. Besides, a system that lets ordinary employees produce good results with the use of tools is far better than a system that relies on old pros. The latter system is not very extensible.

As that example shows, you can develop your own complexity measures for your business. There are a few tools that can help you estimate how complex your process is. In structured program design, some techniques are to count the number of compares in a function. A value less than ten is considered acceptable. Computational complexity analysis focuses on two aspects of system complexity: time complexity and space complexity. Time complexity deals with how long it takes to perform a computation with a given number of I/O. Certain kinds of problem solutions have linear time complexity. That is, if you double the number of I/O you will double the amount of time it takes to do the calculation. Painting a wall has linear time complexity. A wall that is twice the size will take you twice the time to paint it. Looking something up in a dictionary has logarithmic complexity if you use an efficient search algorithm, because you only have to open the dictionary one extra time when you double its size. Space complexity has to do with the amount of space required to perform a function as the size of the I/O increases. In a software environment, this usually relates to the amount of memory it will consume. Whenever you are faced with a process that defies improvement, consider evaluating the complexity of the process steps and looking for ways to simplify them. Besides potential performance improvements, a simpler process is easier to train new people on, is easier to troubleshoot, is less prone to errors, and its CTQs can be made visible more easily.

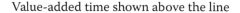

Value-added time shown above the line

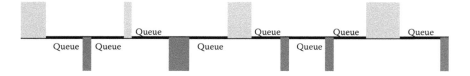

Non value-added time shown below the line

Figure 7.8   A sample time value map.

Time Value Maps

Another useful tool for process analysis is a time value map (TVM). This is similar to the VSM but without many of the details and with a third category of time added. The timeline in a VSM tracks VA and NVA time at the bottom of the map. A time value map distinguishes between NVA time and required NVA time, that is, NVA activities that are required by law, regulation, or contract but that still add nothing to the output. A horizontal line shows all the time that the process output spends waiting, or in a queue. When VA time is spent on it, a line proportional to the time spent rises above the horizontal and when required VA time is spent, a line proportional to the time spent rises below the horizontal. This gives you a simple view of where queues are, where you are adding value, and where you are doing things you must but that don't add value. Figure 7.8 is an example.

Value Add Chart

A value add chart is a bar graph of both VA and NVA time within a process. It can be created from either a VSM or a TVM. It is simply a different representation of the same time data that are on those charts. It is simpler than the others so it is handy for a presentation. It requires that all queuing, waiting, or inventory time (depending on the term you prefer) be associated with a process. This might have to be an arbitrary association, but it really won't affect your conclusions or future action plans. An example is shown in Figure 7.9. In Excel this is called a Column Chart format.

Evaluation Techniques

Besides the standard tools we have discussed already, there are a few other things that can be used to help improve processes. This next batch of topics isn't as crisply defined as the previous tools, but each can play a role in the right circumstances. Process improvement techniques don't lend themselves to much rigor, so the more

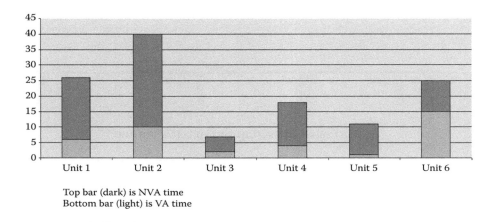

Top bar (dark) is NVA time
Bottom bar (light) is VA time

Figure 7.9   A sample value add chart.

tools you have in your bag of tricks the better equipped you will be to address the problems you see. One of the comments we hear regularly in our Lean and Six Sigma classes is, "Where is the formula to solve my process problems?" Unfortunately there is no formula for solving problems, simply approaches and methods. The DMAIC methodology is a problem-solving framework. Being clear about quantifying the problem is an approach that allows you to use quantitative methods. Having good process performance metrics helps you to evaluate how you are doing, and dozens and dozens of different analysis and measurement techniques are used as they seem appropriate given the circumstances of the problem at hand. There is no substitute for experience when deciding which of the tools should be used when.

Simulation Models

When you are problem solving and understand the root causes and know what to fix, sometimes you can analytically find solutions to the process problems. For that matter, sometimes the solutions are obvious to everyone on the team and no analytics are needed at all, or the solutions might be so inexpensive and fast to implement that you can simply try them out and see what happens. We are seldom so lucky. At still other times solutions aren't obvious but the DMAIC method gives us a framework to systematically generate ideas and assess them, sometimes by conducting experiments and analyzing the resulting data. Sometimes, however, solutions simply do not lend themselves to such linear, analytic thinking because the problems are too complex or nonlinear, or sometimes solutions are expensive or time consuming or both to implement, thus carrying a high risk with trying them out. At times like these, if the problem is worth solving, and it must be or you wouldn't have undertaken it in the first place, we can use dynamic simulation to find good solutions.

Dynamic simulation is the process of creating a model of how the physical process works in a specially designed software application. The simulation model is live, not a static picture of the process, and can be driven with dynamic inputs. Simulations can reflect reality very closely, depending on the level of detail that you model. Often with business problem-solving simulations, the model does not need to be very complex at all. It usually does not need to be any more detailed than our mental picture of how the process works and that is often described in a straight-forward flowchart. For the model to be useful it needs to not only describe how the process is arranged, but it also needs to describe logical conditions in the product or service flow. Dynamic simulation models are driven with dynamic data that simu-lates real input conditions. How do you know what to use to drive the simulation? You simply collect data on what is happening dynamically in the real world and put it into the model. Modern simulation packages make this process straightforward. Other process conditions can also be easily simulated, such as process failures and employee behavior; for example, not everyone comes to work on time. Once you create the process model in the simulator and drive it with realistic dynamic process inputs, the outputs will be simulated. Once you have done this accurately enough to simulate what has happened in the past, you can simply start making changes to the model to simulate changes that the improvement team proposes be made in the real process. Making changes to a simulation model is cheap and fast compared to making the equivalent changes to a real process. Simulation should be considered as a solution-finding tool.

Dynamic simulation software used to require mainframe computers to run, but powerful simulators will run on ordinary desktop PCs today and are far more user friendly than they used to be, complete with dynamic graphics to show you what is happening while the model is running. Typical prices for these packages run from as low as a few hundred dollars for the simplest ones to $15,000 for the most complex and powerful ones. The packages we normally use are in the $3,000 to $4,000 range as we write this. At that price, the software is not the major cost; the cost of the simulation expert to create it is. It is not advisable to attempt to do dynamic simulation with your own staff unless it is something you plan to do regularly because it is really a specialized programming language and is inefficient to do once or twice. For most companies, the practical thing to do is to use a con-sultant who can do it for you the few times you might need it. Typical simulation projects for business process improvement projects take two to eight weeks of effort by experienced simulation users. It can take that long for a new simulation user to be good enough to do his first simple project; to do that, he will be consumed with this new tool and not able to do other work.

Some simple problems and trial solutions can even be simulated in Excel if you are a very strong user of that program. Excel can generate random numbers according to specified distributions so it is possible to create simple but effective static simulations with it that reflect a distribution of outcomes based on a distri-bution of inputs. We once showed a company how they could reduce their lead

time by adding a limited second shift. Their operations people had discussed this
at length and studied this by every means they knew how and were convinced it
was impossible. Adding a second shift that didn't solve the problem would be very
disruptive, so they didn't want to experiment with it, only to have to drop it if it
didn't work. We were there on an unrelated consulting assignment, helping them
to reduce inventory, and had lots of free time in the evenings. We got interested
in their second shift problem and decided to simulate their production flow in
Excel during free evening time. After trying out a few combinations of process
changes and shifts we were able to convince the company operations director that
a limited second shift would help their product flow dramatically. The company
implemented it and was very pleased. As a reward we got a pat on the back from
the company and were yelled at by the owner of the consulting practice for giving
away valuable work despite having proposed this as a project to him earlier and
having it rejected for being out of their expertise. It might have been out of their
expertise, but it was well within ours. He eventually got over it and listened to us
more closely from then on.

What we have been discussing so far is called Discrete Event simulation. In
that kind of simulation, time is a factor. It is used to model the behavior of systems over time with probabilistic inputs that represent real-world randomness.
The simulation tools which do this typically show you a moving picture simulation of how the system behaves over time as an output.

There is another kind of simulation called Monte Carlo. Time is not a characteristic of Monte Carlo simulation. As in Discrete Event simulation, a typical
model replaces point estimates of input, process and environment variables with
statistical representation of those estimates. For example, instead of saying the
average call is 30 seconds long, a point estimate, we model it as a statistical distribution which looks like the distribution of hundreds of call durations we have
measured. Problems that do not involve time can be simpler to describe and don't
need the dynamic pictures so often associated with discrete event simulation.
This kind of simulation is often used for more complex DFSS design decisions.
Some examples are:

- Staffing analysis for operations with highly variable inputs
- Tolerance analysis when specifying system components that have to work
  together
- Design of experiments analysis
- IT project cost and schedule estimation
- System yield or throughput analysis when there is variability in the
  components
- Failure rate or VA/NVA ration calculations that are more sophisticated than
  the point failure rates calculated by most LSS teams

There are many Monte Carlo software tools on the market, many of which work with Excel. Like all simulation packages, they are a specialty tool and take some time and experience to use well. If your need for a tool like this is occasional, you are probably better off to use a consultant to help the team by doing the simulations you need.

Benchmarking

Benchmarking is simply the process of finding out what world-class competitors or similar businesses do and finding ways to emulate them. It is a way of establishing standards. If you cannot get specifications from customers because your customer base is too broad or diverse, then you can imply specifications by studying what specifications other successful companies use and assume those as your customer specifications. You can also use benchmarking to see how other companies organize their businesses and processes and get useful ideas from that. In other words, it can be part of a brainstorming activity to study solutions that others have already implemented.

Benchmarking is a specialty of some consulting firms, who will do these kinds of studies for you. For many problems, however, it can be done by your own team and in fact, we believe that it is more useful when you do them yourselves because the hands-on approach to learning is so much richer and you develop relationships with other companies that can be mutually helpful, not only for your current project, but for others as well. Of course, when the companies and process you want to benchmark against are competitors, you cannot do it yourself, at least not directly. In some cases it is possible to legally "reverse engineer" how competitors do their business and the specifications of their outputs. This is probably most applicable to physical products that are sold via mass distribution networks where you can simply buy their products and study them. An entire formal problem-solving methodology is based on examining how others have solved similar problems. It's called the TRIZ method.

Industry Standards and Internet Research

Industry standards bodies are another source of potentially useful information in our search for specifications and solutions. We covered quite a few standards in Chapter 2. Perhaps you are already familiar with the ones that apply to your industry. On the other hand, maybe you aren't, especially if the market is new to you, or there might be some new standards under development that could be useful for you to know about. If you are going into a new market, becoming familiar with industry standards is essential. While you are at it, don't forget the now ubiquitous Internet. Most of us now use the Internet as a standard part of our research methods. It is simply incredible how much information is available and searchable. When it comes to very specific details, however, the Web is not all it could be.

There are very good reasons to keep information private, and one of them is so that you cannot find it. Internet research is best for getting ideas and finding out what is publicly known about the topic, but it can be a trap. Anybody can publish to it, most people are not experts, and there is no review or rating process for most information there. In addition, because anyone can publish to the Web, there is always conflicting information. There is no way to tell who knows their stuff and who doesn't. A good example of how the Web can be useful is if you want to know more about what TRIZ is and where you can get books or training on it or find consultants who know it. That is such a unique acronym that you will quickly find useful information. Try to search for "problem solving," though, and it is a different story of jumbled, messy hits that go all over the place. If you try another technical term, let's say "histogram," you will get every article on esoteric histogram types that every math graduate student in the world felt compelled to put on the Web. If you start reading them you'll get so confused that you'll give up on process improvement and consider retirement. The savvy Web researcher, however, knows how to use Web searches to find useful information, so it belongs in your bag of tricks. Finally, you can use the Internet to find those industry standards that we mentioned.

Limited Pilots

The last tool we want to mention is simply building limited pilot processes to both experiment when it is difficult, dangerous, or expensive to experiment on a production process, or to try out proposed solutions. Pilot operations can be anything from a full-scale duplicate of all or part of your main process to a scaled-down version. It is common for IT operations to have a full-scale pilot operation to test new releases or changes to their operations because of the huge disruption that changes to their main environment would entail if things went wrong. In manufacturing operations, pilot facilities are less common, but they are there, most often used for R&D purposes, but sometimes also for process improvements. The problem with using an R&D-style pilot line for main operation process improvement is that when the scale changes, so many variables change that it might be difficult to know how the results will transfer. You can get false positive or false negative results. Another common piloting approach is when there are many copies of a process running. There, simply trying out changes on one or a few of them before doing it to all of them makes so much sense that it would be silly not to do that. One of the biggest 3D virtual worlds, perhaps the biggest one, is Second Life™. It is a collection of 3D simulators that can be accessed via special client software over the Internet. Each simulator has a dedicated CPU and there are over 10,000 of these simulated "worlds" interconnected and online at any one time, which are visited by as many as 75,000 people simultaneously. With a megasystem like that, it is easy to pilot changes by trying them out in a few of the worlds or in a group of them disconnected from the main grid. At the other extreme might be a communication company that is essentially driven by a single giant IT system to handle the billions of calls, e-mails, and other media that flow through their systems. Sure there are numerous components to it, but it is essentially one big system. A pilot for that might have to be as large as the production system itself. They might not have any choice but to do that, too, when you consider the cost of shutting off millions of customers for a change gone bad. You can bet that there is a constant stream of changes happening to a system like that, some for process improvement and others as the business model changes or new products are rolled out or discontinued.

We have a word of advice for those who use production systems to conduct experiments. The people in charge of operations will always be against it, as any experimenting is likely to deoptimize the system's performance; even worse; there is a risk of shutting it down. To avoid these risks, the production owner is likely to impose constraints on what you can do. Be very sure that those constraints will not invalidate your entire experiment. In one such disastrous situation, a company needed to conduct experiments to help understand process operations more fully so that they could be mathematically modeled and reengineered to use less energy and space as well as to drive several quality improvements. It was a lofty, multipurpose goal. None of their pilot operations were close enough to their production systems to use, so they used a full production system as a pilot. The operations manager for the target system imposed a constraint, namely that the experimenters could change nothing in the process; they could only collect product samples and process measurements but could not conduct real designed experiments. This was destined to fail from the start, but the team didn't understand data collection, statistics, or the dynamics of processes well enough to know that the right thing to do was to walk away. Instead they spent $250,000 collecting data that in the end told them nothing. Don't do that.

Poka-Yoke: Mistake Proofing

The final topic in this chapter is a design topic. We have so far focused on tools and techniques for finding out what is wrong with processes and eliminating root causes so as to improve how they operate. Process quality variations that are beyond customer specifications are called defects. Why do defects happen? Well, from a very high level there are two categories of defect causes: those caused by people and those caused by the process independent of people. The latter category includes input problems, equipment problems, and environmental problems. Although all defects can be addressed and reduced with the techniques discussed so far, this topic is designed to reduce defects caused by people. Those of you in service businesses should pay close attention to this.

People make mistakes. What is a mistake? You can either perform an action that you are not supposed to do or fail to perform an action that you are supposed to do. Why might someone make one of these mistakes? Here is a list that is far from exhaustive:

- Unclear instructions
- Tiredness
- Physical problems (eyesight, hand–eye coordination, strength)
- Difficult to do (so they do something easier instead)
- Don't care (not motivated to do well)
- Don't know (lack of training or memory)

Whatever the reason, mistakes happen all the time. No one person makes lots of mistakes or you would notice it and do something about it. He or she wouldn't be in that job for long uncorrected if you are doing your job as a manager. Mistakes are therefore fairly rare. But you have lots of people involved in your processes. If each person only makes one mistake a day and you are in a company with 10,000 employees, 10,000 mistakes are made each day. Look at this quote about medical errors: "The most comprehensive evaluation of human error in the ICU used an engineering model and outside observers and reported an average of 178 activities per patient per day and 1.7 errors per patient per day (1%). For this 6 bed ICU, a severe or potentially life-threatening error occurred on average twice a day" (Donchin et al. 1995, 294). Is it a reasonable assumption that 1.7 errors per day is the norm for an intensive care unit, a place where the employees have one of the highest average levels of education in the country, and where there is no denying their motivations to do well, that your company's mistake rate is better than that?

Hopefully you will now agree that your people and you (did you think you were exempt?) are making lots of mistakes every day. Fortunately, not all of those mistakes are harmful. However, some of those mistakes result in errors in the product or service that you are producing and some of those errors will result in customer defects. In this context an error is an output that isn't what it should have been, had the mistake not been made. The mistake changed the output. However, if the output is still within the customer limits, it will not be perceived as a defect. It will affect the overall statistics of the system and so will appear as part of the common cause variation of your system. If the mistake causes an error that results in an output beyond the customer limits, then we have a defect.

Now that we understand that some defects are caused by human mistakes, how can we proceed to reduce the mistakes, which will in turn reduce defects? A simple approach is to design the process, the product, or both so that common mistakes simply cannot happen, despite the presence of all the human frailties listed earlier. The Japanese call this poka-yoke; we call it mistake proofing. The concept is simple, as are many of the process improvement concepts that are part of the Lean thinking method. The poka-yoke concept was formalized, and the term adopted, by Shigeo Shingo as part of the TPS, but engineers have used the concept of mistake proofing for many decades to design things that defy human attempts to use them wrong. What the Lean enterprise advocates did is to simply educate the rest of the business community about this and empower many more employees to poka-yoke their own work processes. This is in line with the concept of pushing the responsibility for much of the system quality and system improvements close to the workers, where they can identify and fix problems much faster than management can because they are in the process every day. Software application interface design has long been an area where these principles have been known and used. Type checking data is a form of mistake proofing. If you are presented with an electronic form to fill in and one of the fields is your phone number, it is a straightforward process to verify that you entered a valid phone number before the form lets you go on to the next field. Even the ubiquitous Excel spreadsheet application has the ability to do this. Just because it is there, however, doesn't mean that people use it. They seldom use it, resulting in messy data to analyze later on.

There is no formal methodology for how to mistake-proof a process element, but there are a few principles that you can think about when attempting to do it. The first is the concept of *elimination*. This means to examine the process step where the error is known to occur and redesign it so that it cannot happen. Eliminate the opportunity. Perhaps the step is redundant. Perhaps it can be done in another place or at another time. Perhaps it can be skipped completely by changing the way the system works. The second method is *facilitation*. When you facilitate a process step, you provide guidance to reduce the chance of an error occurring. Type checking is a kind of facilitation, and so is a mechanical template for placing parts onto an assembly. Pop-up help or examples in context are also types of facilitation. It is frustrating to look at an empty field that you are supposed to fill in and not know what is expected. If a description, example, or both are easily available, or even automatically available, that facilitates your understanding of what to do. The third method is *mitigation*. This means modifying the process so that the mistakes don't affect the outputs, or if they do, they don't exceed customer expectations. Have you ever wondered why there are often extra parts in assemble-it-yourself furniture and things that you buy? One explanation is that the manufacturer knows that their process occasionally packs too many or that the customer often loses a few, or that some of them are likely to be defective. To eliminate the costly and consumer-hostile result of having the customer have to call to request replacement parts and delay assembly by days or weeks, it is simply cheaper to pack a few extras in the package. Another example might be when a database input form automatically reformats inputs to be the format required by the next process. It does it right in front of your eyes so you can see what it did. A telephone number that it expects to be in the form (000) 111–2222 and that is entered 000.111.222 or 000–111–2222 or 0001112222 is reformatted automatically on the spot. This is a form of mitigation and it allows users to detect if it was done right without requiring them to do it over themselves or presenting them with an irritating error message. The last approach is *flagging*. This is to simply detect the error and somehow make note that it is there so that it can be located and removed later. Out-of-range data can be flagged at input, for instance. Perhaps the data were collected and entered correctly and represent a process deviation, or perhaps some digits were transposed or the measuring device was defective or read wrong. The software cannot detect from these alternatives so it does the next best thing and flags it so that someone can notice it and make a decision later. When one of us first got out of engineering school he had a task of designing a sensor to detect holes in toilet paper as it was being made. It was a fascinating project and it worked. At the point where the detector had to be located, the paper was moving at thousands of feet per minute. Paper machines are really, really large to be making products as flimsy as toilet paper. It was impossible to do anything about the hole at that location so we installed a paint gun and used the sensor to spray paint at that spot. Later in the production process where hole detection would have been very expensive to do, color detection was easy to do, so we detected the paint and cut out the bad parts. It was a very rewarding project. After all, nobody wants holes in their toilet paper!

One of the reasons that mistakes happen is because of process complexity. Recall our discussion of complexity reduction earlier. Complexity and mistakes are strongly linked. You can make a good argument that reducing the complexity of process operations will reduce mistakes by people. The mistake-proofing approaches discussed here can be used with simple or complex processes, but every time you have a chance to simplify something, do it. Be aware that some processes and mistakes lend themselves to mistake proofing and others don't, so don't be like the mechanic with only one tool that he tries to use for everything. If the consequences of a mistake are large and the likelihood of the mistake occurring is small, then inspection is not likely to find it. Instead, redesigning your process to include appropriate mistake-proofing elements will prevent it from happening in the first place.

Chapter 8

Working on Ideas

Throughout this book we have discussed the elements of solving problems. One of the frustrating things that some people find with all of this is that all of the problem-solving approaches have at least one, and sometimes several places in the methodology where, like the old mathematics cartoon with a student looking at a board full of equations, there is a note in the middle of the equations saying, "And then a miracle happened!" The miracles in problem solving are the creative ideas that people come up with to verify. The methodologies give us a framework to approach the problems and use logic and data to stay organized and not forget steps. Inevitably, though, there comes a time when we too need a miracle, an idea. This chapter is about how to generate those ideas.

Brainstorming

Brainstorming isn't a very specific term but it can loosely be defined as a creativity technique designed to generate ideas for the solution to a problem. There are as many ways to do brainstorming as there are people, so we won't try to belabor it, but instead present a few ideas that we think are relevant and useful. First, let's describe the typical approach:

- Define the problem clearly.
- Assemble a group that includes SMEs and outsiders.
- Explain the problem and background to the participants.
- Explain the brainstorming rules, typically:
  - No criticism of ideas.
  - Clarification questions are allowed.

    – It is OK to offer an idea that is an extension of another one.
    – It is OK to combine ideas to create new ones.
    – Focus on quantity. We want lots of ideas to start with!

- Hold a warm-up exercise to get people into a creative mindset (many ways to do this).
- Have the group suggest ideas (many techniques for this, too).
- Number and record the ideas as they are presented.
- Stop when the group is worn out (like waiting for the last popcorn kernel to pop, when volume slows way down, stop it).
- Either with this same group or a smaller one you can then categorize ideas into groups, eliminate duplicates and obviously impractical ones, and go through an assessment process to select one or more to work with.

This can be a fun exercise or a very frustrating one. Brainstorming requires some getting used to. If your company has a strong hierarchical structure, the mere presence of a senior manager in the room can kill the process. Nobody wants to say things that might be construed as dumb in front of the big boss in many companies, so think carefully before you invite them, or if you are the boss, before you invite yourself. Be realistic about how you are perceived by your own employees.

Brainstorming was first described as a technique in the 1930s by Alex Faickney Osborn in a book called *Applied Imagination*. It is a controversial process and many people don't agree that it works, or at least that it is the best way to generate ideas. Nevertheless, it is still widely used so should be a part of every problem solver's tool chest. Even if it isn't the best way, it is often fun, so it can help create teamwork and a pleasant workplace. Besides, ideas are not proof, so as a quantitative problem solver all you really need from an idea session are reasonable things to test with data. It will almost certainly do that for you.

Six Thinking Hats

We've been teaching Lean and Six Sigma for years and we always mention the Six Thinking Hats technique without explanation in courses and it almost never fails that nobody in the class has heard of it, yet this technique has been around since the mid-1980s and was developed by Dr. Edward de Bono, who wrote a book by the same name describing it.

The basic idea is that we have different thinking styles and for many of us, one style is predominant. To arrive at good ideas we need to use a variety of thinking styles. Six Thinking Hats describes five different styles of thinking to help ideation. We describe them here and you'll see where the sixth one comes in. The idea behind the technique is that we all tend to have a predominant style and problem solutions can look different from different points of view, so when we can train ourselves to examine the situation from a variety of points of view we are more likely to come up with useful solution ideas. Standard brainstorming does put a group of people in the room, some of whom probably do have different thinking styles, but there is no guarantee of that. Even if this is the case, there is no guarantee that you will cover all of the thinking styles. Six Thinking Hats encourages you to use all of the thinking styles to ponder the problem. It can be used alone as a self-imposed discipline and can also be used as a facilitated group activity, either where the entire group brainstorms five different times, each time using a different point of view, or where the facilitator reminds people to periodically switch views.

When this is used as a group exercise, the facilitator often wears a colored hat (hence the name). Each hat represents a different point of view. When the facilitator is wearing a specific hat, it is a signal for everyone to think like that. This is a simple, effective, and fun idea. Here is a summary of the hats.

- *White hat:* Here you focus on the available data. You summarize what they tell you and look for gaps in your actual knowledge and try to gather data to fill in missing portions or rationalize them. You look at data trends and might extrapolate them as seems appropriate. Much traditional Six Sigma analysis is white hat thinking.
- *Red hat:* When doing red hat thinking you use your intuition, feelings, and emotions. Perhaps you can already start to see the usefulness of this method. All organizations tend to have natural white hat people and natural red hat people. This lets all of the hats have their say, and furthermore, asks each person to try on all the hats. When red hat thinking, you can attempt to predict how your solutions might be accepted by others who might not understand your reasons for choosing them.
- *Black hat:* This is the pessimistic hat. Here you look at the downside of things. You are cautious and defensive. You look for reasons why things might fail. The usefulness of this kind of thinking is that it avoids letting a solution that is proposed by an overly optimistic, rose-colored-glasses team get out the door without taking an opposing look at it. Believe me, no matter how good a job you do, someone will take shots at it when it leaves your team, so black hat thinking is a way of predicting that and not digging yourself into a hole that you are later surprised to have to defend. It makes your solutions more realistic.
- *Yellow hat:* This hat is the opposite of the black hat. Here you focus on the benefits and opportunities that you can see. This kind of thinking helps you sell your ideas and helps you to stay motivated and keep going when there is too much black hat stuff around!
- *Green hat:* The green hat stands for creativity. This is our personal favorite. Here we allow ourselves to be a little wacky. We let the group do some open-ended brainstorming or even get a little wild. One of the more interesting green hat exercises we've done involved making a list of all the things you could do with a paper clip if you had all the time and money you needed.

Our job was to develop a list of imaginative, theoretical solutions. One of the solutions was to create a lighter-than-air balloon that could lift large weights. That's right, out of a single paper clip!

■ *Blue hat:* The last hat is the process control hat. This is the hat worn by people chairing meetings. They can use this hat in various ways. They might use it to direct the group to all think using the same hat, or might switch hats in a free-wheeling discussion to force, for example, some yellow hat thinking when the group is getting worried.

Mind Mapping

A mind map is a graphical diagram used to represent ideas, words, activities, or things around a central theme. Do you like to doodle? If so, a mind map might be just the thing for you to learn to harness your doodling into something useful. Mind mapping was reportedly first used in the third century and has been used in various forms since then, but it was popularized by Tony Buzan in the United Kingdom a few decades ago. Mind mapping is based on the notion that human minds do not think linearly. We form ideas and thoughts that are related to other ideas. Our minds are more like a messy colored picture than an organized database, yet we are taught to read from left to right, from top to bottom, and from front to back; to make lists constantly; to stay within the borders; and so on. If you are of Asian or Middle Eastern descent, you read in different order than Westerners do, but it is still a logical, linear order. Figure 8.1 is an example of a mind map to describe CoBiT.

A mind map starts with a central theme. As you learn more about it, you write words or pictures that represent ideas on the page and connect them to the theme. We call those subtopics. Things that further describe or explain a subtopic are noted similarly and connected to it with lines. Strong connections might be shown with a heavy line, weak connections with a dotted line. If you discover that some subtopics are related to each other in some way, you indicate that graphically somehow, perhaps by lines, by circling all of the related ones, or by adding colors. When you are done you have a nice, colorful, messy mind map that looks like the way your mind thinks, rather than one that looks like a neat table.

Mind mapping is reported to be a better way to take notes, to be an aid to brainstorming, to be a way to study a textbook or course, to outline a novel or book you plan to write, to describe a problem and potential solutions, and so on. We include it in this book because it is a tool that is fairly widely known and we see it a lot. However, we have some reservations about its usefulness. First of all, when using software you need to have a computer, obviously, and being stuck to a computer can inhibit creativity in a group. If you use it to take notes, you need large pieces of paper and several colored pencils. We never have those around, and carrying them is not convenient. Even if we did have them, it is rare to have enough free space on

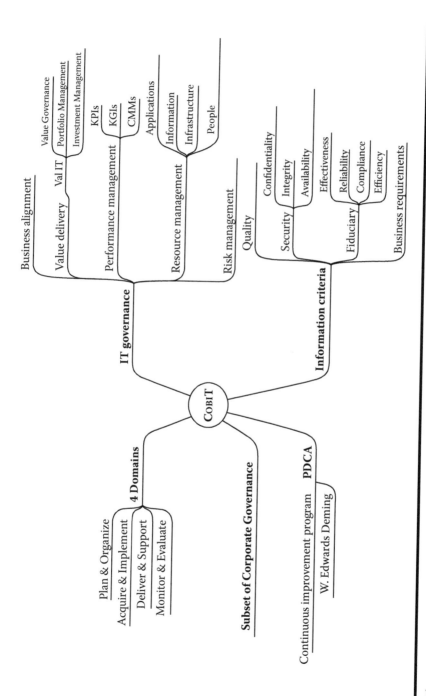

Figure 8.1   A mind map describing CoʙɪT concepts.

a table or desk to use them without tipping over your neighbor's coffee. Still, if you are already skilled at the technique you could use a whiteboard and colored markers to create a mind map of a brainstorming session and later convert it to software or take a picture of it. One of us took a mind mapping course and found it to be fun and interesting. In that course each participant read a business article and created a mind map of it, then presented the mind map to the group. It took less time to convey the idea of the article by showing and explaining the mind maps than it did to read the book and outline it to start with, so it was a fairly efficient way to get a lot of people to understand a lot of articles with each person only having to read one of them.

Affinity Diagrams

If you have ever had the problem of too many ideas, which can easily result from a brainstorming session, then you know that it is helpful if you can arrange the ideas into groupings that have common themes. This allows you to describe the elements in broader terms, lets you identify solutions that might address a number of problems, or lets you arrange topics into logical groups for later study. For example, if you have a group of eighty ideas that need further study, it would be helpful to perhaps sort them into four or five groups by technology content so you can identify the right technology SMEs to look at each group. You could perhaps arrange them into groups that have location in common so that you can have people in different cities deal with a common group of issues that are close to them. That's what an affinity diagram does. It is simply the process of taking lots of things and categorizing them into fewer but common groups. The term affinity diagram is somewhat of a misnomer. The process might better be described as affinity piles because not much diagramming is involved. Table 8.1 is an example from a brainstorming session at a local process improvement professional society that was formed in Atlanta in 2008. The group brainstormed ideas for meeting topics for the coming year, which were recorded on pieces of sticky paper and put on a board. Once finished, there were about forty random ideas. After discussion, these ideas were grouped into six main categories of ideas. This led to a strategy of choosing one topic from each category a month.

Affinity diagrams seem like an organization tool but they can be a creativity aid, too. Once you have the large group of topics you can leave them posted on a wall for a few days and have people come in and rearrange them, allowing them to add, delete, combine, or split categories. This is a way of using the unconscious creative power of the human mind to create order out of chaos. Making an affinity diagram can also identify opportunities to create new topics (or solutions if that is what you are using it for). Simply seeing so many things arranged, first in random piles, and then into increasingly coherent groupings, can often inspire new ideas that can be added.

Table 8.1 Affinity Diagram

		Process Improvement Exchange Group Brainstorming Topics
1.		Process Improvement Strategy
	a.	Process improvement in an organization on steroids (impatient)
	b.	Accelerating process improvement
	c.	Gaining management buy-in
	d.	Integrating process improvement throughout an organization
	e.	How do you sell the concepts and potential benefits before you have actual data
	f.	Change management
	g.	Assessing projects/developing process improvements
	h.	Continuation of process improvement—how to handle PI after the initial project is completed
	i.	Control (as in DMAIC)
2.		Industry
	a.	Six Sigma to improve software development
	b.	Offshore software development; process of transitioning to offshore, what works, what doesn't
	c.	Process improvement development in a fast/changing/growing IT environment
	d.	Process improvement in nonprofits
	e.	Using process improvement to improve public education
	f.	Six Sigma applied to software
	g.	Supply chain—using Lean to analyze and reduce delivery times for overseas suppliers
	h.	Health care—failure mode analysis and process improvement for medical errors in hospitals
3.		Case Studies
	a.	Lean/Six Sigma project—what worked, what did not
	b.	Business success stories with real tangible ROI that persuaded management to embrace Six Sigma

(continued)

Table 8.1 Affinity Diagram (Continued)

4.	Metrics	
	a.	Measuring performance for organization and personal accountability
	b.	Aligning and cascading metrics with strategy
5.	Tools	
	a.	Malcolm Baldrige Performance Excellence Criteria
	b.	Simulation
	c.	Stats refresher
	d.	Minitab (2xs)
	e.	Taguccii DOE
	f.	DFSS
	g.	Value stream mapping
	h.	Project charters
6.	Format	
	a.	Bi-monthly, individual presenter
	b.	If no presenter then panel with defined questions
	c.	Field trips on off months

Multivoting

Another organization tool for ideas is to use multivoting to narrow a large number of choices down to a smaller and more manageable number. It is a prioritization technique that is simple and fast to do. Multivoting is a secondary step after a brainstorming effort has generated a large list of potential options. The voting is normally done by giving each participant a number of votes. Each person can then go to the board where all of the ideas are listed and apply his or her votes by check marks, initials, or colored sticky paper if you have enough colors. If you use check marks, try to have each person use a different color. This lets you verify that each person voted his or her correct amount. The standard method is to give each participant a number of votes equal to one-third of the total items on the list. An alternate way of voting is that each member writes his or her choices on a piece of paper and hands it to the facilitator, who tallies them. This technique is slower but it has the advantage that participants cannot see what the others are voting for. This is a good procedure if you are concerned that some people might be swayed by what others vote for. It eliminates the ability to vote like the boss to get brownie points.

Some facilitators allow the voters to vote several or all of their votes on one or a few items. Others require that they can only apply one vote per item. Once the votes are tallied, there are usually a few clear winners. If there aren't, delete the options with the fewest votes, typically any with two or fewer, and repeat the voting with the remaining options. The goal is to arrive at a group consensus; it is not strictly a democratic process. At any stage people can make arguments that deleting an option is not appropriate and the rest of the group has a chance to hear those opinions before they vote again. This multivoting process normally converges and leads to a consensus conclusion. At the end of the meeting we mentioned earlier where we generated ideas for professional society meeting topics, we used multivoting to decide what topics we would have for the next four months. It was easy to do and allowed us to get to the beer fast. This brings up an important point: Don't try any of these techniques at a bar. They won't work. You'll end up with ideas like chocolate-covered mittens.

TRIZ

In Chapter 7 we mentioned a problem-solving approach called TRIZ, which is based on examining how other people have solved similar problems. TRIZ is the Russian acronym for theory of inventive problem solving, so it would be TIPS in English. TRIZ was developed based on the hypothesis that there are universal principles of innovation that are the basis for most inventions. If you can identify these principles and what classes of problems they solve, and you can categorize your problem into one of those classes, then you merely need to copy solution principles that others have used to solve your problem. The topic is fascinating but not very well known in the business world. It was developed to be applied to engineering problems involving physical things.

The TRIZ technique is based on the observation that technical systems tend to evolve to increasingly ideal states by overcoming contradictions in ways that minimize the introduction of new resources. Humans have been solving problems in this way for long enough that we have faced and solved problems of virtually every type; therefore most innovations are simply transpositions of known solutions from other problems that have already been solved, not necessarily in the same field. TRIZ is based on the detailed analysis of millions of patents and the belief that an old solution can be used to solve a new problem if we look at the problem and solution as fundamental elements. The procedure goes something like this:

1. Identify the characteristic of the system we wish to improve (e.g., make it more complex).

2. Identify a characteristic of the system that tends to get worse if we do number 1 (harder to repair).
3. Use the TRIZ matrix to identify which of the forty fundamental solution principles allow you to achieve number 1 without causing number 2 based on the categorization of those 2 million patents.
4. Study the suggested principles from the solution matrix and use them to suggest solution approaches for your system.

As you can see, TRIZ doesn't tell you how to solve the problem, but it does point out the kinds of solutions that have solved similar problems in the past across a wide range of industries. It can be used to kick-start the solution creativity process when you've reached a dead end. Here is a short example:

■ Suppose we want to make our system more complex to add new functions demanded by consumers.
■ We also need to make our system easier to repair.

This is a contradiction. As we make the system more complex, it inevitably becomes harder to repair. When we put these two things into the TRIZ matrix, it suggests the following solution principles:

Solution principle 1. Segmentation
  − Divide an object into independent parts.
  − Make an object easy to disassemble.
  − Increase the degree of fragmentation or segmentation.

Solution principle 13. The other way round
  − Invert the action(s) used to solve the problem (e.g., instead of cooling an object, heat it).
  − Make movable parts (or the external environment) fixed, and fixed parts movable.
  − Turn the object (or process) upside down.

These solution principles should inspire us to think about things that we can try. Perhaps if our system is a software application, we might apply the first segmentation principle and divide our application into more independent modules than it now has, thus making each module easier to troubleshoot than a combined system might be.

Process Thinking

We have discussed a lot of topics about process improvement so far, including several methodologies and lots of tools. We have mentioned the difference between functional and process orientation a few times but now want to focus on that. When we talk about process performance, we mean the business process that flows from inputs to outputs. Not all companies are organized around processes. More typical is organization around functional lines, believing for some reason that if all the engineers are in one room and all the programmers are in one room and all the accountants are in one room, and so on, they will all be more effective. To some extent that might be true, but when you are only functionally organized, there is a strong tendency to suboptimize your business processes in favor of optimizing functional performance. This is never good for the business but it is easier to manage than true process management so it's common.

Figure 8.2 shows a diagram of a business with five functional areas. Each functional area has performance goals. In general, they aren't related to each other and there is a natural tendency to compete with each other for resources, management time, and money. Figure 8.3 shows the same business but with four key business processes overlaid on the functional organization.

To know what these processes are and describe them is the first step. To have someone in charge of them is the next step. One of our clients was recently at that stage. It is a huge functionally organized insurance company that had recently defined their key business processes and appointed people to manage each one. By manage, we mean report on its performance, identify process performance criteria, and determine ways to improve it. Unluckily for the process manager and the company, those process coordinators had no staff, no budget, and no power. They had to manage by influence. The departments had all the money and staff. The performance of this company's business processes will always be secondary to the performance of their functional departments because their entire reporting and

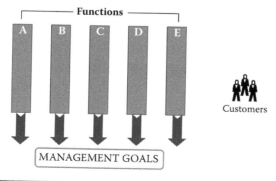

Figure 8.2   A functional organization diagram.

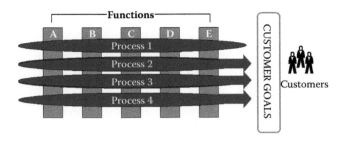

Figure 8.3 A process-oriented organization diagram that also shows the functional areas.

budgeting system has been organized around the departments. Unless they take the next step, it is a wasted effort.

The next step is to make the process managers the ones with the budgets and power. In that case the functional departments become subcontractors that provide expertise to help various parts of the process function. The process manager decides what is needed and what acceptable performance is. In the most efficient case the process manager should not be required to use the internal departments at all if they cannot deliver the performance that is needed. The process performance is controlled by root causes, some of which are internal to the process and some of which are functions of the process inputs. Each department's job is to deliver its part of the process activity and meet the process variable goals that are set by the process manager based on sound, quantitative analysis of the process as a whole. In one sense, the departments are really irrelevant to the performance of the business process. Figure 8.4 shows one of the company's processes with the departments in the background as they should be.

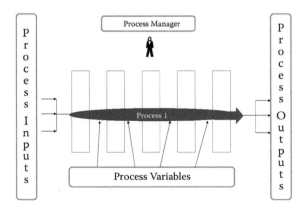

Figure 8.4 A process-oriented organization diagram showing the functional areas as secondary (in the background).

The process outputs go to customers who specify acceptable output parameters. The performance of the process is determined by process variables, some of which are controlled by the departments. The departments are required to deliver key process metrics within appropriate process specs as determined logically by the process manager, who is shown at the top overseeing it all. The performance of each department as a department is irrelevant to the performance of the process. Key company metrics should revolve around how the important company processes are performing and the process managers should have the ability to force changes and responsibilities as needed. Departments have little value in this model unless their participation leads to great process performance.

When a company starts thinking about their key processes in this way then everyone in the chain is focused on how the process is doing, not how they are doing. This state of process nirvana cannot be achieved without a strong process-oriented senior management team who works tirelessly to ask the right process questions all the time. There is no substitute for leadership by example.

Chapter 9

Lean Six Sigma Projects

At this point we trust you have adopted and adapted some guidance and you have started training your various belts. Now it is time to think about potential quality improvement projects. There are literally hundreds of opportunities in your organization. Perhaps that is your problem: You are paralyzed in the face of all the choices. You don't need a scytale to decode or a crystal ball to see the endless possibilities. What you do need is a process. We can help. In this chapter, we provide some suggestions regarding improvement projects.

Before providing you with some suggestions, we think it is important that you consider the following ten pitfalls when embarking on Lean Six Sigma initiatives:

1. *Lack of vision:* All the guidance we have shared with you either implies or requires that you have a vision and that you share it with your customers and employees. Any projects you select must relate directly to your business goals and objectives; otherwise they don't provide real value. Don't substitute the LSS tools and techniques for planning. Executive management must set the direction, create the vision, and then get out of the way.

2. *Lack of commitment and leadership:* If you are not going to lead the charge, you should get out of the way. You must show your staff you are serious about taking the lead to get things done. You need to create a vision for your staff and to create a plan for achieving your goals. You should know by now that Lean Six Sigma requires real commitment by everyone in your organization. For example, sponsors and champions must show for report-outs and all process owners must demonstrate buy-in.

3. *Lack of communication:* You need to communicate effectively your deployment plans throughout the organization. People are uneasy during periods

of change, so you need to keep them in the loop. If you choose to not communicate, you choose to fail.

4. *Lack of practical training:* Lean Six Sigma success relies heavily on trained staff to lead the projects. You cannot expect success unless you invest heavily in your people. Make sure you tap motivated individuals to receive LSS training: It produces a high-performance team and it indicates to others that their involvement is a good way to get ahead. Your training program should also include an employee retention plan. What's more, you should provide JIT LSS training rather than providing all the training up front. Otherwise, you have at least two problems. First, your staff will forget everything you taught them unless they get the opportunity to apply what they learned without delay after the training. Second, your staff might leave for more money, as they did at one company we know. We have found it very beneficial for your staff to take a project with them into training or to start a project right away.

5. *Lack of respect:* You must respect individuals and their expertise and experience. Your staff knows the right things to do and they are just waiting to tell you. Go ahead and ask them: They might amaze you. Similarly, your customers know what they want and will tell you should you ask them. Your customers and employees must believe that you are humble enough to listen to them. Also, you should assure your employees that no layoffs will occur due to any productivity improvements from any Lean Six Sigma projects.

6. *Lack of understanding of the customer:* Voice of the Process is important but the VOC is more important. You must understand that the customer decides what is right. Spend more time up front talking to your customers. Resist the urge to jump in and do something until you are absolutely sure what your customers want or need. As part of understanding your customers, your organization must have a procedure for determining the cost of poor quality. You should also understand that your employees are your customers as well.

7. *Lack of realistic expectations:* Before you jump in, ensure that everyone knows what to expect. Tell them there is going to be change and hard work. If you want to introduce a quality initiative into your organization, you need to work out how to do it in a way that won't disrupt or slow down the normal workflow. Otherwise, you better know how to deal with the objection that it costs too much or will disrupt operations.

8. *Lack of consensus:* You must get everyone to agree on your IT governance framework and the tools and techniques to use. If you don't get consensus, people will work to ensure you fail.

9. *Lack of persistence:* You need to keep at it; anything worth having is worth working for.

10. *Lack of performance measures:* You need to decide on how you will measure the performance of your LSS initiatives. Put in place metrics for sponsors, Champions, and belts. Even with metrics in place, you must provide feedback

to all involved parties. Performance measures should include an incentive, rewards, or recognition program.

We can summarize these important points by reminding you of the ABCs of Lean Six Sigma: aptitude, behavior, and culture. You need the right skills, you need to do something, and you need to share beliefs and practices in your organization. Don't even think about defining problems until you have given considered thought to and expended energy on these ten potential traps.

Potential IT Projects

One of the authors was fortunate to attend one of W. Edwards Deming's seminars. He said, "Don't tell me ten ways I can't do something; tell me one way I can! It's so easy to do nothing!" You could decide at this point that it is too hard and you will do nothing, or you can read the rest of the chapter and find out about some potential projects. We have intentionally kept the descriptions simple: one or two things you should think about. The ideas are ones that should help you take the theory and turn it into successes in practice.

Ensuring Compliance

Every CIO should have compliance as an IT goal. Compliance could mean conformity with the organization's policies and standards or external laws and regulations. Let's look at a simple example. You might have a "clean desk" policy or a legal requirement to store sensitive documents (for example, credit card numbers per PCI DSS). To ensure compliance, you need to ensure that employees store sensitive documents accordingly. Your data collection process would involve doing a "midnight audit" or an after-hours walkthrough to discover sensitive documents. When you find noncompliance, you need to document it. Now you need to capture the various document-handling processes before you can work on their improvement. Your assessment of these processes would involve mapping the document's life cycle from creation to destruction. Every time someone touches the document, there is an opportunity for noncompliance. When you find noncompliance, you need to look at the noncompliance and determine the factors that contributed to it. Does the person not understand the requirements for storage? Does the person not have sufficient storage space? Does the person know of the methods for destruction? Has someone classified the document? Is the classification visible to the person handling the document? You need to understand how attacking any of these problems will affect compliance. Additionally, you might find that one office has a bigger compliance issue than another. Understanding why will help you to work on the problem. Don't forget to check to see whether your improvements fixed the noncompliance issue.

You might think that noncompliance is a minor issue in your organization, but Accenture reported differently.* In a November 5, 2008 news release regarding their survey, they stated that 60 percent of millennials either are not aware of their organization's IT policies or are not inclined to follow them. You therefore face a significant educational and compliance challenge going forward.

IT Security

If you are looking for help with respect to IT security, good resources are available. You should check out the Six Sigma Security group on LinkedIn[†] for starters. Compliance with most security guidance, such as ISO 27001, necessitates process mapping. IT security really benefits from business process improvement and starts with a thorough understanding of your processes. Remember you can basically measure anything when you define it. If you need help with measurements, look at the book *How to Measure Anything* (Hubbard 2007). IT security is rife with potential projects.

Deactivating Employees' Access

People leave your organization on a regular basis: They retire, they get a new job, or you terminate them. In addition, you sometimes reassign them and they have new duties. These actions require that someone change employee access rights. In a large organization, making these changes is a full-time job. In some cases, the person you are terminating has network, system, or application authority and you are worried they could have backdoors installed.

First, you need to map the existing process. This step alone will point out weaknesses in your employee termination process—it is usually in the notification subprocess. Gather some data on how long it takes and discover where the bottlenecks are. Does the problem lie with the manager's notification? Does the problem lie in the human resources group? Does the security group respond quickly enough? Have you given people individual rights that you must remove? Have you given rights to groups and put the employee in the groups? Is there a way to inform everyone who needs to know? Establish a policy, develop a process and metrics, and measure and report. Doing nothing can compromise the security of your organization.

Data Accuracy

A favorite chestnut of any auditor is application controls. CobiT Application Control AC3 Accuracy, Completeness, and Authenticity Checks offers: "Ensure

---

* http://newsroom.accenture.com/article_display.cfm?article_id=4767.
[†] http://www.linkedin.com/groups?about=&gid=1396997&trk=anet_ug_grppro.

that transactions are accurate, complete and valid. Validate data that were input, and edit or send back for correction as close to the point of origination as possible." Should you choose to not do accuracy, completeness, and authenticity checks, you should expect missing or inaccurate data due to insufficient controls on inputs. You can calculate approximations about the number of errors in your data. Of course, you might have approximation errors, but without real data, it will do. Then you need to study why there are errors. Do you perform any input checks on data entry? Do you validate key fields? Do you use drop-down menus? Do you do range checks? Do you do reasonableness checks on the data? Do you do transaction totals? Do you validate postal or zip codes to addresses? Do you validate Social Security numbers?* Do you validate credit card numbers?† Don't allow your employees to enter inaccurate data. Reducing the percentage of errors results in real savings, but also allows your managers to make better decisions as they have better data. Better data result in better decisions—it makes sense.

Password Reset

We have heard people complain that it takes too long to get their password reset when they cannot remember it. When you map the process and start to collect data, you should find that it doesn't take very long to reset a password. After all, it takes the security administrator just seconds to actually do the reset. All the NVA activities consume the time. The request sits with the person's supervisor, then it is in transit, and finally sits in some queue awaiting action by the security administrator. This is a project that leans toward Lean more than Six Sigma. In fact, the Five Whys probably would solve your problem.

1. Why does it take so long to reset a password? Because the supervisor has to approve it and send it to security.
2. Why does it have to go to security? They have to do the reset.
3. Why do they have to do the reset? They are the only ones with the authority to do it.
4. Why are they the only ones to have the authority? We wanted to centralize security tasks and we didn't give the supervisor the authority when we set up our rules.
5. Why did you want to centralize password resets? No particular reason. Supervisors could reset passwords when we give them the authority. It makes more sense to do it this way as the supervisor personally knows the person, whereas the security administrator might not.

---

* See http://www.breakingpar.com/bkp/home.nsf/0/87256B280015193F87256F6A0072B54C for an example.
† See http://javascript.internet.com/forms/credit-card-number-validation.html for an example.

There are many other things you could fix with password resets, but this is one of the biggest problems. Cutting any time creates real value and adds to the bottom line. If you have an interest in an automated process for resetting passwords, you should check out FrontRange Solutions HEAT.* Not setting passwords in a timely manner affects user productivity.

User Account Creation

Talk about wasting time: You have a new employee who cannot use the applications she needs when she comes on board. One of the authors recently started a contract and spent four hours cooling his jets while waiting for them to properly set up Active Directory for him. This costs the client money and provides no one value. In the same way, you create the user's account with the wrong privileges and he cannot access the right applications or data. This situation is very similar to the password reset problem: You are wasting productive time while the employee waits for the right privileges.

Improving Network Security

Consider the mountain of data available at your network perimeter. You have packets flooding in from all over. Suppose you intercept a packet that looks like a threat to your organization. Your network access control device needs to make a quick decision on whether to discard the packet or not. Discarding good packets (Type II error) is bad business.

You might have ten points where software makes such pass–fail decisions about the usefulness of data, transactions, packets, or frames. In Six Sigma speak, we call these points decision nodes. When these ten nodes pass judgment on 100,000 requests each day, you have 1 million opportunities for a decision error each day. Should your decision nodes average 99.38 percent accuracy, you are at four sigma—about the accuracy of airline baggage handling. If you could improve your accuracy to six sigma or 99.99966 percent, you would only discard 3.4 per million legitimate requests. At six sigma, there is a 99.9 percent chance that all 1 million decisions are accurate on any given day. Furthermore, there is a 97 percent chance that all decisions in a month are right. There is only a 15 percent chance at four sigma that all decisions are right on a given day, whereas there is a 15 percent chance at six sigma that all decisions are right over a five-year period. Such efficiency is invaluable when protecting your organization from people who mean you harm. It therefore behooves you to ensure your rules are adequate to prevent both Type I and II errors. You need to digest the mountain of mostly benign data, analyze the malicious data, and adjust your rules accordingly.

---

* http://www.frontrange.com/ProductsSolutions/Detail.aspx?id=3122.

Improve Application, Server, and Network Uptime

Who doesn't have some outage: application, server, or network? Every minute of downtime costs you money. Downtime refers to the period when a system is unavailable or fails to perform its primary function. ITIL provides excellent advice on availability management and IT business continuity management. LSS can help you improve the performance of these processes.

Improving Personal Productivity

Personal productivity is something that affects everyone. Almost everyone has at least one e-mail account and wastes time every day reading and deleting e-mail. Why not use Lean techniques on your e-mail inbox? You can use the Five Ss we covered in Chapter 5 as follows:

1. *Sort:* Create folders and use rules to sort your incoming e-mail. You can also sort by importance. Obviously, you will tackle those e-mails with the highest importance based on your group and personal goals. If the e-mail is spam or phishing, delete it immediately.
2. *Set in order:* If the e-mail is not of high importance but needed, place it in a pending folder. You should create a task for the e-mail with an action date. If you still use paper, you could print off the e-mail and place it in your "to do" file. If it is a progress report or another document not requiring immediate action, file it so that you can easily retrieve it at a future date.
3. *Shine:* Yes, your e-mail client probably archives old e-mail periodically, but do you want to bet your career on that working? You should back up your e-mail on a regular basis and you should move e-mails on a project to an archive when you finish the project.
4. *Standardize:* You need to develop a naming standard for your e-mail folders. It needs to make sense to you and not us. You could organize around projects, people, or dates—your choice. Just don't make it too complex.
5. *Sustain:* Pick a time everyday (perhaps the end of the day to prepare for the following day) and go through your e-mails. Action those requiring immediate action. As a rule of thumb, never handle your e-mail more than twice. Either action it when you receive it or file it for posterity or future action. If it helps, you can assign different colored flags with most e-mail clients.

You could apply the Five Ss to the e-mail you send. The most important thing to do is to decide whether the people to whom you address the e-mail really need to see the message.

Software Development

As software becomes more complex, the probability of exposing end users to application defects increases exponentially. Subtle quality problems can cause unexpected failures, potentially leading to lost business and a damaged reputation for product quality.

Consider the applications in your organization, and you will discover that they are constructed of many thousands of lines of code. You can inspect the final code to death, but this is not the way of Lean Six Sigma. Software quality begins as soon as you start writing code. You need to bake it in from the start rather than relying on functional and performance testing. Typically, you'll find that many errors come early in the development process, perhaps from a misunderstanding of the customer's requirements.

Software development is an excellent candidate for applying the tools in this book. The DMAIC methodology provides a good roadmap as follows:

- *Define:* Project charter, stakeholder analysis, SIPOC diagram, VOC, affinity diagram, Kano model, and CTQ tree
- *Measure:* Prioritization matrix, process cycle efficiency, time value analysis, Pareto charts, control charts, run charts, and FMEA
- *Analyze:* Five Whys analysis, brainstorming, C & E diagram, affinity diagram, control charts, flow diagrams, Pareto charts, regression analysis, and scatter plots
- *Improve:* Brainstorming, flowcharting, FMEA, stakeholder analysis, setup reduction, queuing methods for reducing congestion and delays, Five Ss method, and Kaizen
- *Control:* Control charts, flow diagrams, charts to compare before and after, such as Pareto charts, quality control process charts, and standardization

The following metrics are appropriate for development. You should establish a baseline, gather trend data, and review after you make an intervention.

- Appraisal cost per defect by phase (by project and total)
- Rework cost per defect by phase (by project and total)
- Rework as a percentage of effort (by project and total)
- Defect containment effectiveness (by project and total)
- Total containment effectiveness (by project and total)
- Effort variance normalized for size (by project and total)
- Schedule variance normalized for size (by project and total)
- Defect density, or defect per size (by project and total)
- Effort per size, or productivity
- Duration per size, or cycle time

Based on experience with sustained application of these metrics, most organizations should see a shift from 10 percent to 20 percent of NVA work to VA within two years.

DFSS

Most of our discussion so far has revolved around approaches to solving problems that already exist. That makes sense, because most of the world is here, right in front of us, and much of it doesn't work right so we have much to do. When we open our eyes we can see what isn't working right and we can work to improve it. Most of the Lean and Six Sigma methodologies focus on fixing things that exist and are broken. But what if you want to create something new, like a new application? Something that doesn't exist today? You are probably wondering whether you can use these same tools and techniques to improve existing processes to design something from scratch that meets customer expectations right out of the box so you don't have to go through the cycle of build, study, and fix. Can you just build it so it works right the first time? Well, the answer is an emphatic yes, and you can use Six Sigma techniques to do it. When you use Six Sigma this way, it's called Design for Six Sigma (DFSS). DFSS is a lot less formal than Six Sigma problem solving. It is better described as a system design approach and philosophy than a methodology. Before you jump down our throats, though, various people have developed quasi-methodologies to implement DFSS. The more noteworthy are the following:

- *DMADV:* Define, measure, analyze, design, verify
- *DMADOV:* Define, measure, analyze, design, optimize, validate
- *IDOV:* Identify, design, optimize, validate
- *DMEDI:* Define, measure, explore, develop, implement
- *DCCDI:* Define, customer, concept, design, implement

The very fact that there are so many methodologies attests to the fact that it is not a very commonly understood or accepted approach. Part of the reason there are so many flavors of DFSS is that organizations do not attempt to bake in Six Sigma as often as they use it for problem solving. Should you think about how many people in your own organization sell, produce, deliver, or support existing products or services compared to how many develop new ones, you'll realize that far fewer people are involved in designing processes than fixing processes. To add to this, generally management has considered design of anything a creative endeavor, so attempts to formalize design processes have long been resisted, or perhaps more accurately, not widely accepted. As well, consulting companies touting clients by aggrandizing their expertise with DFSS took the opportunity to create and market their particular version of the methodology.

Another occasion where you might want to choose to apply DFSS tools and techniques is on regular DMAIC-type improvement projects when you require a very high Sigma level and you find that you simply cannot get there with improvement projects. Let's say that you need to reach a Sigma level of 5.0 to be world class and that is your goal, but you are stuck at 4.0 and have run out of ideas. Rather than give up, you can switch to a DFSS thinking style. In other words, pretend your existing process does not exist and that you have a blank sheet of paper. Design a new process that does what you need and demonstrate it. Assuming you could do that, look at your existing process and see how you can turn it into what you have designed. Sometimes this is nothing more than a conceptual problem. The existing problem is "in your virtual way" and you keep assuming limitations, which you could overcome were you only clever enough to do so. When you put a team in a room with an infinite pot of virtual money and no restrictions, they won't be encumbered with the limitations of reality. Once they have a process that works, it is often a much simpler task to see how to convert your existing process to the new one than it is to transform it through incremental improvements. Now you can actually see a process that works. Keep in mind that just because you want a Sigma level of 5.0 doesn't mean it is even possible. If you know that others have done it, then perhaps it is. It is important that you set goals that are possible to reach. Sometimes your existing technology or untrained staff impose performance limitations that you simply cannot overcome by improvement type projects. Unless you are willing to start from scratch, your process performance will have a limit. This is always a problem for large businesses with huge investments in technology. Suddenly a new breakthrough can make your entire infrastructure obsolete. Unfortunately for them, telecommunication companies are constantly in that position. One of the authors spent years of his life building systems only to find them replaced a year or two later by entirely new systems when the market shifted. As an employee in the middle of those projects, it seemed wildly wasteful at the time. Now that we're older, wiser, and a stockholder, we have a broader viewpoint and we're glad they did. These companies ran as hard as they could down the path they were on, but were smart enough to recognize that there was a limit that they could only overcome by changing horses when the new horse was ready to run.

Really these methodologies use the same set of tools, many of which are the same as the Six Sigma tools, to achieve their ends. The idea behind DFSS is simple: If you do a careful job of defining customer requirements and potential root causes that might affect those requirements, and should you make appropriate use of available data and new data through correct experimenting, you can design a process that meets those requirements out of the box the first time. In other words, when you develop all processes using DFSS techniques, you could make the claim that you would never have any need for DMAIC-style problem solvers. We only have problems to solve because most design processes are haphazard and incomplete. Of course, these last few statements are naive and simplistic because as Six Sigma practitioners like to say, "Shift happens," but certainly the world would need fewer problem solvers if there were more designers. It is not in human DNA to spend a lot

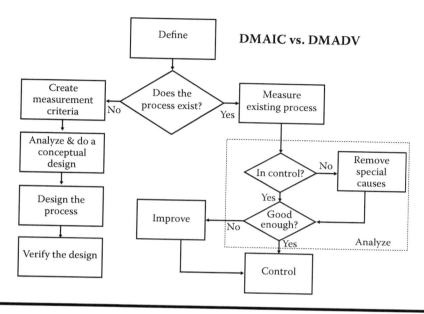

Figure 9.1   DMAIC and DMADV.

of time doing the tough stuff, the up-front work. Figure 9.1 provides a simple chart to help you decide whether to use DMAIC or DMADV.

So how does DFSS work? How can you design something right the first time when others who create designs cannot do it right? What does it mean to be wrong? Being wrong could mean several things. At the customer level, it simply means that the process is producing too many defects. But why did our brand new design do that? Most likely for one of the following reasons:

1. You did not account sufficiently in the design for the actual environment.
2. You designed in some conceptual flaws so that it violates a basic principle.
3. You did not capture correctly or in sufficient detail the customer CTQ metrics.

You can use many standard Six Sigma tools to address the first and last of these three reasons and the DFSS methodologies are designed to use them for that purpose. The middle reason is another story. To create a conceptually correct design is an interesting problem. We're familiar with two tools that could help. There are certainly others and we don't claim that these two are all you have available. The first we mentioned earlier in the book, TRIZ. This is simply (but brilliantly) using the combined experience of those who came before us. It is experiential. The other is axiomatic design, which is a mathematical method of describing design parameters and process functions and mapping them in an ideal way such that there is no interaction between them and that you minimize the information required for each step. Axiomatic design is a much more complex technique to learn and understand. It was developed by MIT's Dr. Suh Nam Pyo in the early 1990s. Dr. Suh and his team have developed a software package that helps people do axiomatic design.*

DMADV Methodology and Tools

We believe that DMADV is the most popular of the DFSS methodologies, but whether it is or not, we use it to demonstrate briefly how you would use DFSS. The DMADV phases are as follows:

- *Define:* This is virtually identical to the same phase in DMAIC. You should end up with a charter that defines the scope of your project, an understanding of your customers, and the key quality and production parameters that you need to meet.
- *Measure:* What are you going to measure? Didn't we say that we are designing a new process that does not yet exist? Just as in a DMAIC project, sometimes the metrics that you are given by your customers aren't specific enough to take action on, so we need to detail them. We might have to do a QFD matrix exercise (see a description later in the chapter) or similar activities to determine the real CTQ variables. At the output of the measure phase, you should have a clear, quantitative understanding of all of the CTQs. While you are in this phase, there might indeed be data worth collecting. What if your project was to develop a new cell phone and one of the CTQs is that the mean battery life needs to be 500 hours? What characteristics of cell phones affect their battery life? It would be useful to have data on those things. What about the habits of your users? It would be useful to have data on how your users actually use their cell phones, right? What about the environment? Will you sell your phones in Costa Rica? Will you sell them in Chicago? Do you expect the batteries to last the same 500 hours in both places in the summer and the winter? The ambient temperature matters a lot for battery life, as any of you who have lived in colder climes know. Collecting data on the known environments will prove useful. You can do all of this as part of the measure phase.
- *Analyze:* In a DMAIC project, you use the analyze phase to discover and prove the root causes for failures. In a DMADV project, there is no process yet, so you gather, armed with knowledge of the goal, the CTQs, and as much relevant data as you can. You also develop design concepts for your new process. This is a high-level, functional type design, but one with specifications for each of the functional blocks. For your 500-hour cell phone, your high-level design block diagram might include a new heat transfer holder to

---

* For more information on this concept and the software, contact Axiomatic Design Solutions in Brighton, MA.

transfer body heat from the user to the cell phone so that the Chicago user's batteries stay warm enough to function. Your design might also include an onboard solar battery charger that serves to constantly recharge the battery when it is used outdoors. It was your knowledge of the goal and limitations of the environment that would drive you to put those functional requirements into the design because you would know that without heat and without some way of recharging on the fly, no existing battery could handle the typical customer usage, which we have good data on, remember?

■ *Design:* You now design the actual system in enough detail to build it. Here you would choose the actual components, the heat transfer technology, solar cells, case, battery, and all the other components. Because you are designing this product to meet statistical performance criteria, in other words, not only to perform, but to fail in mass usage at a known rate (determined by your agreed on Sigma level), you are also likely to do failure analyses of the design using whatever tools are useful. You might want to use FMEA to evaluate all the things that could go wrong, find out the probability that they will, and determine the effect on battery life should they happen.

■ *Verify:* You next verify that your design works. You could do this by building prototypes, by simulation, or by trials. You most likely would build prototypes of cell phones and test them for reliability. You would probably simulate a complex new business process using a dynamic simulator. You most likely would do a pilot of a new food production line where there are dozens of the lines needed for full production. Your pilot might involve converting one line or building one line per your new specifications and verifying that you can operate it to meet your goals before switching everything else over. Where the process is large enough to warrant it, you might first simulate it and then build a pilot. Once you have confirmed that the process works as designed, you are done.

Here is a list of some of the common and not-so-common tools that you can use in a DFSS project. Like other improvement projects, we only use tools that seem to fit the problem at hand, but it's useful to know several of them so that you have choices.

■ *QFD matrix:* A method for analyzing customer needs and process functional requirements. The output of the exercise is a list of functions, parameters, and variables that you have prioritized in terms of how they affect your customers' needs. We have provided a detailed description of this tool later in this chapter.

■ *FMEA:* A method for analyzing potential failure modes within a product or service and classifying the defects by severity or determination of the effect of failures on the product or service. Table 9.1 gives you a sample FMEA worksheet and completion instructions.

■ *TRIZ:* We discussed TRIZ in Chapter 8.

Table 9.1 FMEA Example	
Consecutively number the steps.	#
What is the step?	Process function (step)
What can go wrong?	Potential failure modes (process defects)
What is the impact on the customer if the failure mode is not prevented or corrected?	Potential failure effects (KPOVs)
What is the severity of the defect (1–5)?	SEV
What is the class of the defect? (e.g., business, security, etc.)	Class
What causes the step to go wrong? (i.e., How could the failure mode occur?)	Potential causes of failure (KPIVs)
What is the likelihood of the defect occurring (1–5)?	OCC
What are the existing controls that either prevent the failure mode from occurring or detect it should it occur?	Current process controls
What is the ability to detect the defect (1–5)?	DET
Risk Priority Number = (SEV*OCC*DET)	RPN
What are the actions for reducing the occurrence of the cause or for improving its detection? You should provide actions on all high RPNs and on severity ratings of 4 or 5.	Recommend actions
Who is responsible for the recommended action? By what date should it be completed?	Responsible person and target date
What were the actions implemented? Include completion month/year (then recalculate resulting RPN).	Actions taken
What is the severity of the defect after the action (1–5)?	New SEV
What is the likelihood of the defect occurring after the action (1–5)?	New OCC
What is the ability to detect the defect after the action (1–5)?	New DET
New Risk Priority Number = (SEV*OCC*DET)	New RPN

- *Design of experiments (DoE):* Methods for minimizing the number of experiments needed to determine how processes work.
- *Design optimization tools:* Optimization techniques to determine by calculation or simulation where you might find the best region to operate a set of variables.
- *Tolerance design:* Methods to analyze how variability in components of a system all add up to create variation in the final output. You can use this technique to predict performance or to find tolerant resistant designs.
- *Axiomatic design:* We discussed this earlier in the chapter.
- *Reliability analysis:* Calculation methods to estimate how reliable a system will be given knowledge of the reliability of the components and how they are functionally arranged.
- *Simulation tools:* We discussed these earlier in the book.
- *Benchmarking:* We discussed this earlier in the book.

There are many books on DFSS and you should get one should you want to design a new system or application. It is better to bake quality in than to try to retrofit it later.

QFD and House of Quality

We mentioned FMEA earlier as a good system and application development tool, especially for assessing project and product risks. Another excellent tool is QFD, or House of Quality (HOQ), which is an assembly of related tables and hierarchies intended to assist a designer in building a product or service to meet market demands. You could use it for process improvement as well. Simplistically, you iteratively use HOQ matrices, along with an associated assembly of tools, to go from high-level customer requirements to a very detailed process or part specification. QFD and HOQ are related but not widely understood and have tended to become synonymous, so people often interchange the two acronyms. We use QFD to describe this entire process because people commonly use it that way and many of the tools and templates sold for this purpose are called QFD templates.

You use the QFD as a tool to translate customer requirements (that is, the VOC), market research, and technical characteristics of products or services into a prioritized list of targets that your new or improved process or new product design must meet. It looks a little intimidating at first, but once you understand how it works, it is fairly straightforward and clever, although it can take a lot of time to work through for a complex problem. Figure 9.2 is a graphic depicting the components.

We've numbered the components in Figure 9.2 so that we could associate the numbered components with the following numbered paragraphs.

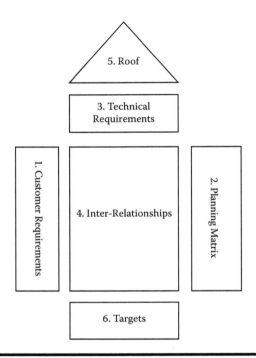

Figure 9.2 QFD components.

1. *Start with customer requirements.* After all what is the point of building something when you don't know what's expected? You gather information through structured conversations with your customers. In those talks, you get your customers to describe what they need and what kinds of problems they face. As you collect these data, it is likely to be free-flowing and unstructured like you would expect from a group of talks with many people, so before you can use it, you need to organize it. You can build affinity diagrams for each customer to help and then build master affinity diagrams for all of them as a group to arrive at common themes and wording. When you are done with this exercise you will have a tree diagram that shows a hierarchy of customer needs. The tree could be flat (all on the same level) or could have several levels to it, depending on the complexity of the problem. We use a simplified example of the design of a hardware and software application for a mobile dispatching system for a telecommunications company to demonstrate. As a result of customer interviews, we concluded that the customer has the functional needs shown in Table 9.2. This is the VOC.

2. Next you address the planning matrix on the right side of the diagram. Here you quantify the priorities of the customer requirements because everything cannot be top priority. You also adjust these priorities based on design issues.

Table 9.2   Voice of the Customer

		Customer Requirements (VOC)	Customer Importance
Program is easy to use	Program is fast	Can find items in database quickly	5
		Cursor is responsive	4
		Interfaces to existing database	4
	Commands are easy	Customizable icons	3
		Can do things with one click	5
		Icons are clear	3
	Fonts are flexible	Can see fonts before choosing	3
		Changing fonts won't scramble text	5
		Lots of options	3

The information that you need to complete this portion also comes from customer interviews or questionnaires. First, you have the customer weigh the importance of each documented characteristic. There are many ways to arrive at these weightings. We are not going to delve into them here, but regardless of the method you use, you need to rank them numerically. A common approach is to use a five-point Likert scale* where each item is ranked from one to five. Should it turn out that you have different markets for this service or product, you might need to complete a QFD for each market when values are likely to be very different between them. Another component of this part of the matrix is to measure how happy customers are with existing or competitive solutions by ranking the performance of those products against the same requirements. Optionally, you could also establish the rating that you plan to have for your product, and then you could calculate the improvement factor for each one by subtracting it from your current product should you have one. You could also create a sales point measure to weight what characteristics are useful to market the product. Later on, you can add factors as the situation warrants. For instance, when environmental considerations are relevant, weigh those. The QFD is a general approach that you modify for each situation so often no two of them look exactly alike.

3. Now that you have the customer and the market views, you need to look at the technical requirements for what you are making or defining. You describe

---

* http://en.wikipedia.org/wiki/Rensis_Likert.

the product or service from the point of view of the company and how you will create or deliver it. Start by creating a list of all of the measurable characteristics that you think affects how well it meets customer requirements. You can use the same methods for doing this as you used for determining customer requirements. People find affinity trees useful for organizing the information. It is then common to add a row to show the direction of change of each of these variables that improves performance. Use the arrow to show the direction that the measurable characteristic needs to go in to make your major category of product or service better.

4. Next you address the interrelationship matrix at the center of the QFD assembly. Remember, you make use of the matrix to transform customer requirements (VOC) into technical characteristics (voice of the process). Each cell is an intersection of a VOC and a voice of the process. The QFD team looks at each cell and asks, "How significant is this technical requirement (on the top) to satisfying this customer need (on the left)?" Usually you display the answer as a four-point scale of high, medium, low, or not at all. Represent the high, medium, and low answers with different shaped and colored symbols to make them easy to pick out. If you use a red circle to mean high, a blue square to mean medium, and a green triangle to mean low, each cell will have one of those in it or be empty, meaning that the voice of the process doesn't affect that VOC at all. In addition, you assign each of the four levels a numerical value: 9, 3, 1, and 0 are common, but you can use scales that fit your business. Because of the process complexity, we recommend that you employ software to do the mapping. After you complete the exercise, you could vary those scales to see whether slight variations affect your main conclusions. This is a form of sensitivity analysis and shows how critical your scale assumptions are to your final result. This tool, like many process improvement tools, attempts to quantify opinions. As you might appreciate, this is often an inexact process so a sensitivity analysis helps to give you confidence in your answer.

5. You complete the triangular roof next. This is a triangle because it is designed to show where process or product characteristics fight each other. It is a matrix of intersections of every voice of the process with all the other voices of the process. In a similar fashion to the interrelationship matrix, for every cell in this matrix, the team asks the following question: "Does improving one of these requirements make the other requirement better or worse?" When the answer is that when one is made better the other is made weaker, put a minus sign in the cell. When making one better also makes the other one better, put a plus sign in the cell. When they are unrelated to each other, leave it blank. You can indicate the strength of interactions with positive and negative numbers or colored symbols as well, should you have the data to support it. You do not fill the half-cells directly above each voice of the process because they don't represent any intersection: You only fill the squares. The roof information can help to highlight what design improvements might lead to a wide

range of improvements. It also points out conflicting requirements in the proposed design. These are opportunities for creative problem solving to find other ways of doing this process without having to make those trade-offs. It is better for you to understand the limitations of your design early than to discover them after you have spent most of your budget building it.

6. Finally, you fill the bottom matrix to summarize what you have learned in the form of targets for each voice of the process requirement. There are usually three parts to it: technical priorities for the voices of the process, competitive benchmarks, and targets. You can calculate a priority by summing down each column the product of the interrelationship ratings (in the interrelationship matrix) and the overall ratings (in the planning matrix). These technical priority ratings tell you how important each voice of the process element is relative to each of the others. Use this to allocate staff and budget to ensure attention to the most important ones and to tell you what characteristics need the most improvement when compared to competitors. In the benchmarking row, fill in the specifications for each of the competitors you are benchmarking against, as well as the values for your existing process (should you have any). Finally, looking at all of the information in the QFD, set target values for each of your voice of the process specifications. There is no algorithm for doing this, just the combined judgment of your team. However the QFD matrix now has a lot of useful information in a compact form, to form the basis of discussions that should enable the team to come to a consensus on targets.

Congratulations! You have now completed an HOQ and more important, you now know the component priorities and have a clear direction on how to design your product or process. This is still a fairly high-level process view, however. The "whats" are on the left in the form of VOCs and the "hows" are on the top in the form of voices of the process. You can express more and more detail when necessary by making what we have just described the first of a four-phase process. We call this the four-phase QFD model, and it is shown graphically in Figure 9.3.

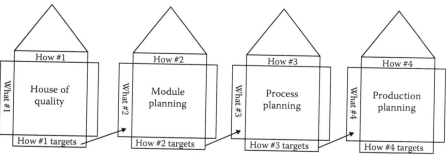

Figure 9.3　Four-phase QFD model.

When you are developing a complex system like a new enterprise resource planning system or an automobile, you might find this approach appropriate. With the four-phase system, once you have completed your initial HOQ, you then proceed to do another one, this time the "how targets" of the first exercise become the "whats" of the next one. They become the new VOC and you design the modules for your system with those as inputs. In so doing, you create new and more detailed "whats." Those, in turn, become the "hows" for the third, usually the process stage. The last step is the production stage, where you establish operational metrics or the results of this entire process.

As you can see, QFD is a design aid. It helps you determine what to do based on what the customer needs in a complex, multivariable environment where there are many factors to consider and many potential interactions among them. QFD is not an optimizer. There is no guarantee that it will lead to an optimal, or even a useful solution, but like many of the tools described in this book, you can apply QFD analysis to organize the collective genius of your teams to make decisions that have a logical basis. And unlike the gut-feel approach, it leaves records for a peer review.

Other IT Improvement Projects

Eric Lundquist (2008) wrote that CIOs should consider the SWAT model. He suggests that CIOs should save it, whack it, assess it, and trash it when deciding what projects to kill, to do or not do. Look around your organization and think SWAT. Other potential projects to consider include the following:

- *Improve portfolio management:* Determine why the process to evaluate, approve, fund, prioritize, and monitor IT investments is not in place or doesn't produce adequate results.
- *Improve the process of logging in to the network from remote locations:* Determine why it takes so long or why it is so difficult to log in remotely to gather e-mail or support applications and systems.
- *Improve staff retention:* Determine why your development and retention program is not working.
- *Improve efficiencies:* Determine why all tasks are performed in-house and why you are not leveraging third-party resources where core competencies are not best of breed.
- *Avoid being caught when the market shifts:* Determine why the current planning cycle is not acceptable.
- *Improve IT audit findings:* Determine why the IT group is getting or has unresolved security deficiencies.
- *Improve application performance:* Determine why an application is available but not responsive or exceeds user expectation.

- *Reduce data center resource consumption:* Determine why the data center and its various components consume so much power, water, and other renewable and nonrenewable resources.
- *Improve change management:* Determine why there are so many unscheduled changes and why you need to back out so many changes.
- *Reduce the number of people bypassing security controls:* Determine why people bypass basic physical and logical safeguards.
- *Reduce the number of servers:* Determine why the organization has so many servers and consolidate them.
- *Improve business continuity planning:* Determine why all parts of the IT infrastructure are not covered.
- *Reduce disaster recovery time:* Determine why the recovery time objective is not being met or is too high.
- *Improve Web site traffic:* Determine why your Web site doesn't rank in the top ten on all major search engines and directories.
- *Improve Web site usability:* Determine why the Web site has usability problems; for example, missing links, finding product or service information, finding contact information, failed contact e-mail, failed subscription requests, or failed sign-ups.
- *Reduce the number of errors in batch processes:* Determine why batch processes don't complete on time.
- *Improve backup cycle time:* Determine why backups cause application performance issues.
- *Improve Internet network uptime:* Determine why your Internet connection goes down.
- *Reduce network monitoring tools:* Determine why you have so many network monitoring tools that you use.
- *Improve wait times while calling the help desk:* Determine why help desk agents take a long time to answer the phone.
- *Improve resolution on first call with the help desk:* Determine why users' issues don't get resolved the first time they call the help desk.
- *Reduce the time to resolution and response for user requests:* Determine why turnaround time for application enhancements or changes is long.
- *Reduce the overall software spend:* Determine why you are paying software maintenance on software that you don't actively use.
- *Improve the forecast of the monthly IT budget:* Determine why the IT budget varies from the forecast.
- *Reduce the cycle time for laptop provisioning:* Determine the number of instances where the SLA was exceeded and determine why.
- *Improve laptop security:* Determine why hard drive encryption is not deployed on laptops.
- *Reduce the cycle time for cell phone provisioning:* Determine the number of instances where the SLA was exceeded and determine why.

■ *Improve the quality of software rollouts:* Determine how software rollout impacts other applications and infrastructure.
■ *Improve the cycle time of software rollouts:* Determine why it takes too long to deploy software when it is ready for deployment.
■ *Improve schedule achievement for each phase of development projects:* Determine why you did not meet a phase schedule.
■ *Improve the reliability of new software:* Determine why new software rolls out but is unusable because of bugs.
■ *Reduce malware outbreaks:* Determine why protection is not sufficient to prevent the introduction of viruses, worms, and other malware.
■ *Automate manual processes:* Determine why every human touch point increases the likelihood of failure.
■ *Migrate platforms and applications flawlessly:* Determine why application performance before and after the migration is different.
■ *Project life cycle management:* Determine why each application is undergoing a platform change (platforms can be database, operating systems, or hardware related).
■ *Cell phone usage and billing:* Determine why you have cell phone billing inaccuracies.
■ *Consistent infrastructure patch management:* Determine why servers are on different levels of patches and the number of vulnerabilities identified due to incorrect patching.

Generating Project Ideas

The preceding list is just the tip of the iceberg. Where do you get more project ideas? It's easy: Just ask yourself the following questions and the ideas should pop out:

■ Where do you spend most of your budget?
■ Where are your mission-critical applications?
■ Where are the 20 percent of the applications that generate 80 percent of the revenue?
■ Where are the service level gaps?
■ Where do you spend time fighting fires?
■ Where are your pain points?
■ Where is the largest volume of data?
■ Where is the greatest transaction volume?

Well that's it. You should have plenty to think about. To quote Deming again, "I hope what you have heard here today will haunt you the rest of your life."

Call to Action

As we write this book, every pundit is talking doom and gloom about the world economy. There is no question that some of us might face adversity. Undoubtedly, this adversity will force some of us to confront difficult issues in our organizations and in our markets, issues that we would rather avoid and probably have managed to avoid for a long time. It is time for *hansei* (or critical self-reflection). Hansei, a core part of the Japanese ethos, requires that you acknowledge your mistakes and pledge improvement. When you reflect carefully, determine root causes, and take focused, creative actions, your future should shine brighter. In the end, you need only follow these simple steps for success:

1. Reflect on any problem you face.
2. Trace the problem to its root cause.
3. Take bold action.
4. Check to verify you did something of value.
5. Make adjustments when necessary.
6. Start all over again.

Appendix A: Guidance

Corporate Governance

1. Cadbury Committee: http://www.fsa.gov.uk/pubs/ukla/lr_comcode.pdf
2. Capacity Check Diagnostic Tool: http://www.tbs-sct.gc.ca/emf-cag/risk-risques/tools-outils-eng.asp
3. Committee of Sponsoring Organizations of the Treadway Commission (COSO): http://www.coso.org
4. Criteria of Control Board (CoCo): http://www.cica.ca
5. Financial Management Capability Model: http://www.oag-bvg.gc.ca/internet/English/meth_gde_e_19740.html
6. GAO Green Book: http://www.gao.gov/special.pubs/ppm.html
7. OMB Circular A-123: http://www.whitehouse.gov/omb/circulars/a123/a123_rev.html

IT Governance

1. Applied Information Economics (AIE): http://www.hubbardresearch.com/
2. Australian Standard for Corporate Governance of Information and Communication Technology (AS 8015): http://www.standards.org.au
3. Business Information Services Library (BiSL): http://www.aslbislfoundation.org/uk/bisl/index.html
4. Business Value Index: http://ipip.intel.com/go/category/topics/business_value/
5. Control Objectives for Information and Related Technology (COBIT): http://www.isaca.org/cobit
6. Corporate governance of information technology (ISO/IEC 38500:2008): http://www.iso.org
7. Information Assurance Compliance Maturity Model Index (IA-CMMI): http://www.unifiedcompliance.com/it_compliance/iacmmi/
8. Information Services Procurement Library (ISPL): http://projekte.fast.de/ISPL/
9. Total Economic Impact (TEI): http://www.forrester.com/TEI
10. Val IT: http://www.isaca.org/valit

Information Management

1. Application Services Library (ASL): http://www.aslbislfoundation.org/uk/bisl/index.html
2. Fault, Configuration, Accounting, Performance, Security (FCAPS): http://www.iso.org
3. Generic Framework for Information Management (GFIM): http://primavera.fee.uva.nl/PDFdocs/99-03.pdf
4. IAITAM Best Practice Library (IBPL): http://www.iaitam.org/Best_Practice_Library.htm
5. Information Technology Infrastructure Library (ITIL): http://www.itil-officialsite.com/home/home.asp
6. Information Technology Investment Management (ITIM): http://www.gao.gov/new.items/d04394g.pdf
7. OBASHI Framework: http://www.stroma.eu/Slayers.asp

Quality Management

1. European Foundation for Quality Management (EFQM): http://www.efqm.org/
2. Information technology—Service management—Part 2: Code of practice (ISO 20000-2): http://www.iso.org
3. Information technology—Security techniques—Information security management systems—Requirements (ISO 27001): http://www.iso.org
4. Quality management systems—Requirements (ISO 9001): http://www.iso.org
5. TickIT: http://www.tickit.org/
6. Total Quality Management (TQM): http://www.managementhelp.org/quality/tqm/tqm.htm

Quality Improvement

1. Applied Information Economics (AIE): http://www.hubbardresearch.com/
2. Balanced Scorecard (BSC): http://www.balancedscorecard.org/
3. Capability Maturity Model Integrated (CMMI): http://www.sei.cmu.edu/cmmi/
4. Enhanced Telecom Operations Map (eTOM): http://www.tmforum.org/browse.aspx?catID=1647
5. eSourcing Capability Model (eSCM): http://www.ceiamerica.com/cei/why_cei/escm.asp
6. Information Security Management Maturity Model (ISM3): http://www.ism3.com/
7. Information technology—Process assessment—Part 2: Performing an assessment (ISO 15504-2): http://www.iso.org/iso/iso_catalogue/catalogue_tc/catalogue_detail.htm?csnumber=37458
8. IT Service Capability Maturity Model (ITS-CMM): http://itservicecmmwebsite.googlepages.com/
9. Six Sigma: http://www.asq.org/sixsigma/
10. Lean: http://www.lean.org/

Project Management

1. Business Analysis Body of Knowledge (BABOK): http://www.theiiba.org/
2. IPMA Competence Baseline (ICB): http://www.ipma.ch/certification/standards/Pages/ICBV3.aspx
3. Managing Successful Programmes (MSP): http://www.msp-officialsite.com/home/Home.asp
4. Organizational Project Management Methodology Model (OPM3): http://opm3online.pmi.org/
5. Project Management Book of Knowledge (PMBOK): http://www.pmi.org/
6. Projects in Controlled Environments (PRINCE2): http://www.prince2.org.uk/home/home.asp

Risk Management

1. Management of Risk (M_o_R): http://www.apmgroup.co.uk/M_o_R/MoR_Home.asp
2. Operationally Critical Threat, Asset, and Vulnerability Evaluation (OCTAVE): http://www.cert.org/octave/

Architecture

1. Engineering Principles for Information Technology Security (A Baseline for Achieving Security) NIST Special Publication 800-27: http://csrc.nist.gov/publications/nistpubs/
2. Extended Enterprise Architecture Framework (E2AF): http://www.enterprise-architecture.info/
3. Federal Enterprise Architecture Framework (FEA): http://www.cio.gov/Documents/fedarch1.pdf
4. Information processing systems—Open Systems Interconnection—Basic Reference Model—Part 2: Security Architecture (ISO 7498-2): http://www.iso.org/
5. Moriconi, Xiaolei and Riemenschneider Methodology: http://citeseer.ist.psu.edu/moriconi97secure.html
6. Sherwood Applied Business Security Architecture (SABSA): http://www.sabsa.org/
7. The Open Group Architecture Framework (TOGAF): http://www.opengroup.org/togaf/
8. Whitman & Mattford Methodology: http://www.amazon.com/Principles-Information-Security-Michael-Whitman/dp/0619216255/sr=8-1/qid=1168271358/ref=sr_1_1/105-8440691-5565264?ie=UTF8&s=books
9. Zachman Framework for Enterprise Architectures: http://www.zifa.com/

Software Development

1. Dynamic Systems Development Method (DSDM): http://www.dsdm.org/

2. Guide for Developing of System Requirements Specifications (IEEE 1233): http://ieeexplore.ieee.org/Xplore/login.jsp?url=/iel1/3731/10912/00502838.pdf?temp=x

3. Software engineering—Guidelines for the application of ISO 9001:2000 to computer software (ISO/IEC 90003:2004): http://www.iso.org/iso/iso_catalogue/catalogue_tc/catalogue_detail.htm?csnumber=35867

4. Software engineering—Product quality—Part 4: Quality in use metrics (ISO/IEC TR 9126-4): http://www.iso.org/iso/iso_catalogue/catalogue_tc/catalogue_detail.htm?csnumber=39752

5. Standard for Software Test Documentation—Description (IEEE 829): http://standards.ieee.org/reading/ieee/std_public/description/se/829-1983_desc.html

Appendix B: Shewhart Constants for Control Charts

n	A2	D3	D4	d2	A3	B3	B4
2	1.88	0	3.27	1.13	2.66	0	3.27
3	1.02	0	2.57	1.69	1.95	0	2.57
4	0.73	0	2.28	2.06	1.63	0	2.27
5	0.58	0	2.11	2.33	1.43	0	2.09
6	0.48	0	2	2.53	1.29	0.03	1.97
7	0.42	0.08	1.92	2.7	1.18	0.12	1.88
8	0.37	0.14	1.86	2.85	1.1	0.19	1.82
9	0.34	0.18	1.82	2.97	1.03	0.24	1.76
10	0.31	0.22	1.78	3.08	0.98	0.28	1.72

Note: n is the sample size. This sample chart only goes to $n = 10$. Values for larger values of n exist.

Appendix C: Table of z Values

- This table has pairs of columns.
- The left-hand table value is the z value.
- The right-hand table value is the fraction of the total area of the histogram that is to the right of the z value. It is also called the tail area.
- The z value is the number of standard deviations to the right of the mean (on the horizontal axis).
- The table assumes a standard normal distribution with a mean of 0 and a standard deviation of 1.

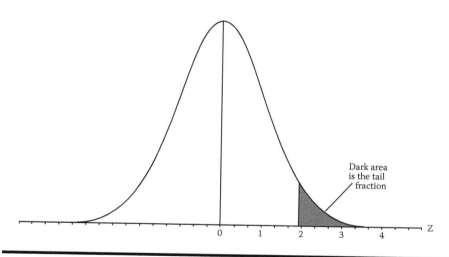

Figure A.1   Standard normal distribution.

Z Value	Tail Fraction	Z Value	Tail Fraction	Z Value	Tail Fraction	Z Value	Tail Fraction
0.00	0.5000	0.56	0.2877	1.12	0.1314	1.68	0.0465
0.02	0.4920	0.58	0.2810	1.14	0.1271	1.70	0.0446
0.04	0.4840	0.60	0.2743	1.16	0.1230	1.72	0.0427
0.06	0.4761	0.62	0.2676	1.18	0.1190	1.74	0.0409
0.08	0.4681	0.64	0.2611	1.20	0.1151	1.76	0.0392
0.10	0.4602	0.66	0.2546	1.22	0.1112	1.78	0.0375
0.12	0.4522	0.68	0.2483	1.24	0.10.75	1.80	0.0359
0.14	0.4443	0.70	0.2420	1.26	0.1038	1.82	0.0344
0.16	0.4364	0.72	0.2358	1.28	0.1003	1.84	0.0329
0.18	0.4286	0.74	0.2296	1.30	0.0968	1.86	0.0314
0.20	0.4207	0.76	0.2236	1.32	0.0934	1.88	0.0301
0.22	0.4129	0.78	0.2177	1.34	0.0901	1.90	0.0287
0.24	0.4052	0.80	0.2119	1.36	0.0869	1.92	0.0274
0.26	0.3974	0.82	0.2061	1.38	0.0838	1.94	0.0262
0.28	0.3897	0.84	0.2005	1.40	0.0808	1.96	0.0250
0.30	0.3821	0.86	0.1949	1.42	0.0778	1.98	0.0239
0.32	0.3745	0.88	0.1894	1.44	0.0749	2.00	0.0228
0.34	0.3669	0.90	0.1841	1.46	0.0721	2.02	0.0217
0.36	0.3594	0.92	0.1788	1.48	0.0694	2.04	0.0207
0.38	0.3520	0.94	0.1736	1.50	0.0668	2.06	0.0197
0.40	0.3446	0.96	0.1685	1.52	0.0643	2.08	0.0188
0.42	0.3372	0.98	0.1635	1.54	0.0618	2.10	0.0179
0.44	0.3300	1.00	0.1587	1.56	0.0594	2.12	0.0170
0.46	0.3228	1.02	0.1539	1.58	0.0571	2.14	0.0162
0.48	0.3156	1.04	0.1492	1.60	0.0548	2.16	0.0154

Z Value	Tail Fraction	Z Value	Tail Fraction	Z Value	Tail Fraction	Z Value	Tail Fraction
0.24	0.0152	2.80	0.0026	4.40	0.0000054125439	7.20	0.00000000000030
0.26	0.0119	2.82	0.0024	4.50	0.0000033976731	7.30	0.00000000000014
0.28	0.0113	2.84	0.0023	4.60	0.0000021124547	7.40	0.00000000000007
0.30	0.0107	2.86	0.0021	4.70	0.0000013008075	7.50	0.00000000000003
0.32	0.0102	2.88	0.0020	4.80	0.0000007933282		
0.34	0.0096	2.90	0.0019	4.90	0.0000004791834		
0.36	0.0091	2.92	0.0018	5.00	0.0000002866514		
0.38	0.0087	2.94	0.0016	5.10	0.0000001698267		
0.40	0.0082	2.96	0.0015	5.20	0.0000000996443		
0.42	0.0078	2.98	0.0014	5.30	0.0000000579013		
0.44	0.0073	3.00	0.0013	5.40	0.0000000333204		
0.46	0.0069	3.02	0.0013	5.50	0.0000000189896		
0.48	0.0066	3.04	0.0012	5.60	0.0000000107176		
0.50	0.0062	3.06	0.0011	5.70	0.0000000059904		
0.52	0.0059	3.08	0.0010	5.80	0.0000000033157		
0.54	0.0055	3.10	0.0010	5.90	0.0000000018175		
0.56	0.0052	3.20	0.0007	6.00	0.0000000009866		
0.58	0.0049	3.30	0.0005	6.10	0.0000000005303		
0.60	0.0047	3.40	0.0003	6.20	0.0000000002823		
0.62	0.0044	3.50	0.0002	6.30	0.0000000001488		
0.64	0.0041	3.60	0.0002	6.40	0.0000000000777		
0.66	0.0039	3.70	0.0001	6.50	0.0000000000402		
0.68	0.0037	3.80	0.0001	6.60	0.0000000000206		
0.70	0.0035	3.90	0.0000	6.70	0.0000000000104		
0.72	0.0033	4.00	0.0000	6.80	0.0000000000052		

Appendix D: Useful Microsoft Excel® Statistics Functions

STDEV()	Returns the standard deviation of the values referred to in the parentheses.
AVERAGE()	Returns the arithmetic mean of the values referred to in the parentheses.
MEDIAN()	Returns the median of the values referred to in the parentheses.
MODE()	Returns the mode of the values referred to in the parentheses.
MAX()	Returns the largest of the values referred to in the parentheses.
MIN()	Returns the smallest of the values referred to in the parentheses.
RANDBETWEEN(x,y)	Generates one random number between the integers x and y.
Menu: /Tools/Add-Ins	To add additional statistical and other functions into Excel.
Menu: /Tools/Data Analysis/Histogram	To create histograms and Pareto charts.

Appendix E: Bibliography

Architecture

Carbone, Jane. 2004. *IT architecture toolkit.* Upper Saddle River, NJ: Prentice Hall.

Krafzig, Dirk, Karl Banke, and Dirk Slama. 2004. *Enterprise SOA: Service-oriented architecture best practices.* Upper Saddle River, NJ: Prentice Hall.

Ross, Jeanne W., Peter Weill, and David C. Robertson. 2006. *Enterprise architecture as strategy.* London: McGraw-Hill Europe.

Corporate Governance

Beniger, James R. 1986. *The control revolution.* Cambridge, MA: Harvard University Press.

Calder, Alan. 2008. *Corporate governance: A practical guide to the legal frameworks and international codes of practice.* London: Kogan Page.

Colley, John L., Wallace Stettinius, Jacqueline L. Doyle, and George Logan. 2004. *What is corporate governance?* New York: McGraw-Hill.

Hubbard, Douglas W. 2007. *How to measure anything: Finding the value of intangibles in business.* New York: Wiley.

Kaplan, Robert S., and David P. Norton. 1996. *The balanced scorecard.* Boston: Harvard Business School Press.

———. 2004. *Strategy maps.* Boston: Harvard Business School Press.

———. 2006. *Alignment.* Boston: Harvard Business School Press.

Moeller, Robert R. 2008. *Sarbanes–Oxley internal controls: Effective auditing with AS5, CobiT, and ITIL.* New York: Wiley.

Niven, Paul R. 2006. *Balanced scorecard step-by-step.* New York: Wiley.

Root, Steven J. 1998. *Beyond COSO: Internal control to enhance corporate governance.* New York: Wiley.

IT Governance

Grünendahl, Ralf T., and Peter H. L. Will. 2006. *Beyond compliance: 10 practical actions on regulation, risk and IT management.* Wiesbaden, Germany: GWV-Vieweg.

ItSMF—The IT Service Management Forum. 2007. *IT governance based on COBIT 4.0.* Zaltbommel, Netherlands: Van Haren Publishing.

Keyes, Jessica. 2005. *Implementing the IT balanced scorecard: Aligning IT with corporate strategy.* Boca Raton, FL: Auerbach.

Van Bon, Jon, ed. 2006. *Frameworks for IT management.* Zaltbommel, Netherlands: Van Haren Publishing.

Weill, Peter, and Jeanne W. Ross. 2004. *IT governance.* Boston: Harvard Business School Press.

Information Management

Behr, Kevin, Gene Kim, and George Spafford. 2004. *The visible ops handbook: Implementing ITIL in 4 practical and auditable steps.* Eugene, OR: ITPI.

OGC. 2007. *The official introduction to the ITIL service lifecycle.* London: TSO.

Steinberg, Randy A. 2006. *Measuring ITIL: Measuring, reporting and modeling—The IT service management metrics that matter most to IT senior executives.* Victoria, BC, Canada: Trafford.

Van Bon, Jon, ed. 2005. *Foundations of IT service management based on ITIL.* 2nd ed. Zaltbommel, Netherlands: Van Haren Publishing.

Quality Improvement/Management

Breakthrough Management Group with Neil DeCarlo. 2007. *The complete idiot's guide to Lean Six Sigma.* New York: Alpha Books.

Brue, Greg. 2005. *Six Sigma for managers.* New York: McGraw-Hill.

Brue, Greg, and Rod Howes. 2006. *The McGraw-Hill 36-hour course: Six Sigma.* New York: McGraw-Hill.

Brue, Greg, and Robert G. Launsby. 2003. *Design for Six Sigma.* New York: McGraw-Hill.

Brussee, Warren. 2006. *All about Six Sigma: The easy way to get started.* New York: McGraw-Hill.

Chowdhury, Subir. 2003. *The power of design for Six Sigma.* Chicago: Dearborn Trade Publishing.

Chrissis, Mary Beth, Mike Konrad, and Sandy Shrum. 2003. *CMMI: Guidelines for process integration and product improvement.* Boston: Addison-Wesley.

Damelo, Robert. 1996. *The basics of process mapping.* New York: Productivity Press.

Davidow, William H., and Bro Uttal. 1990. *Total customer service: The ultimate weapon.* New York: HarperPerennial.

De Bono, Edward, 1985. *Six Thinking Hats.* NY: Little, Brown and Company.

Deming, W. Edwards. 1982. *Quality, productivity, and competitive position.* Cambridge, MA: MIT Press.

———. 2000. *Out of the crisis.* Cambridge, MA: MIT Press.

den Boer, Sven, et al. 2006. *Six Sigma for IT management.* Zaltbommel, Netherlands: Van Haren Publishing.

Donchin, Y., D. Gopher, M. Olin, Y. Badihi, M. Biesky, C. L. Sprung, R. Pizov, and S. Cotev. 1995. A look into the nature and causes of human errors in the intensive care unit. *Critical Care Medicine* 23:294.

George, Michael L., David Rowlands, Mark Price, and John Maxey. 2005. *The Lean Six Sigma pocket toolbook.* New York: McGraw-Hill.

Goldratt, Eliyahu M., with Eli Schragenheim and Carol A. Ptak. 2000. *Necessary but not sufficient.* Great Barrington, MA: North River Press.

Goldratt, Eliyahu M., with Jeff Cox. 2000. *The goal.* 3rd revised ed. Great Barrington, MA: North River Press.

Gupta, Praveen. 2007. *Six Sigma business scorecard.* 2nd ed. New York: McGraw-Hill.

Gygi, Craig, Neil DeCarlo, and Bruce Williams. 2005. *Six Sigma for dummies.* Indianapolis, IN: Wiley.

Harmon, Paul. 2007. *Business process change: A guide for business managers and BPM and Six Sigma professionals.* Burlington, MA: Morgan Kaufman.

Harry, Mikel, and Richard Schroeder. 2005. *Six Sigma: The breakthrough management strategy revolutionizing the world's top corporations.* New York: Currency.

Hayler, Rowland, and Michael D. Nichols. 2007. *Six Sigma for financial services.* New York: McGraw-Hill.

Jaca, J. Mike, and Paulette J. Keller. 2002. *Business process mapping: Improving customer satisfaction.* New York: Wiley.

Lepore, Domenico, and Oded Cohen. 1999. *Deming and Goldratt.* Great Barrington, MA: North River Press.

Liker, Jeffrey K., Michael Hoseus, and The Center for Quality People and Organizations. 2008. *Toyota culture: The heart and soul of the Toyota way.* New York: McGraw-Hill.

Osborn, Alex Faickney, 1953. *Applied imagination: Principles and procedures of creative problem solving.* New York: Charles Scribner's Sons.

Pande, Peter S., Robert P. Neuman, and Roland R. Cavanagh. 2002. *The Six Sigma way: Team fieldbook.* New York: McGraw-Hill.

Siviy, Jeanne M., M. Lynn Penn, and Robert W. Stoddard. 2007. *CMMI and Six Sigma: Partners in process improvement.* Boston: Addison-Wesley Professional.

Tayntor, Christine B. 2007. *Six Sigma software development.* 2nd ed. Boca Raton, FL: Auerbach.

Walton, Mary. 1986. *The Deming management method.* New York: Putnam.

Wedgwood, Ian D. 2007. *Lean Sigma: A practitioner's guide.* Upper Saddle River, NJ: Prentice Hall.

Wheat, Barbara, Chuck Mills, and Mike Carnell. 2003. *Leaning into Six Sigma: A parable of the journey to Six Sigma and a Lean enterprise.* New York: McGraw-Hill.

Portfolio/Program/Project Management

Lundquist, Eric, 2008. http://blogs.cioinsight.com/lundquist/content/business_applications/remember_the_swot_analysis_before.html

Maizlish, Bryan, and Robert Handler. 2005. *IT (Information technology) portfolio management step-by-step: Unlocking the business value of technology.* New York: Wiley.

Morris, Peter W. G., and Jeffrey K. Pinto. 2007. *The Wiley guide to project, program & portfolio management.* Hoboken, NJ: Wiley.

OGC. 2007a. *For successful project management/Prince2.* London: TSO.

———. 2007b. *Managing portfolios of change (with MSP for programmes and Prince2 for projects): Integrating MSP and Prince2.* London: TSO.

———. 2007c. *Managing successful programmes 2007 edition.* London: TSO.

Project Management Institute. 2003. *Organizational project management maturity model: Knowledge model.* Newtown Square, PA: PMI.

————. 2004. *A guide to the project management body of knowledge.* 3rd ed. Newtown Square, PA: PMI.

Software Development

Dickinson, Brian. 1989. *Developing quality systems: A methodology using structured techniques.* 2nd ed. New York: McGraw-Hill.

Dunn, Robert H. 1990. *Software quality: Concepts and plans.* Englewood Cliffs, NJ: Prentice Hall.

Grady, Robert B., and Deborah L. Caswell. 1987. *Software metrics: Establishing a company-wide program.* Englewood Cliffs, NJ: Prentice Hall.

Graham, Dorothy, Erik Van Veenendaal, Isabel Evans, and Rex Black. 2007. *Foundations of software testing.* London: Thomson.

Kan, Stephen H. 2002. *Metrics and models in software quality engineering.* 2nd ed. Boston: Addison-Wesley Professional.

Data Analysis

Ayres, Ian. 2007. *Super crunchers: Why thinking-by-numbers is the new way to be smart.* New York: Bantam Dell.

Davenport, Thomas H., and Jeanne G. Harris. 2007. *Competing on analytics.* Boston: Harvard Business School Press.

Koomey, Jonathan G. 2008. *Turning numbers into knowledge: Mastering the art of problem solving.* 2nd ed. Oakland, CA: Analytics Press.

Levitt, Steven D., and Stephen J. Dubner. 2006. *Freakonomics.* New York: Morrow.

Prahalad, C. K., and M. S. Krishnan. 2008. *The new age of innovation: Driving cocreated value through global networks.* New York: McGraw-Hill.

Redman, Thomas C. 2008. *Data driven.* Boston: Harvard Business School Press.

Rowntree, Derek. 1981. *Statistics without tears: An introduction for non-mathematicians.* London: Penguin.

Schmuller, Joseph. 2005. *Statistical analysis with Excel for dummies.* Hoboken, NJ: Wiley.

Surowiecki, James. 2005. *The wisdom of crowds.* New York: Anchor Books.

Appendix F: Lean and Six Sigma Resources

American Society for Quality (http://www.asq.org/): Provides Six Sigma certification.

Axiomatic Design Solutions, (http://axiomaticdesign.com): Provides Axiomatic Design software and consulting.

Curious Cat (http://management.curiouscatblog.net/): Management improvement blog.

David M. Lane Web page (http://davidmlane.com/hyperstat/Statistical_analyses.html): Free statistical software.

Discover 6 Sigma (http://www.discover6sigma.org/): Six Sigma resources.

eVSM (http://www.evsm.com/?gclid=CLykrOzQ5ZICFQksswodcSIn5g): Value stream mapping software.

FMEA Info Centre (http://www.fmeainfocentre.com/): Everything you want to know about failure mode and effect analysis.

Implement Lean Manufacturing (http://www.implement-lean-manufacturing.com/lean-lego-game.html): Lean Lego game.

i Six Sigma (http://www.isixsigma.com/): If you are only going to look at one link, this is the one.

International Society of Six Sigma Professionals (http://www.isssp.com/): If you are a joiner, this is the site for you.

John R. Grout Web page (http://facultyweb.berry.edu/jgrout/everyday.html): Mistake-proofing example.

Lean Enterprise Institute (http://www.lean.org/): Lean training and resources.

Lean Institute Canada (http://www.leaninstitute.ca/index.htm): Source for consulting and training. One of the authors' sites.

Lean Six Sigma Academy (http://lssacademy.com/): Lean and Six Sigma information.

Lean Supermarket (http://www.leansupermarket.com/servlet/StoreFront): One-stop shopping for all your Lean needs: posters, tags, task sheets, value stream mapping tools, and much more.

LodeStar Institute (http://www.lsixsigma.com/): Lean and Six Sigma training.

Makigami Info (http://www.makigami.info/): Learn about Makigami mapping.

MAMTC (http://www.mamtc.com/lean/links.asp): Lean links.

Minitab (http://www.minitab.com/): Data analysis and statistics software and training.

MoreStream (http://www.moresteam.com/toolbox/t405.cfm): 5 Why analysis.

Ocapt Business Books (http://www.ocapt.com/search/?link=6&q=lean+enterprise+institute): Lean books.

Onesixsigma (http://www.onesixsigma.com/): Lean and Six Sigma resources.

Poppendieck (http://www.poppendieck.com/lean-six-sigma.htm): Lean definition.

ProcessModel, Inc. (http://www.processmodel.com): Provide discrete event simulation software for LSS projects.

Productivity Press (http://www.productivitypress.com/): Lean publishing site.

Pyzdek Institute (http://www.pyzdek.com/DMAICDMADV.htm): DMAIC and DMADV explained.

Qimacros (http://www.qimacros.com/index.html): Lean Six Sigma software, training, and consulting.

Quality Council of Indiana (http://www.qualitycouncil.com/CSSBB.asp): Six Sigma cortication information.

Robert Niles (http://www.robertniles.com/stats/): Statistics everyone should know.

SigmaFlow Process Management (http://www.sigmaflow.com/): Lean Six Sigma tools.

Six Sigma & Process Excellence IQ (http://www.sixsigmaiq.com/index.cfm): Lean and Six Sigma networking, tools, and information.

Superfactory (http://www.superfactory.com/): Resources for lean manufacturing and lean enterprise excellence.

TreQna (http://www.treqna.com/): Open source Six Sigma.

Truth to Power Association (http://www.t2pa.com/cores/gov-risk/process-improvement): Process improvement discussion site and blog.

University of Texas at Austin (http://lifelong.engr.utexas.edu/sixsigma/index.cfm): Six Sigma training.

Value-Train (http://www.value-train.com/): Lean and Six Sigma training and useful links. One of the authors' sites.

Westgard (http://www.westgard.com/SixSigCalc.htm): Online Six Sigma calculators.

Wikipedia (http://en.wikipedia.org/wiki/List_of_Six_Sigma_software_packages): List of Six Sigma software tools.

Appendix G: Acronyms and Initialisms Used in This Book

AIE: applied information economics
ANSI: American National Standards Institute
ARC: Appraisal Requirements for CMMI
ARCI: accountable, responsible, consulted, informed
ASL: Application Services Library
BSC: Balanced Scorecard
CEO: chief executive officer
CFO: chief financial officer
CIO: chief information officer
CLT: Central Limit Theorem
CMMI: Capability Maturity Model Integration
COBIT: Control Objectives for Information and related Technology
COPQ: Cost of Poor Quality
CPM: Critical Path Method
CRM: customer relationship management
CSA: Canadian Standards Association
CTQ: Critical to Quality
DCCDI: define, customer, concept, design, implement
DFSS: Design for Six Sigma
DMADOV: define, measure, analyze, design, optimize, validate
DMADV: define, measure, analyze, design, verify
DMAIC: define, measure, analyze, improve, control
DMEDI: define, measure, explore, develop, implement
DoE: design of experiments
DSDM: Dynamic Systems Development Method
DSS: Data Security Standard

eTOM: enhanced Telecom Operations Map
FMEA: failure modes and effects analysis
GLBA: Gramm–Leach–Bliley Act
GQM: Goal-Question-Metric
HOQ: House of Quality
ICT: Information and Communications Technology
IDEAL: initiating, diagnosing, establishing, acting, leveraging
IDOV: identify, design, optimize, validate
IEEE: The Institute of Electrical and Electronics Engineers
ISACA: Information Systems Audit and Control Association
ISO: International Organization for Standardization
ISPL: Information Services Procurement Library
IT: information technology
ITGI: IT Governance Institute
ITIL: Information Technology Infrastructure Library
ITIM: Information Technology Investment Management
ITUP: IBM Tivoli Unified Process
JIT: just-in-time
KGI: key goal indicators
KPI: key performance indicators
LSS: Lean Six Sigma
MIPS: Millions of instructions per second
MOF: Microsoft Operations Framework
MSA: Measurement Systems Analysis
NVA: non-value-added
OGC: Office of Government Commerce
OPM3: Organizational Project Management Maturity Model
PA: process area (CMMI)
PCI: Payment Card Industry
PDCA: Plan-Do-Check-Act
PERT: Program Evaluation and Review Technique
PMBOK: A Guide to the Project Management Body of Knowledge (PMBOK®
    Guide)
PMI: The Project Management Institute
PSM: Practical Software Measurement
PSP: personal software process
QFD: Quality Function Deployment
QMS: quality management system
RACI: responsible, accountable, consulted, informed
RACIO: responsible, accountable, consulted, informed, omitted or out-of-the-loop
RASCI: responsible, accountable, supportive, consulted, informed
ROI: return on investment
ROIC: return on invested capital

RPM: resource project management
RTP: Risk Treatment Plan
RUMBA: reasonable, understandable, measurable, believable, achievable
SCAMPI: Standard CMMI Appraisal Method for Process Improvement
SDLC: system development life cycle
SDP: Service Design Package
SIP: Service Improvement Program
SIPOC: suppliers, inputs, process, outputs, customers
SLA: service level agreement
SMARRT: specific, measurable, actionable, realistic, results-oriented, timely
SME: subject matter expert
SoA: Statement of Applicability
SOX: The Sarbanes–Oxley Act of 2002
SPC: statistical process control
TOC: Theory of Constraints
TQM: Total Quality Management
TRIZ: Theory of Inventive Problem Solving (in Russian)
TSP: team software process
TVM: time value map
VA: value-added
VOB: voice of the business
VOC: voice of the customer
VOE: voice of the employee
VOP: voice of the process
VSM: value stream map
WE Rules: Western Electric Rules (for control charts)
WIP: work in process

Index

Page numbers followed by f indicate figures.
Page numbers followed by t indicate tables.